Yourself
First

A Commonsense Guide
to Life-Cycle
Retirement Investing

Timothy W. Cunningham and Clay B. Mansfield

John Wiley & Sons, Inc.
New York • Chichester • Brisbane • Toronto • Singapore

Copyright © 1996 by John Wiley & Sons, Inc.
Published by John Wiley & Sons, Inc.

Library of Congress Cataloging-in-Publication Data:
Cunningham, Timothy W.
    Pay yourself first : a commonsense guide to life cycle retirement
investing / Timothy W. Cunningham, Clay B. Mansfield.
       p.   cm.
    Includes bibliographical references.
    ISBN 0-471-16248-5 (pbk. : alk. paper)
    1. Finance, Personal.   2. Retirement—United States—Planning.
  3. Investments.   I. Mansfield, Clay B. II. Title.
HG179.C845   1996
332.024—dc20   96-29256
                                      CIP

Printed in the United States of America

10 9 8 7 6 5 4 3 2 1

DEDICATION

A dream is but a dream until someone finds the courage to take a chance and make that dream a reality. Rare is the man who has done this in his own life. But even rarer is the man who believes in others and fosters that same courage in them by his willingness to stand with them and put his money behind their dream. Such a man is Benjamin B. Cohen. Two guys in a rented room owe this man so much. In some small way we hope to honor Buddy by dedicating this book to him.

CONTENTS

Contents

Contents

FOREWORD

THE SUM TOTAL of human knowledge continues to expand in all directions ever faster and farther like a celestial supernova. But as the sum total of human knowledge expands toward an infinite horizon, the finite nature of the individual human mind can absorb in a lifetime only a smaller and smaller percent of that total information. Hence, the birth of the expert, whose specialized knowledge of a single narrow subject soars out to the farthest limits, even farther away from the human center and the broad population.

There is good news and bad news about the increasing specialization of expertise. The good news is that experts can help us manage and direct specialized information. This has the potential of filtering today's deluge of information wisely and thus discriminating between that which is important and that which is not. Under ideal conditions, this helps us solve problems more effectively. The bad news is that the price of expertise is our loss of the ability to appreciate the interconnectedness of things. Experts are like the blind men examining the elephant. One holds its tail and says the elephant is like a rope. Another embraces an elephant leg and says the beast is like a tree. The third man touches the elephant's ear and declares it to be an animal shaped like a giant leaf. Who is right? They all are—but they are also all wrong. That's why the definition of an expert is someone who knows more and more about less and less until they know absolutely everything about nothing at all.

Not surprisingly, the investment profession has become increasingly specialized. Experts have come to dominate the field, speaking their own language and following their own customs. Each expert claims superior knowledge and wants others to purchase that knowledge in one form or another (present company included, thank you very much). Specialized expertise is not always easy to understand. While this may not be a conscious attitude on the part of the expert, the result is that the average fellow on the street is sometimes left confused about how to handle his money.

It is symptomatic that purveyors of specialized expertise have a tendency to speak in tongues. Over time, they have developed a lexicon of terms and phrases that makes the conveyance of that specialized knowledge to the uninitiated all but impossible. This leads to a widespread phenomenon perhaps best expressed as follows: "If I can't understand what he's talking about, he must be an expert and therefore worth what I am paying him."

I have always felt that value of knowledge is best gauged by its ability to improve the human condition. To do so, specialized knowledge must meet two conditions. First, it must be accessible to a broad audience. Second, it must be usable by members of that audience to solve their problems. In other words, knowledge must be conveyed so that large numbers of individuals can willfully choose to act upon it and thereby effect a change in their lives.

As a supplier of specialized knowledge (also known as a consultant), I have always personally believed that my job was not to make simple issues complex and thereby justify my fee, but rather to make complex issues simple and hence usable and thereby justifying my worth.

When I first read *Pay Yourself First,* I was struck by a resonant chord of kinship. Here was a book on investing, a vessel of specialized knowledge, that met the two conditions. Written in plain English, it is a book that non–investment professionals can read and understand. This book contains clear and complete information that can be implemented by broad numbers of people to form a concrete plan of action. Perhaps most important, it is specialized knowledge whose use will lift the human condition.

Last, like finding three prizes in a Cracker Jacks box where you thought you would find none, the two authors have managed to make the consumption of their specialized knowledge both entertaining and enjoyable. To the authors, my congratulations and admiration. To the readers, may you live long and prosper, because this book may help you accomplish the latter, which can't but help the former.

RICHARD P. GLEASON, Senior Vice President
Director, Consulting Group
Smith Barney

PREFACE

MANY PEOPLE BUY BOOKS on investing looking for a way to make lots of money—and the sooner the better. Neither the financial services industry nor the media has helped matters much. The reams of what we call financial pornography spew forth from the printing presses in a seemingly endless torrent. This stuff comes in two varieties. First, we have the promotions for mutual funds and investment products that appeal to our greed. "Number one performer!" "Best mutual fund in its class!" "Up 600% in last seven years!" Then there is the popular financial press. This material often titillates more than just our greed. It seeks to feed our egos. Many times, books and magazines tell us that all of us can pit ourselves against the capital markets and come out on top. "The ten hot stocks to buy now!" "How to outperform the markets forever!" "We beat the market and you can, too." "Secrets of the investment gurus!"

While it's obvious that sensationalism sells, the reality of investment promises are rarely as satisfying as the come-ons imply. Many seem to have forgotten that money and savings are difficult to come by. This means we must be wise in how we handle them. Nowhere is this more important than investing for retirement. That's because we all have limited amounts of time and money in our lives, so financial mistakes must be kept to a minimum.

It is our view that life is pretty simple when we understand the basic rules. Retirement investing is no exception. The problem is that most of us either didn't learn the basic rules of investing, forgot them, or figured we just could plain ignore them. This is one reason why we so easily fall prey to the sensational investing messages strewn across our paths. So, at the risk of giving away a Big Secret in the Preface, here is one basic rule that applies to every investment circumstance and should be memorized by every investor: It is easier to *stay* out of trouble than it is to *get* out of trouble.

To succeed in retirement investing, people must understand what the problem is and how to go about finding a solution. We hope this book will help serve that function by acting as a useful primer. We have tried hard to pull all the elements together—from defining the retirement problem to laying out a reality-based solution and then showing how the pieces fit together.

ACKNOWLEDGMENTS

THERE ARE THREE great lessons that come from the Old Testament story of David and Goliath. The first is never be afraid to trust an unknown future to a known God. The second is Goliath wasn't too big to hit. He was too big to miss. The third lesson is found in David's rejection of choice weapons from the Israelite soldiers. That lesson is that sometimes what you know is enough. Anyone launching a new enterprise should remember this story and its lessons.

We are especially fortunate. Unlike David, when we went out to do battle, on the lips of all our shareholders was one word: WIN! For their steadfast support, we would be remiss if we didn't recognize and thank all the shareholders in Benson White & Company.

ONE

Let's Get a Few Things Straight Right off the Bat

NOBODY HAS PERFECT KNOWLEDGE

There is no easier way to illustrate something than to tell a tale. We suspect that this idea prompted Bill Bennett to write his best-selling compendium of stories entitled *The Book of Virtues*. Of course, the original book of virtues is the Bible. One story from Genesis seems particularly important for our time. It is the story about the tree of knowledge of good and evil. This is not an easy story to understand. We can't tell you that we have quite put all the pieces together ourselves. But we are sure of at least one thing—without the critical distinction between good and evil, there can be no virtue.

The Genesis story is set in the Garden of Eden where God introduced His creation to humankind. Adam and Eve found Eden to be the ultimate playground. There, they explored the innocence of unquestioning consciousness while basking in God's love. The sole admonishment humans received from God was not to eat the fruit from the tree of knowledge of good and evil. But human beings are restless and never satisfied with mere paradise when there are rules

1

to be tested. So it should come as no surprise that trouble began when consciousness gave way to curiosity.

The lightbulb went on first in Eve's head. Why not try the fruit, she thought. It looked delicious. She wanted to be more than she was, and the key to fulfilling that desire had to be the special and forbidden knowledge of good and evil. Besides, it was hanging on the tree, there for the taking. All she had to do was pluck it and take a bite. What possible reason could God have to object to her having knowledge of good and evil? It made no sense.

Eve may have been bright but she wasn't bold enough to defy God all by herself. First, she had to be prodded by the snake, and then she had to find an accomplice. Adam was easy to recruit, to put it mildly. He was the guy and she was the gal. One look at her, and it was all over for him. Eve had her man and the first wheel was about to come off creation.

Well, you know what happens next. They do the deed. Self-consciousness opens their eyes to good and evil. They see themselves as they are. Guilt lives. Sin exists. And God was so displeased that He banished Adam and Eve from Eden.

Now you might well ask why this act angered God so much that He sent the two original humans out of heaven. Aren't good and evil merely a part of creation? Don't they qualify as something that makes us distinctly human? Doesn't humankind require this knowledge to evolve to a higher plane? The answer is yes—but here's the rub. Humans lack the ability to see knowledge in its fullness or completeness. Maybe God was upset because Adam and Eve jumped the gun. Perhaps God knew humans did not yet have the capacity to handle the power of knowing good from evil without doing great harm to themselves and others. We just can't say.

But one thing seems especially clear. Many modern humans seem to believe that good and evil are merely alternative interpretations of equally valid perspectives. But if, in the final analysis, good and evil are relative, then nothing is true and nothing is false. However (and this is important), merely because good and evil are sometimes hard to discern does not mean they do not exist. It simply means that we are unable to have perfect and definitive knowledge of what truth is and what it is not. This fact should not prevent us from trying to sort out good from evil. But what we must understand is that the very essence of our search for truth resides in an attitude of humility, for humility is the currency of human wisdom. Despite our pretense to the contrary, we do not have ultimate knowledge. We cannot fathom the mind of God. We do not seem ready to do so.

Our purpose behind starting with this story is simple: Humility is not found on Wall Street where smugness is the hallmark. Everywhere in the investment world there is a great pretense that the unknowable can be known and defined—all for a price. Look at all the stock market strategists and pundits. Call a crash or pick a market turn and you're a genius. In this way, certain people are anointed geniuses during every market upturn and others deemed prophets just before things start to slide downhill. Humility is in decidedly short supply—replaced by puffed-up posturing and preening. But do not be fooled by the financial world's Street performers as they strut around making pronouncements about the true nature of things. Humility is the only path that leads back to God, if not to the Garden of Eden itself, and to the true meaning of the stewardship of life as well as our pocketbooks.

This is the spirit of this book. We are going to try to steer you through the reefs and shoals of retirement investing to the best of our ability. We don't pretend to have all the answers. We don't view ourselves as standing on a pedestal to address you, the inquisitive, yet perhaps confused, reader. Rather, we encourage you to join us as a partner in trying to make sense of our topic: a commonsense guide to life-cycle retirement investing.

MORE CHOICES DO NOT AUTOMATICALLY MAKE FOR BETTER DECISIONS

The well-known Steven Spielberg film, *Indiana Jones and the Last Crusade,* tells a great action and adventure story. The plotline is simple. Indiana Jones, played by Harrison Ford, and his father, played by Sean Connery, are two archeologists who set out to find the sacred goblet known as the Holy Grail. The Grail is the cup said to have been used by Christ at the Last Supper. Finding the cup would establish the accuracy of the Bible and confirm the existence of the Nazarene. Additionally, legend had it that whoever drank from the cup would have eternal life.

The plot unfolds in dramatic fashion with heroes and villains both consumed by the search for the Grail. The climactic scene comes near the end when Indiana Jones is pursued into a cave where the Grail is supposed to be found. He makes his way through all manner of booby traps and crosses a bridge over a high canyon to arrive at the sacred grotto where the Grail is kept. The villains are hot on his heels, though, and arrive at the grotto shortly after Indiana. The grotto is not what any of them expected. Instead of a single goblet on a prominent pedestal, there are literally scores of goblets arranged on several ledges. Virtually all the cups were made of gold or silver and lavishly bejeweled. How does one know which is the true Grail? There are so many to choose from. Undaunted, the villain chooses a goblet that seems especially beautiful. Expecting eternal life, he fills the cup from the basin of water in the grotto and drinks deeply. At once, instead of eternal life, the villain ages quickly, becoming elderly in a matter of seconds and then dying a horrible death from accelerated old age. This fellow chose the wrong cup and drank from it, and the legend exacted its penalty. Now it was Indiana's turn.

He was staggered. The choice was nearly impossible. How could he distinguish between the true Holy Grail and the impostors? Then a solution dawned on him. He had to define his problem in simple terms. The key to finding the cup was to understand the nature of Him who had used it last. Christ was a humble carpenter from Nazareth. He was most certainly not part of the ruling class. This meant that the Grail was likely to be a simple carpenter's cup, unpretentious in design. In this way, Indiana chose a small earthen goblet that was, in fact, the Holy Grail, and by doing so reminded us that simple things can have great value.

Choice need never be confusing if we know what we are looking for. However, if we have no clear idea of what we seek, then choice not only can be overwhelming, it can actually become debilitating. The financial services industry doesn't make things easy. There is an overwhelming number of investment products offered in the financial markets. You can buy stocks, bonds, options, futures, commodities. There are mortgage-backed securities such as GNMAs and FNMAs, and FNMLCs. There are REITs and UITs, and a slew of other oddities.

Mutual funds were supposed to make investing easier by allowing ordinary investors to acquire professional management and diversification. However, there are now so many mutual funds that investing has once again become difficult because there are too many choices. There are stock mutual funds, bond mutual funds, big company funds, small company funds, technology funds, utility funds, global funds, emerging country funds, and on and on. It is more than confusing—it's terrifying. And if the sheer number and variety of funds weren't bad enough, the industry makes it even more difficult to choose because every single fund claims to have the best returns available. It is sort of like Garrison Keillor's fictional Lake Wobegon, a town where all the children are above average.

What investors need is a way to make sense of all the choices. They need to understand that there is more to investing than the latest hot stock or mutual fund. But, at the same time, investors need to remember that much of life is not all that complicated— that simple and straightforward things do indeed have merit and deserve careful attention. In this book, we will try to untangle a few of these investment knots, and, along the way, we hope to make sense out of the seemingly chaotic and complicated world of retirement investing. It's really quite simple when you start at the beginning, and that means defining the problem before solving it.

YOU NEED A YELLOW BRICK ROAD TO FIND OZ

Kids love coloring books. There are probably several reasons for this. Coloring books allow a kid to participate in the creation of art, even if it is just a bunch of scribbled lines. When very small, kids have little self-consciousness about coloring within the lines (or outside the lines, for that matter). They color the pages almost at random, choosing all sorts of wacky colors. That's part of the fun. Grass becomes orange, and water is colored red. At a young age, the sense of power that comes from unlimited self-expression is undeniable. However, as children grow older, they want to act more grown up and draw more realistically. Typically, though, they lack the motor skills and experience required to create realistic-looking pictures.

This is the age when connect-the-dots coloring books are especially popular. The picture is hidden on the page, and the child has to connect the dots to render the figure visible. There is great satisfaction in connecting the dots and seeing the outlines of a picture emerge. All kids have to do is draw a line from one number to the next, and before they know it, they have drawn, say, a horse or a dog. Next, they can choose the colors to use in finishing the picture.

At this age, kids often demand more realism in their art, and a connect-the-dots coloring book allows them to get there with a minimum amount of skill.

Unfortunately, there are no connect-the-dots coloring books to help retirement investors, and, frankly, that's too bad because people could sure use one. In fact, what investors really need is to see a picture of what the retirement problem is. If investors could see such a picture, they could successfully deal with what they would need to do to invest for their retirement. Of course, nobody wants to do a poor job of investing. However, many individuals just lack a meaningful approach, together with the necessary skills and knowledge to successfully accomplish their retirement investing objectives. If there were a connect-the-dots kind of strategy available, then people could learn how to attack the problem and solve it. Instead, what exists is just a bunch of unconnected retirement investing concepts, many of them contradictory and inconclusive.

Human pursuits have no meaning when performed in a vacuum. A coloring book has figures to color in, a tennis court has lines, and a baseball field has bases to tag. Rules give definition to every game. However, in the field of investing, we are led to believe that the only things that count are the capital markets and returns. With great fanfare, we are sold on the "pile" theory—the bigger the pile, the better, forgetting that there is a human purpose that has to be served along the way. Now, there is nothing wrong with achieving high investment returns, but these returns must be connected with a human financial objective (such as funding a retirement benefit) to make any sense. Therefore, we are going to try to connect the dots to tease forth a picture of the retirement problem as it relates to the human condition. And that is what is important if we are to solve the retirement investing problem.

BEWARE OF CREDENTIALISM

To the best of anyone's knowledge, the following are true statements: Cleopatra was rather plain looking and had a large hooked nose. The Vandals were a mostly respectable group of seagoing trading people. Nero didn't own a fiddle (they didn't exist, as such) and set up homeless shelters for the poor after the great fire that ravaged Rome during his rule. Queen Victoria was anything but a prude. Indeed, she enjoyed the bawdiest of jokes and had an open affair with a commoner who lived with her for many years.

Niccolò Machiavelli was a Florentine political philosopher who was known for his writings about the darker side of the use of power, yet he was never a powerful and crafty ruler himself. Instead, by all contemporary accounts, Machiavelli was a pleasant, mild-mannered diplomatic bureaucrat. Yet his understanding of people was nothing if not insightful. He wrote: "For the great majority of mankind is satisfied with appearances, as though they were realities, and is more often influenced by things that seem than by those that are."

Credentialism is but another offshoot of our reliance on appearance. By credentialism, we mean the tendency to judge things not on merit, but on the presumption of merit accorded on the basis of appearance as defined by the supposed significance of the credential. Thus, large management consulting firms can charge small fortunes for the advice of inexperienced but well-educated young men and women. And even the worst lawyer in the world will be afforded more courtesy in a courtroom than a better-prepared nonlawyer. The same principle holds true for the dilettante who graduated from Harvard as compared to the harder-working and better-prepared graduate of an obscure but excellent small college. In a stack of resumes, that of the Harvard graduate will probably make the shortlist, while that of the obscure graduate, despite representing the more effective candidate, will most likely languish in the circular file.

To be sure, credentials are an important way to discriminate among alternatives, but they are no substitute for sound judgment and careful consideration. True, we must organize and categorize experience to deal with the world. Without mental cubbyholes in which to place things, every waking moment would overwhelm us. It is only when the categorization is taken too far that it becomes dangerous. Credentials can lead us astray as often as they can lead us in the right direction.

How can we avoid an overemphasis on credentials in making decisions? It's not easy. We can start by asking just how the credentials being offered help solve the problem at hand. Of course, to accomplish this task, we must define the problem—in itself, a difficult task. However, the only sure cure for misguided credentialism is to focus on those critical factors that have nothing to do with credentials. This means paying closer attention to defining the problem and selecting a solution than to credentials that have little to do with the real issues at hand.

Recently, we had the good fortune to once again talk with a man who represents many of the best qualities to be found in a human being. This guy is trustworthy, courageous, loyal, kind, and, above all, generous. Jim is a former U.S. Marine who hails from the northeastern Pennsylvania coal country and doesn't apologize for his humble roots or ways. These people have a down-to-earth view of life and its struggles. They are strong willed and self-reliant, and they know that success in life comes from making do with what you've got. And this describes big Jim to a T.

Jim told us the story of Anthony Pizzone. Tony Rose, as he was called (he wore a rose in his lapel everyday), was a first-generation Italian who arrived in the Wyoming Valley of Pennsylvania in the late 1930s. Tony brought with him no education, zero money, and only the desire to work hard. The man believed in the American dream—that initiative and hard work will be rewarded. With that thought firmly held in his mind, over the next three decades Tony Rose built a very successful asphalt-paving company. At the height of his success in the paving business, he was accorded the highest flattery that could be given by his peers—he was asked to explain the secret of his good fortune and how he managed to accomplish so much without any formal education. He replied, "When you ain'ta gotta no education, you gotta use-a you noggin!"

College degrees don't get things done. People do. Credentials indicate only that a person has successfully completed the work necessary to have the degree granted. However, what is more important is that a degree does not tell us about an individual's ability to think clearly. Degrees and titles are just labels. The ability to think clearly is not certifiable. Consequently, people should never confuse the two things.

Furthermore, there are times when ignorance is your best weapon against the sophisticated. Higher education, for all its benefits, often promotes goofy ideas. When all the academics are saying that something is true, there are many times when it actually isn't. Such people each see their little world through a straw. Want proof? Just think about the silly, narrow topics that pass for legitimate inquiry in university-land, then turn to the world of the financial statisticians and observe direct parallels that purport to frame some sort of reality. But when this sort of thing becomes translated from the world of the academic into the real world (and this occurs regularly), people become confused. The only antidote is common sense.

YOU ALREADY HAVE THE TOOLS YOU NEED TO DO THE JOB

During the late 1950s and early 1960s approximately 3,000 people lived in Clarks Summit, Pennsylvania. One thing about the town that stood out was the number of churches that existed in this little pea patch at the end of the Northeast Extension of the Pennsylvania Turnpike. There must have been at least seven different faiths in Clarks Summit, but one Presbyterian minister, the Reverend Robert Lukens, was especially well known. Reverend Bob, as folks called him, was a plain man, neither handsome nor homely. He was a remarkably decent fellow who liked and respected everybody. When the pastor preached, he spoke to his congregation like the neighbors that they were. The people of Clarks Summit liked that.

One Sunday, Reverend Bob gave a sermon on the story of David and Goliath. Most folks know the gist of this story about how David, as God's anointed, takes on the Philistine giant, Goliath. It's a story about how faith and courage win the day. But Reverend Bob put another twist on the tale. As David prepared to face Goliath, Solomon's soldiers made great sport of the event. They knew Goliath's physical strength and skill in the art of combat were sure to overpower young David, who had a mere sling for a weapon. To make the contest a bit more evenly matched, the soldiers offered the young fellow the pick of any sword or spear he wished. But David was unfamiliar with the sword or lance. So he stuck with what he knew best—a simple leather sling. And herein lies a great message for us all.

Many of us feel inadequate when faced with a difficult task or job. We sometimes lack confidence in our own judgment and capabilities. In such situations, folks often look for a crutch to lean on. Sometimes, we crave more experience or special knowledge. Sometimes we think if we had just one more fact, we could make a better decision, even though gathering more facts does not automatically improve the decision. Or we are eager to use other people to fight our difficult battles. Surely, we think, the experts know more than we do and have special tools or knowledge to fix what ails us. So it is that, regardless of the form it takes, when faced with thorny decisions, we often get a sinking feeling that something outside of ourselves is needed to handle the problem. Reverend Bob's sermon tells us that often, as with David in his fight with Goliath, simply being who you are and using what you know is enough to win the day. It was for David.

When it comes to investing, many people have the disturbing sensation of not being up to the job at hand. How we cope with this personal challenge varies from person to person and from situation to situation. Certain occasions do call for special information or special tools. Otherwise, we are simply flying blind. But more often than not, it isn't another tool or opinion that we need to make a good decision. Instead, we need only the courage to weigh the evidence at hand, ask questions, listen to the debate, and decide what makes sense by using the simple deliberative tools that each and every one of us already has inside.

This means that we shouldn't allow ourselves to be baffled by things we don't understand. In the world of investing, if it cannot be explained easily, then it probably is not worthy of continued pursuit and should be dropped like a bad habit.

A SHORT REVIEW

Wall Street has deliberately complicated what is a fundamentally simple matter. Given the right information, anyone can understand retirement investing. This book is based on a number of simple principles that might best be called the fundamentals of retirement investing. Understanding the fundamentals requires the right frame of mind. That's because our experiences often blind us and prevent us from seeing important truths. Before we get into the fundamentals of retirement investing, keep in mind the following:

- Nobody knows everything. It's good to remember this as you go about any pursuit—especially investing.
- You have to define a problem before you solve it. It helps to have a good set of lines and boundaries, so you can focus your energies on solving the problem before you.

- You don't have to get overly fancy or complicated about your investment approach. Simple things are almost always better. They are certainly easier to understand, and there are fewer things to go wrong.
- Credentials can mask faulty thinking and blind us to the straightforward realities of life. Beware of the expert who cannot explain things in a clear and straightforward manner.
- You ought to be able to understand everything you are doing and explain it to somebody else. Otherwise, you do not understand it and it is something you shouldn't do.

TWO

The Foundations
of Life-Cycle
Retirement Investing

WHAT IT MEANS TO BE AN INVESTOR

Investing is what you do with money that is left over after you have
paid your bills. An investor uses this "excess" money to solve his or
her financial objectives, such as funding a retirement or financing a
child's education. Investing must serve a human purpose to be
meaningful. Those who attempt to manage assets without serving a
human purpose have no way to define what they need to accomplish. They have no way to know what is an acceptable risk or an
acceptable return. The result is confusion and perhaps an unmet
financial need, which could be disastrous for an individual.

The subject of this book is retirement investing. The sole objective of retirement investing is to fund the expenses of retirement.
The entire investing process must serve and solve this objective.
This means that the focus of our attention must be on solving the
problem rather than on beating the capital markets (i.e., the stock
and bond markets). Returns, and returns alone, are not the solution
to a problem. Merely chasing higher returns in the capital markets

can and does lead many of us down the wrong road. That so many people focus solely on the capital markets is a measure of how far we have strayed from purposeful, solution-based investing. The capital markets form the arena in which investments are purchased or sold. They do not form the essence of investing any more than the supermarket forms the essence of eating.

By its nature, investing involves risk. Risk comes in any number of forms, and it pervades every nook and cranny of the investing process. Risk is about loss—of income, of principal, or of purchasing power. Do what you will, your investments are always at risk. The biggest heartaches for investors are caused by mistaking what risk is and by taking on risks that are inappropriate to one's life circumstances. Most often these heartaches and failures come from greed—mindlessly chasing higher investment returns. This reckless investing behavior results in losses that can be difficult, if not impossible, to recover from.

All investors have two critical limits: time and the ability to produce wealth for investing. Every individual investor is limited by the mortal constraints inherent in the human life span—none of us lives forever. This is a fact lost in most financial decision making. As with every book on investing, we will cite investment averages taken from many decades of history. In doing so, it is intimated that investors have unlimited time. This is not so. In reality, most people have a far more limited real-time horizon than the averages would suggest. If a person begins investing for retirement at age 23, he or she may have some 40 to 45 years of investing ahead before being ready for retirement and another 15 to 20 years of continued investing during retirement. Mortal limits impose a boundary to all individual investing.

Investment capital is created by not spending everything we earn. The ability to save therefore provides the other critical limitation for every investor. The ability to save is conditioned by things we control and by things we cannot. For instance, most young people don't earn much money. This means their savings potential is limited. This is a situation that most young people cannot control. They may have time on their side, but their small income gives them little ability to save much money. When people become parents, they have financial obligations to their children that make it again hard to save. This is a natural part of most people's life cycles. Once retired, our ability to save falls off rapidly, because during retirement we are no longer earning money from full-time employment and must live off our savings.

Investors see themselves differently from those who do not save and invest. They view themselves as people saving for the day when their money will earn their living for them, rather than living on their employment income. Plus, investors know the magic of compounding, a universal principle that can be employed wherever one invests. Compounding is easy to illustrate. Consider the following story. The other day we saw two brothers bickering with each other. They were about 11 and 15 years old, and they were fighting as only brothers know how. Finally, the older one said, "OK, if I'm right, you have to pay me once a day, every day for the whole month of June."

"How much?" shot back the little brother.

"A penny a day the first day, two pennies the second, four the third, and double the pennies each day for the whole month," said the older kid, who had obviously been studying compounding in school.

"You're on," said the 11-year-old.

The argument went on until it was shown that the older brother had won. He then started to crow about his victory.

"The way I figure it," he said, "you're going to owe me forever."

"No way," said the younger boy, "It's only going to be a few pennies."

"Yeah, a few pennies in your dreams. Try $21,000,000 and change, little guy. But, just to show you I'm a pal, I'll let you slide and we can round it off to $20 million."

Ah, yes, the magic of compounding. Those people who have not learned about it and then experienced it first hand will have a hard time grasping its importance. Folks who spend everything they make and then go into debt for even more can't begin to understand the magic of compounding. Most important, compounding is the forgotten secret of retirement investing, and it is the retirement investor's most reliable friend. Compounding requires time and patience. While it requires the disciplined engine of savings to make it work, it is the surest way to financial independence.

THE INVESTING TRIANGLE

To put things in their proper perspective, let's start with a concept called the *investing triangle,* illustrated in Figure 2.1. The three basic parts to the investing triangle are: emergency cash reserves and insurance, serious money investments, and speculation.

Emergency Cash Reserves and Insurance

Emergency cash reserves are intended to provide a cushion for unforeseen events (such as a furnace that gives up the ghost). When an unexpected minor disaster hits, it is far better to be safe than sorry. That means always having the readily available cash necessary to meet the crisis. An emergency cash reserve should equal 3 months to 18 months of cash family living expenses, depending on your circumstances. The primary purpose of your cash reserves is to provide a means of support in the event of a job loss or other unforeseen family emergency. The other typical use of emergency cash reserves is to stand ready to take advantage of personal opportunities that require cash. These short-term savings should form the foundation of every person's financial plan.

However—and this is extremely important—don't touch the money in your emergency cash reserve, unless it is a true emergency. Don't be tempted to spend your emergency cash on this and that. Otherwise, it won't be available at full strength when you need

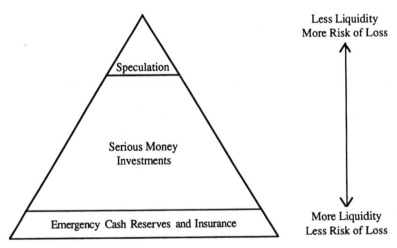

Figure 2.1 The investing triangle.

it. This means that your emergency cash reserve is not for clothes or vacations, or even to pay down credit cards. These expenses should be paid from your income, not your emergency reserve.

Thus, your cash reserve is rainy-day money. It expenses is a financial life preserver to be used only when needed.

By all means, make it a standard practice to put money away in an emergency cash reserve. The requirements for investing this type of money are simple. Emergency cash must be available at a moment's notice. It must be safe. Safety of your principal is more important than yield or return. This means that your emergency cash should be kept in the bank or in a conservative money market mutual fund that invests in federal government obligations. These monies must be readily available for emergency but are not appropriate for inclusion as a separate security in a life-cycle retirement portfolio. That is because cash reserves are to be used in the event of a financial emergency, such as the loss of a job, and not merely as another part of a long-term investment program.

Adjustments to the size of your cash reserve depend on a variety of factors. If you have a spouse who earns a sizable percentage of the family's income, then this will relieve you of the need for as large a cash reserve as would otherwise be necessary. If you have dependent children, then your cash reserve will generally be larger. If your income is secure, then you will require less of a reserve than if your income were unstable. For example, a commissioned sales-person might well want to have a greater emergency cash reserve than that of a salaried employee.

An emergency cash reserve is not a substitute for insurance. A cash reserve is there to overcome emergencies that are important but not catastrophic. For true catastrophes, you must have adequate insurance coverage. Insurance to cover your health, life, house, and possessions is an essential component of your financial well-being. Thus, insurance should be right at the bottom of your investing triangle along with your emergency cash reserve. A detailed discussion of your insurance needs is a subject that is beyond the scope of this book. However, because of the possibility that many types of unforeseen, yet insurable, events could destroy your family's financial stability, having the right type of insurance in force is an important part of your overall investing effort.

Serious Money Investments

Once your emergency cash reserves are in place, you can prepare for your desired financial goals by saving and then investing those savings wisely. For most people, the single most important and long-term component of serious money investing will be devoted to retirement. Retirement funds are monies that are not consumed on a current basis but are set aside and invested today, so as to provide a means of support when you are no longer working. Other serious money investments would be for children's tuitions or a down payment on a house, or simply to build a secure base of assets for peace of mind. Most of this book is devoted to the serious money topic of creating and managing a secure and well-funded retirement nest egg.

You will notice that serious money investing is generally less liquid than emergency cash reserves and also carries a somewhat higher degree of risk to principal. Conceptually, as you move upward in the investing triangle, even serious money investing will become somewhat riskier and less liquid. That's because investments are not like bank deposits that are insured by the FDIC. Investments require the presence of buyers to be liquid. The absence of buyers, by either legal restriction or adverse market conditions, makes investments inherently less liquid and therefore riskier. This means that a firm line must be drawn between speculation and serious money investing.

Speculation

The most common understanding of speculation is that it involves the assumption of a risk in anticipation of a larger-than-average return, while also carrying a higher-than-average possibility of loss. Speculation implies that the riskiness of an investment operation can be analyzed, measured, and understood. The implication here is that speculation involves the exact same elements as investing and differs only in the degree of risk undertaken.

As you go upward within the investing triangle, you increase your risk of loss and decrease the liquidity of your investment. That is, you face a higher risk of loss and less chance that you will be able to convert your assets into cash. The trade-off for the assumption of higher risk is the possibility that you might be able to earn a higher return. However, just because something is risky does not mean the higher return is likely or even possible. Most investment managers consider it their duty to deliver investment results that outperform the standard indexes—a task that rarely meets with long-term success. Many individual investors have also been conditioned to believe that getting the maximum return is the single most important thing about investing. The central idea behind this popular belief is to make as much money as you can, as fast as you can, and then call it investing. However, the more you reach for additional return, the more likely it is that you will engage in speculation and place your investment at risk.

Most of the professionals in today's financial services industry focus on generating the highest rate of return as quickly as possible, within their special discipline. There is nothing wrong with this approach except that it is one-sided and, as such, without balance. Imbalances lead to extremes, and investing is no exception. That is, with the sole attention given to generating higher returns, many investment professionals sometimes overstep the bounds of good judgment and make investments that are fundamentally speculative in nature. Thus, while the industry likes to talk about how to manage serious investments for its clients, it often acts differently with the customer's money. Consider the major mutual fund group that allows its portfolio managers to try to boost returns by borrowing money to make additional investments while using their shareholders' invested capital as collateral.

The real issue for a retirement investor is whether speculation has a role to play in the average person's investment strategy. We conclude that it does not. It makes no sense to gamble with your future rent money. The definition of speculation given above leaves us with the conclusion that speculation could possibly be a perfectly appropriate activity if the risks could be measured carefully. Unfortunately, speculative risks are practically impossible to measure carefully in a world that makes no distinction between speculating and investing in the first place. That's because there is no balance to the discussion. Let us explore this issue more fully.

INVESTMENT VERSUS SPECULATION

In the mid-1960s, the National Basketball Association was entering its golden era. Players with names like Chamberlain, Russell, West, and Robertson were playing the game. The bounce pass was still a fundamental. Clyde "the glide" Frazer was introducing hand checking to the defense. And the '67 Knicks were showing the beauty of team defense and hitting the open man in NBA play.

About this time, the American Basketball Association decided it wanted to elbow its way into professional basketball. To compete with the established NBA, the ABA aggressively bid for the top college talent of the day. The league signed such stars as Doctor J, Dan Issel, and Artis Gilmore. But the owners knew that to be successful they were going to have to make their product more exciting in comparison to the NBA. So the ABA introduced a jazzed-up version of the game, and the "run and gun" was born.

You might remember seeing an old ABA game played. Up and down the court the teams would go, gunning away, each trying to put up more points than its opponent. The only game that counted in the ABA was offense and scoring. It was amazing to watch—your team could score 141 points and still lose! How on earth is it possible that a basketball team can score 141 points and still lose? Simple—the ABA game was predicated on offense, rather than on a more balanced combination of offense and defense. The fact that defense was neglected permitted teams to score big numbers and still come up empty-handed.

The world of investing has a grand and overwhelming obsession with total return. Investors are inundated with investment ideas that boast of being able to provide increased returns. An enormous amount of time is spent in this single-minded pursuit. To our way of thinking, this is just the old ABA strategy—plenty of offense, without any defense to speak of. And anyone who watched the old ABA soon realized that there was only so much offense that could be squeezed out of four quarters of playing time.

Chasing returns has taken on too much importance. Investors have all but ignored the time-honored dictum that the first priority of investment management is to control risk, not necessarily to maximize returns. The investment game has always been both offense and defense, but somehow we've lost sight of this. Many investors today assume that if they pile up enough investment "points," they really don't need much defense. But nothing could be further from the truth.

The essence of retirement investors' mission is to pay themselves adequate retirement benefits without fail. To accomplish this objective, one must not pursue higher returns without maintaining a generous margin of safety. This margin of safety must be included in each and every aspect of a retirement investor's portfolio. Almost by definition, speculation eliminates a margin of safety.

Not surprisingly, others have already traveled down this road. In 1934, Benjamin Graham and David Dodd published the landmark book, *Security Analysis,* and launched the then new profession of the same name. Since this book remains the seminal work in the field, we thought it would be wise to see what it had to say. After considering the matter, Graham and Dodd conclude that one must first define investment and then allow a definition of speculation to emerge as a consequence. Graham and Dodd wrote as follows: *"An investment operation is one which, upon thorough analysis, promises safety of principal and a satisfactory return . . . [as] justified on **both** qualitative and quantitative grounds. Operations not meeting these requirements are speculative."*[1] The most important words in this definition are in the phrase "promises safety of principal and a satisfactory return." Let's explore these terms further.

How safe is an investment? How risky is a speculation? As with many ideas, the dividing line between entirely clear, but opposite, poles provides boundaries to the problem. In matters of safety, as with all the elements of investing, an emphasis must be placed on study and reasonable expectation. So if, after study, we conclude that we can't reasonably expect that an outlay of money will return at least what we paid, we are speculating. If we conclude that we have a reasonable expectation that our principal is safe, we are investing. Between these two extremes is a multitude of variations and shadings.

Messrs. Graham and Dodd go to some length to emphasize the importance of the price of an investment, as well as its quality in determining the safety of principal. They note that when the price of a common stock rises beyond the underlying fundamentals of the issuing company, that stock ceases to be an investment and becomes speculative in nature. Quoting again from their book, "In our opinion the great majority of common stocks of strong companies must be considered speculative a good part of the time after a bull market is well under way, simply because their price is too high to warrant safety of principal in any intelligible sense of the phrase."[2] This means that the purchase of securities at one price may be an investment but at a higher price constitutes speculation.

As is always the case in matters of finance, we must consider the element of time itself. If, over the course of time, we can reasonably expect that a particular investment will return at least its cost, what happens if it loses value in the interim? The answer to this question resides in our need for liquidity. When we invest in something that may reasonably be expected to decline in value before we need to sell it, we have speculated instead of invested.

Similarly, we must consider the portfolio effect. If we purchase a portfolio of investments and see a single investment decrease in value, we may still reasonably anticipate that the portfolio will return our principal. Classification of an entire portfolio as an investment portfolio or as a speculative portfolio depends on the nature and the prevailing market prices of each underlying investment as well as the need for liquidity. If, taken as a group, a portfolio of individual investments cannot reasonably be expected to return at least our original outlay in accordance with our need for liquidity, again, we are speculating, not investing.

We must also note that the more speculative an activity, the less valuable and the more difficult it is to analyze the chances for success or failure. This means that professional speculators, by definition, cannot materially and consistently analyze their speculation to provide themselves with a margin of safety. Gut feelings and intuition do not constitute a careful analysis, because, as Graham and Dodd state: "Even if we grant that analysis can give a speculator a mathematical advantage, it does not ensure him a profit. His ventures remain hazardous; in any individual case a loss may be taken; and after the operation is concluded it is difficult to determine whether the analyst's contribution has been a benefit or detriment. . . . It is as though the analyst and Dame Fortune were playing a duet on the speculative piano, with the fickle goddess calling all the tunes." If professionals cannot retain any control over what they are doing through study and experienced analysis, why should the average retirement investor believe that he or she can speculate with impunity? Speculating is like hopping a moving freight train: Either you make it or you don't, but the risk is great either way. If you lose, you can lose everything.

Turning our attention to the other key phrase, let's look at what is meant by "satisfactory return." Graham and Dodd state: " 'Satisfactory' is a subjective term; it covers any rate or amount of return, *however low*, which the investor is willing to accept, provided he acts with reasonable intelligence."

It is essential to note that the concept of *maximized* returns isn't the same as the concept of *satisfactory* return. In this day and age of trying to squeeze every penny until Lincoln gets a headache, it is important to remember that a satisfactory return is all we should expect from a prudently managed investment program. However, to more fully understand the word *satisfactory*, we have to probe even deeper.

Something that is satisfactory is literally that which gives satisfaction. The dictionary says that the word *satisfaction* means "fulfillment of a need or want." This definition relates directly to the retirement investor. A satisfactory return for a retirement investor is that return that satisfies a need to create and then generate an acceptable retirement benefit. Not surprisingly, this notion of satisfactory return depends on the element of time. Each retirement investor's portfolio has both time and return components. When retirement falls closer to the present, the investor must be satisfied with lower returns. When retirement falls further into the future, we may require somewhat higher returns to be satisfied. Thus, a satisfactory return for an investor at one point in time may be too low or too high for the same investor at another point in time.

Speculation has no place in retirement investing. It is an activity that can't provide a meaningful margin of safety, cannot be analyzed properly to increase the chance of a desirable conclusion, and is subject to additional emotional factors that arise from uncertainty.

The other day, we got a call from a close relative. Bill was a little upset. Recently, he had been dabbling in small company stocks in his retirement account. Not wanting to take any undue risks, Bill had made sure that his stocks had at least the capitalization of Aunt Lucy's grocery store. For a while, things went swimmingly, as the stocks in this segment of the market went great guns. At one point, Bill's portfolio value was up an incredible 46 percent. As you can imagine, he was very pleased with himself, since making money in small company stocks seemed as easy as shaking a stick. Then he hit the hard brick wall of reality as the bubble burst and his entire portfolio slammed down almost 60 percent from its high point. Now he was beside himself. How could he have lost all his profit and put a dent in his portfolio's principal to boot? More important, what should he do now? Should he sell? Should he buy more because the prices had gone down so much? Should he sit tight and wait? One thing's for sure: Any decision was sure to be gut-wrenching.

Bill's experience is hardly exceptional. To qualify as an investor you need only one thing—money. That's all. For darn nearly everything else, you need a license to practice, but that's not the case with investing. What's missing are two important requirements. The first is a basic knowledge of the fundamentals of investing. The second is the expectation of reasonable returns rather than the expectation of a ticket to ride the gravy train.

The central principle of investing is simple. For most investors, it is hard enough setting aside money to invest. So it is important not to get stupid with these precious few dollars. But how do we keep ourselves from getting reckless? The answer begins with an understanding of the direct link between savings and investment. Since savings for investment are difficult to acquire, retirement portfolios must be designed and built conservatively right from the start. Savings are difficult enough to scrape together without having to make up for speculative losses.

The base of the investing triangle (Figure 2.1) is for cash and insurance necessary to meet emergency needs. The next level up the triangle is for what we have called serious money investing. The investment triangle begins with the most conservative securities and follows a gradual transition up to its apex where speculation might (or might not) enter the picture. It is only at the very tip of the portfolio that the "big game" and large risks to principal should be hunted. The fundamental goal is to build and grow retirement investment portfolio, not to gamble with it. The rationale behind this conservative approach comes from knowing that permanent losses are difficult to make up through investment returns alone. Therefore, if you don't have the extra money to replenish the shortfall, your retirement portfolio may suffer permanent damage. The message is clear: We must be careful and purposeful from the start.

As we look out over the financial landscape, it's easy to see how the activity of investing demonstrates a singular confusion of purpose. For example, many people and institutions rely on money market funds to manage their emergency cash. It is axiomatic in money market investing that safety of principal is more important than yield. Yield is important; it is just that it is not the primary objective that safety is. Against this backdrop, the financial press has reported instances in which managers took extra risks in a quest for incremental yield and now find themselves under water with principal losses. Ouch! Other well-publicized problems have surfaced in the use of derivative securities in various mutual funds that presented themselves to the investing public as safe. When market forces went against the managers' derivatives positions, some of them were forced to put up millions of dollars to make good on shareholder losses. Clearly, in the quest for higher returns, these fund managers neglected to pay sufficient attention to their reason for existence. To paraphrase Will Rogers, the first job of money market managers is to ensure the return *of* invested capital, not to boost the return *on* invested capital.

It is a confusion of purpose coupled with unrealistic expectations that lead many investors astray. As we move up the investment triangle, other lessons become important. One such lesson is that you have to build the base of the triangle before you can begin hunting for the exciting big game. For a retirement investor, this means securing the ability to pay yourself retirement benefits in cash.

Deciding whether or not to speculate is a difficult call for a retirement investor. If a retirement account is fully funded and the investor has a well-thought-out financial plan, it still might be a poor idea to dabble in exotic investments. The reason is that most people are ill-equipped to deal with speculative investments. Speculative investments are complex. Like a combination lock, many elements have to come together in sequence to unlock the glorious returns. The average investor (as well as many professionals) just does not know how to evaluate the risks and assumptions in speculative investments. Speculative investors also face special emotional adversities that most people do not relish. When a high-powered investment goes funky, the reaction of most speculative investors is to bail out. Such panic almost always ensures a loss. Plus, the average retirement investor's resources are often insufficient to properly monitor speculative investments. In short, there is often little to be gained with a lot to be lost when the retirement investor tries to hunt for big game.

Many of the issues facing Bill apply equally to any investor who has suffered a speculative loss. Setting aside the fact that Bill made the cardinal error of investing at the apex of his investing triangle before building a solid base of conservative investments, once he lost money, what should he do? The answer isn't obvious. The first thing any investor must do is revisit the reason for having made the investment in the first place. What was the deliberative process that accompanied the initial decision? Did the investor buy on impulse after hearing a good "story"? If the investor was sold a bill of goods by an enterprising salesperson, is there sufficient cause to continue to work on the original premise? Or was the sizzle sold instead of the steak? Was a careful and reasoned analysis carried out prior to having made the investment? If so, do the fundamentals remain solid? How comfortable is the investor with the loss? And, if it's uncomfortable to sit on a losing position, how much is this lack of comfort worth, and what are the consequences of the discomfort? Most important, when does the losing asset need to be converted to cash to meet a financial obligation? In other words, will a losing investor be forced to sell the position and realize the loss, or is there the luxury of waiting? And if selling is necessary, will there be a willing buyer ready to buy?

There are other issues that require exploration. Usually, after a loss, the question arises of whether one should put more money into the losing position. The reasons presented for additional investment are varied. In small company stocks, for example, if investors have studied the fundamentals and believe they have not changed, they may end up deciding to put up more money. After all, they reason, the price is now lower than ever. But watch out! This can be a prescription for disaster. To follow this path, after already having lost money, an investor has to be willing to lose even more. And, since generating the money to invest in the first place is so difficult, a losing circumstance may call for caution rather than boldness.

So the message is as it has always been: first things first. Monies in excess of expenses are the only funds available for investment. This money is hard to come by. It doesn't matter if you are an individual or a pension fund, the principle is the same. Rationally, most speculation is hard to defend. Because if you speculate and lose, the consequences can often be hard to stomach, and the hole you dig may be too big to climb out of. So our advice is: Don't do it.

SOLUTION-BASED INVESTING

If the foregoing provides a thoughtful discussion of what it means to be an investor as opposed to being a speculator, then how does contemporary investment theory stack up? Not too well, as it turns out. Prevailing wisdom dictates that investors are supposed to maximize returns against a market index and minimize the volatility of those returns. This view is quite different from the idea of an investor whose purpose is to preserve principal and generate a return that satisfies a human need.

Placing the capital markets at the center of the investment world does nothing to help a retirement investor solve the retirement investing problem. For many, today's capital markets are like a big lazy Susan. Everybody around the table takes things off and puts things back on, in the never ending search for the highest return. Capital markets don't define financial problems—investors do. And when it comes to the retirement problem, it is defined as: building retirement assets when younger, generating withdrawals when retired, and making careful investment and risk management decisions all along the way. What the capital markets provide are raw materials to solve the problem. However, don't confuse the markets with a solution. Contemporary investment theory simply does not address itself to the solving of normal human financial objectives.

Before we get into the particulars of how to develop a retirement investing solution, let's take a look at the overall environment of retirement investing in the United States. All in all, it's not a pretty picture.

OVERVIEW OF RETIREMENT INVESTING IN THE UNITED STATES

Longevity and Inflation

Americans are living longer. The U.S. Census Bureau estimates that males who reach the age of 65 will have a life expectancy of 80 years. Females who reach the age of 65, on average, will have a life expectancy of 84 years. Improvements in diet and lifestyles will probably increase average life spans in the future. Finally, medicine will continue to advance, pushing the average mortality age even further. This increase in longevity has important implications for retirement investing.

By living longer, you could very easily have a prolonged period of retirement, which would increase the chance that you might outlive your retirement assets. This makes it more important than ever to begin your retirement savings and investing immediately, and supports putting as much money away for the future as possible. As we will discuss later, increased longevity also has important implications for how you invest your retirement assets.

Inflation remains another important issue for retirement investing. The United States has seen relatively low inflation during the twentieth century, averaging approximately 3 percent per year. However, as low as this figure seems, 20 years of 3 percent inflation will turn the buying power of $100,000 into $54,379. And, since 1965, the inflation rate has been about 6 percent—double that of the historic average. Twenty years of 6 percent inflation will turn the buying power of $100,000 into $29,011. While the Consumer Price Index may not be an accurate indicator of inflation for any given individual, it does illustrate the corrosive effects that inflation has on the buying power of assets.

The combination of increased longevity and the long-term persistence of inflation produces a troublesome environment for the average retirement investor. If you prepare poorly for these conditions, you may find yourself being unable to retire when you want to, retiring with less than you need, or outliving your retirement assets.

Social Security

Over the last 40 or 50 years, retirement income has come from several distinct sources. The first source is Social Security, which many people consider to be the foundation of their retirement income. That's because most people think of the Social Security System as a type of government pension fund. But Social Security is not really a pension fund at all. There is a popular misconception that Social Security taxes are collected from an individual's paycheck and placed into a special trust fund. This misunderstanding is then compounded by the belief that Social Security retirement benefits are paid from the monies set aside for this purpose in this trust fund.

However, this is not how Social Security works. It is true that there is a Social Security Trust Fund. But the "assets" in this trust fund are simply debts of the U.S. Treasury. If the Social Security Administration were to pay your benefits directly out of the so-called trust fund, it would send you Treasury debts as a substitute for cash benefit payments. If you held these Treasury obligations until they matured, you would expect the government to give you cash. But where would the government get the cash to pay you? Simple—either it would borrow the money from someone else or it would tax the working population to raise cash to pay your benefit.

In point of fact, from the start, Social Security has always been paying the "benefits" of retirees from the taxes collected from those who are not retired. Any excess of taxes collected from the working population is then lent to the U.S. government, which immediately spends these monies.[3] However, the taxes that are spent on retirees' benefits don't merely go away. An entry is made into the books of the Social Security Trust Fund to record the future obligation to the taxpayer. But when the time comes to pay retirement benefits to that taxpayer, the U.S. Treasury must borrow, collect taxes, or print new money to make good on Social Security payments.

The structure of Social Security would not be as much of a problem if you always had enough people in the workforce to foot the bill. Since the inception of Social Security, this has been the case. That is, there have always been enough younger people working to support the older folks who receive Social Security checks. But, on the whole, the American population is getting older. This means that down the demographic road, an increasing number of people are being paid from Social Security than are paying into the system. As the baby-boom generation of people born from 1946 through 1964 continues to age and retire, the demands on Social Security will become increasingly intense. The number of people in the working population will also increase, but not by nearly as much as the increases in the number of people who are retired. Put simply, the Social Security system will not be able to support all those who will demand Social Security payments because there will not be enough working people to foot the bill. And, despite the myths popularized by the media and the politicians, the so-called Social Security Trust Fund does not exist in any real sense. Again, there is no pool of assets waiting to be distributed to you when you retire, apart from the ability of the U.S. government to borrow and tax in order to raise enough money to pay all retired Americans the benefits that have been promised.

Consider the following. In 1950, there were a little more than 12 people of working age for every person over 65 years old. In 1960, there were approximately six Americans of working age for every American over the age of 65. In the year 2030, it is projected that there will be only two workers for every person over the age of 65.[4]

Put another way, the number of beneficiaries per 100 members of the workforce will increase dramatically from the inception of the program in 1945 to the projected level by the year 2030. What's more, this projection (shown in Figure 2.2) is based on the Social Security Administration's intermediate assumptions regarding income, inflation, immigration, fertility, and mortality. The pessimistic assumptions would have each 100 workers supporting 56 beneficiaries by the year 2030. The optimistic assumptions would have each 100 workers supporting 43 beneficiaries by the year 2030. Any way you look at the Social Security problem, the future is not bright.

The implications of this are clear for all those who are planning for their retirement. Barring a major overhaul that includes privatization of Social Security, there will either be large reductions in Social Security benefits or massive increases in Social Security

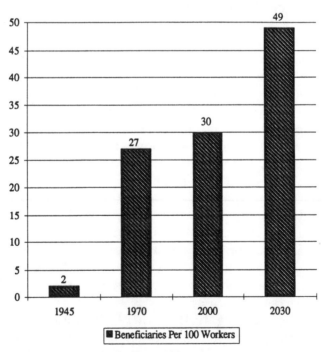

Figure 2.2 Number of Social Security recipients per 100 workers. (SOURCE: Social Security Administration, 1994 Annual Report to the Trustees.)

taxes—or perhaps both. Reductions in benefits could take the form of later retirement ages, smaller retirement payments, income thresholds to qualify for benefits—or a combination of all three.

If present benefits remain unchanged, how many new taxes will be required to pay for Social Security once the baby boomers reach their peak retirement years? Today, Social Security claims 12.4 percent of every payroll, while Medicare costs another 2.9 percent. It has been estimated that these payroll taxes would have to increase until they took 35 percent to 50 percent of all payrolls, just to take care of the retired baby boomers.[5]

There is probably a point at which younger working Americans would protest significantly higher Social Security taxes. Plus, there is a double impact on these younger workers because increased taxes will reduce employees' incomes, thus diminishing their ability to save and invest for their own retirement. Given the political landscape in the United States, it does not appear likely that a resolution to the Social Security problem will be forthcoming any time soon. This lends an additional urgency to the necessity for individuals to take charge of their own retirement investing programs.

Employer-Sponsored Pension Plans

The inevitable decline of Social Security means that prudent individuals should start planning for retirement *now* and try to invest as much as they can. There are other important trends that have profound implications for retirement investing, particularly involving employer-sponsored pension plans. These plans come in two basic varieties: defined-benefit plans and defined-contribution plans.

Defined-benefit pension plans are retirement plans that offer a retirement income guaranteed by a plan sponsor, usually an employer. If the employer is a government, then contributions into these kinds of pension funds come out of tax collections. If the employer is a corporation, then contributions come out of corporate profits.

These plans place the risk of coming up with the cash to pay pensions squarely on the backs of the plan sponsor. Many pension sponsors in the private sector have come to the decision that they are not willing to continue to shoulder the risk of guaranteeing pensions and thus have eliminated or wound down their defined-benefit plans. In 1983, the number of traditional defined-benefit plans was 175,000. By 1990, this number had declined to 113,000, and estimates by actuaries indicate that the number of defined-benefit plans may have dropped to as few as 83,000 by 1993.[6]

In 1974, almost 29 percent of the private sector labor force was covered by a defined-benefit plan. By 1990, that number had dropped to under 21 percent and continues to decline. The decline in the defined-benefit plan has been mirrored by rapid increases in the number of employers offering defined-contribution plans. By the count of the U.S. Department of Labor, from 1984 through 1992 the number of participants in defined-benefit plans decreased by 4.8 million workers, while defined-contribution plans picked up more than 14.9 million new participants.[7]

Defined-contribution plans do not guarantee a fixed retirement benefit to the participant. In the most common of such arrangements, the employee contributes into a retirement account, and the employer matches those contributions up to certain defined limits. Not only is this account the property of the employee, who may choose not to participate, but the employee must also decide how to invest the contributions and bear the consequences of those investing decisions. This choice is made from a group of investment choices offered by the plan.

Defined-contribution retirement plans almost seem designed to set up retirement investors for failure. They do this in several ways.

- First, participation in defined-contribution plans is not automatic or mandatory. Often, employees simply elect not to save and invest anything for their retirement, even when their employer will compensate them to do so.
- Typically, defined-contribution plans are not as generous as defined-benefit plans. Even if the participant elects to save as much as possible and the employer contribution is relatively large, the final retirement benefits will often be lower than they would have been with many defined-benefit plans.
- Defined-contribution plans often allow participants to borrow from their retirement accounts. While this is a popular option, it is also irresponsible. Retirement assets must remain invested over the long term to be able to take advantage of the power of compounding. Borrowing from these accounts defeats their purpose.

- Many defined-contribution participants have difficulty choosing among competing investment alternatives and make investing mistakes that cost them dearly in terms of the size of retirement income they can hope to achieve.

In two important aspects, though, defined-contribution plans are superior to defined-benefit plans. Defined-contribution plans are the private property of the participant. This makes these assets portable: When an individual leaves an employer, he or she can take the retirement account along by rolling it over into an individual retirement account (IRA). However, on average, less than one-third of all employees actually roll over their defined-contribution retirement assets into IRAs once they leave an employer-sponsored retirement plan.[8] Furthermore, because these retirement accounts are private property, they are controlled and directed by their owners who are no longer at the mercy of employer-managed plans. This advantage can be either a blessing or a curse, depending on whether the owners save and invest wisely.

THE IMPORTANCE OF SAVING AND INVESTING CONSISTENTLY

Things seem to move more quickly these days. The rhythms of life have assumed a hectic pace that leaves many of us wondering whether we can keep up. Were things really simpler 30 or 40 years ago than they are today? Or is it just our memories that make them appear that way? It seems as though life's lessons used to come from more traditional and steadfast sources than they do today. Do we really learn the important things from a sound bite on CNN or a three-minute segment on the *Today* show? Probably not. We like to think the time-tested sources of insight offer us more.

Remember the biblical story of Noah? Noah was commanded to build an ark to preserve life on earth during a great flood. It seems that, in those days, folks had gotten off to a bad start, and God meant to set things straight by starting over. Noah's neighbors ridiculed him for building this huge ship when it was obvious that it wasn't really going to rain for 40 days and 40 nights. It is true that it wasn't raining when Noah built the ark. Thus, the night before the rains started, we imagine that most of Noah's neighbors went to sleep entirely satisfied with the state of the weather.

How many of us believe that everyone else needs life's lessons more than we do, or that everything's fine and dandy right up to the minute that it isn't? We guess that's just human nature. Tomorrow does come, though, and you must be ready for it. Simply trying to pile up your assets isn't the same thing as having a plan and a method to save and invest for retirement, and then to actually generate a retirement benefit for yourself. Maximizing returns simply does not meet the financial objective of paying yourself a retirement benefit. They are two interrelated but separate activities.

It may seem elementary, but to be able to invest you must first save. This means you must set aside some of what you earn for future needs and not consume every penny you make as fast as you make it. Money should not burn a hole in your pocket. It is absolutely essential that you begin to save early and then save and invest regularly if you want to achieve retirement security. The longer you wait to begin saving and investing, the harder it is to accumulate enough money to help support you in your retirement. The importance of starting your investment program early cannot be overemphasized. To demonstrate the effect of time and compounding on the value of an investment program, consider the following example.

Suppose two people each want to start a retirement account. The first person, Ann, invests $1,000 per year at an 8 percent annual compound return, starting when she is 25 years old. She continues to invest for a total of ten years until she reaches the age of 35. This means she will have put a total of $10,000 into her retirement account. Her account earns 8 percent per year for each year until she is 65 years old, and she doesn't invest another cent for the entire 30-year period from age 35 to age 65. When Ann turns 65, she will have a total of $167,498 in her account. That is over 16.7 times her original investment of $10,000.

The second person, John, doesn't begin his retirement investing program until he turns 35 years old. At this point, he decides to invest $1,000 per year at 8 percent annual compound return every year until retirement at age 65. This means that John will be investing a total of $30,000 into his retirement account over the course of 30 years. When John turns 65 years old, he has a total of $123,346 in his account, but he has earned only 4.1 times his investment of $30,000. The results of this example are shown in Table 2.1 and Figure 2.3.

Table 2.1 The Importance of Starting to Invest Early in Life

Age	Ann starts at age 25 and invests $1,000/year until she is age 35	John starts at age 35 and invests $1,000/year until he is age 65
35	$ 16,645	$ 1,000
40	24,458	7,336
45	35,936	16,645
50	52,802	30,324
55	77,584	50,423
60	113,996	79,954
65	167,498	123,346

Think about it. Ann invested $10,000 and ended up with $167,498. John invested $30,000 and ended up with only $123,346. Although Ann invested only a third as much money as John, she ends up with 36 percent more dollars in her retirement account at age 65. This is a testament to the power of compounding. What a difference a few years can make. This is a lesson worth remembering.

While it is important to start a retirement investing program early, your first priority must be to accumulate enough savings to

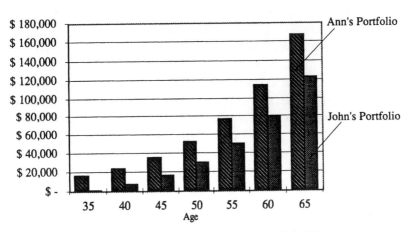

Figure 2.3 The importance of starting to invest early in life.

have cash reserves available if you need them. This will put first things first and get you started off on the right foot. And what matters about this money is that it is safe and available—not how much it will earn. Emergency cash reserves must be safe and liquid.

But savings alone will not help you achieve retirement security. The reason is clear: While your cash reserves are safe, the returns on this money will probably be low. In fact, savings alone rarely outpace inflation, even when inflation is very low. As we will examine later, the only way to keep ahead of inflationary erosion of your money is to invest carefully in high-quality stocks. Investment returns from common stocks do not come free from the risk of loss. However, while both stocks and bonds carry the risk of loss, only investing in common stocks offers the long-term opportunity to outpace inflation through participation in the growth in the earnings of corporate America.

The historically higher long-term compound returns available from common stock investing can actually end up paying for a good deal of your retirement. But this will happen only if you get in the habit of putting money away into your retirement investing account on a regular basis and if you follow a clear and disciplined approach to the management of that account.

Taking Charge of Your Future by Paying Yourself First

What can we conclude about retirement investing in the United States? People are living longer. Inflation exists, and no matter at what level, it will erode the value of retirement assets. Social Security is on shaky ground. Defined-benefit plans are in decline. And for a variety of reasons, ample retirement benefits from defined-contribution plans are less certain to be there when you retire. The conclusion is obvious: To ensure a secure retirement, each individual must take charge of his or her own future.

Taking charge of one's own retirement investing means first learning how to save. In learning how to save, there is nothing as important as learning how to pay yourself first. Sitting down to pay the bills is not fun. There's the rent or mortgage, the electric bill, the telephone bill, the car payment, the insurance bill, and, of course, the credit cards.

For many people, it seems as if there's nothing left over to save. But whenever people have income, they should always put part of it away for later and resist the temptation to spend it all. Even people with modest incomes will have a literal fortune pass through their hands during their working lifetimes. Think about it—a family that averages $35,000 a year in income throughout 40 years of their working lifetime will have earned a total of $1.4 million!

If you find you have no income left to save after you pay the bills, then you must cut back on your expenditures to free up some money for savings. So when you sit down to pay the bills, remember to make a check out to yourself first. The bigger the check, the better, but the amount is not as important as the practice. This means that even a few dollars a week is better than nothing at all because saving money must precede investing it. Now paying yourself first seems like an easy step to take. But to pay yourself first means that you have less money to live on today so that you may have more to live on tomorrow. That means doing all the little things that constitute careful underspending. You can't have everything you want exactly when you want it. You have to adjust today's spending habits to make room for savings that will help support you tomorrow.

If you have trouble putting money aside for your retirement, here are a few tips on how to increase your ability to pay yourself first and then have enough left over to meet your expenses:

- Supplement your income with a part-time job. Encourage your children to take odd jobs such as yard work and baby-sitting and then to pay for as many of their own purchases as possible.
- Ask yourself whether each purchase is what you merely want or what you really need. Buy only what you really need.
- Don't pay for things on credit. You not only end up with high interest payments to make, but you take away from future income by spreading your current expenditures into the future.
- Don't make more than one automatic teller withdrawal per week. The more money you have in your pocket, the more money you will end up spending.
- Don't eat out at restaurants as often. Bring your lunch to work.

- Rent videos instead of going out to the movies frequently.
- Don't spend large sums on extravagant vacations. Drive instead of fly.
- Settle for fewer rounds of golf each season. Don't attend live sports events as frequently.
- Don't purchase or lease an expensive luxury car. Settle for a more moderately priced vehicle. Better yet, try buying a good used car instead of a new one.
- Don't splurge as frequently on new clothes.
- Shop around for the best price for big-ticket purchases, but don't buy something just because it is on sale.
- Whenever possible, make automatic deposits into your retirement account to ensure that you pay yourself first, especially if amounts are withheld from your paycheck.
- If you receive any kind of windfall, resolve to save a portion of it for your retirement.
- If you leave a job and get cashed out of a retirement plan, by all means, roll over the balance into an IRA for yourself.
- If you are carrying high-rate debt from credit cards, do not use the cards until they are fully paid off. Paying credit card balances off is like investing your money and earning 18 percent per year.

And, above all, start now and invest as much as you can as often as you can. Make it part of your financial life. These are obviously just a few suggestions among the multitude of spending habits that define careful underspending. The important point is that you make room in your life for saving money—regardless of your income. An important final note: Once your savings program is established, don't touch it. You have to develop a certain attitude toward this process. Instead of constantly raiding your pool of savings to make purchases, consider leaving the pool alone and starting a separate savings program to put away funds for a purchase you can make with cash. The ability to save and invest varies with age and circumstance. Before we can consider how to invest for retirement, we have to know how these variations impact the overall process. That brings us to the life-cycle theory of savings and consumption.

OVERVIEW OF THE LIFE-CYCLE THEORY OF SAVINGS AND CONSUMPTION

At its core, retirement investing is not just about the capital markets where stocks and bonds are bought and sold. It is also about how investors can meet their retirement investing needs through use of securities purchased in the capital markets.

No single factor is as important in determining an appropriate retirement investing strategy as a person's age. As a matter of law, age-based rules and regulations govern tax-advantaged retirement accounts. However, as a matter of finance and common sense, an age-based approach also allows for tailoring the retirement investment portfolio to the age-specific needs of every retirement investor. Other than age, many other factors in a person's financial situation are extraneous to the retirement investing strategy. These other factors (e.g., financing a child's education, maintaining a household, increases and decreases in income) will influence how much money a person can invest for retirement and when that person is able to invest those monies. However, once money is invested for retirement, most other factors cease to be involved in the analysis.[9]

As people age, so do their retirement investing requirements. These changes are the result of different needs evidenced during different stages in the normal human life cycle. The economist, Franco Modigliani, won the Nobel Prize in 1985 in part for his work on the life-cycle theory of savings and consumption. The main tenet of Modigliani's theory is that humans defer consumption from their younger years to pay for future consumption when they are older. In practice, people do tend to demonstrate this behavior in their savings patterns as they invest for retirement. But the level of savings is not spread evenly across the years. Figure 2.4 illustrates the pattern of human life-cycle savings by tracking the percentage of personal income represented by the personal savings rates of heads of households in the United States.[10]

Extrapolating from the data shown in Figure 2.4, when under the age of 25 most Americans are just entering the workforce or still attending school. They save less than 5 percent of their income. Two factors appear to influence savings and investment behavior during this period in a person's life. First, most young people do not earn very much because they are just entering the workforce.

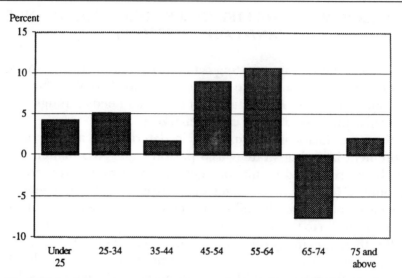

Percent

Figure 2.4 Average personal savings rate by age of household head in the United States.

Additionally, their consumption and savings patterns reflect a similarly low level of expenses.

Between the ages of 25 and 34, people frequently earn more than they did when they were younger. This increased income more than makes up for their increased expenses during this stage of their life cycle. Much of the time, these expenses are associated with the very early stages of household formation, an activity that includes having children as well as purchasing and furnishing a residence. Thus, savings rates rise slightly from the earlier age group and go above 5 percent of income.

The savings situation changes dramatically during the years when most households have growing children. Expenses associated with raising children most dramatically impact the savings rate when the head of the household is between the age of 35 and 44. During these years, expenses rise faster than income, and savings fall to less than 2 percent of income. Once children grow up, however, the situation again changes dramatically. From ages 45 through 64, incomes rise while expenses decline, and the savings rate climbs steeply, to almost 11 percent of income.

However, the savings pattern reverses at retirement, when most people begin to draw down savings and spend more than they save.

During this period, personal savings can be considered as negative. This condition continues until you get to those people over the age of 75. During this period of life, we speculate that aggregate expenses decrease faster than aggregate income, possibly due to the death of a spouse or a move to less-expensive housing.

This normal human life-cycle pattern of savings and consumption is shown in terms of the amount of assets in a typical retirement account in Figure 2.5.

The asset balances in a typical retirement account change during a lifetime of saving and investing. Broadly speaking, the retirement account has two major periods. The first period is when you are earning money and saving for retirement. The second period is when you have retired and are spending the money that you have saved during your working life. As noted above, during your earning years, your ability to save and invest varies, depending on your life circumstances. Once you retire, not only does your savings capacity drop off, but you begin to draw down on the retirement account that has taken a lifetime to build.

Figure 2.5 is not meant to be an illustration of everyone's exact life circumstance. For instance, some people do not have children. These people should not have as much difficulty saving when in their 30s and 40s as those who do have children. Plus, most folks

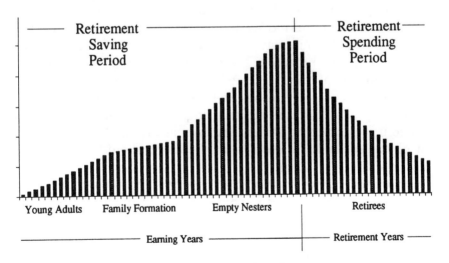

Figure 2.5   Asset balances in a typical life-cycle retirement account.

have ups and downs in their incomes depending on their employment situations. So, while Figure 2.5 does not take into account individual variations in the human life cycle, the general pattern holds true for the vast majority of people.

TYPICAL APPROACH TO RETIREMENT INVESTING

The implications of human life-cycle patterns of savings and consumption are important to consider when investing for retirement. The first and most important implication is the commonality of economic circumstance among people of widely varying backgrounds when retirement investing is considered. This commonality stems from the similarity of age-based events experienced during the course of normal human lives. These common elements circumscribe the problem of successful retirement investing.

The solution to the retirement investing problem requires that people build retirement assets when younger, generate sufficient withdrawals when retired, and make careful asset allocation and risk management decisions during every phase of their life cycles. Moreover, each retirement investor must accomplish this task in a way that is consistent with his or her ability to generate sufficient income for savings and investment.

Figure 2.6 illustrates a common experience many people go through when thinking about the problem of retirement investing. The pre-retirement period is often considered to be a single period of time, in which an investment objective consists of trying to outperform the capital markets. But this approach does not fully consider the impact of time or the ability to save relative to either losses or investment choices. During pre-retirement, many investors have no strategy at all. Others select a single investment strategy and stick to it over a period of decades, even as they go through different phases of their life cycles and, therefore, should be adjusting their investing accordingly.

Approximately five years before retirement, people typically confront the reality of their retirement finances for the first time. Practically nobody intends to wait until they are so close to retirement before they consider the problem more carefully. But that's what happens just the same. People get lost in their busy lives and time seems to slip by without notice. Before you know it, you are 60 years

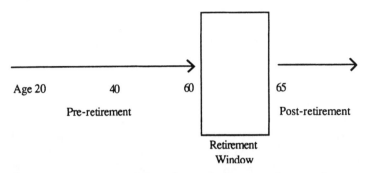

Figure 2.6 Conceptualizing the typical approach to retirement investing.

old and finally ready to seriously consider what specific resources you can count on when you retire. When facing this retirement window, many folks discover that now their glass looks half empty when, just a short time before, they were sure the glass was half full. Often, a sense of urgency will accompany contemplation of the retirement window, brought about by the pressing desire to make up for lost time and opportunity.

The problem with this approach is that by the time someone is five years from retirement, it is too late to accomplish much in the capital markets. Waiting until this period in one's life to address retirement often results in making bad investments by reaching for extraordinary returns. That's a fool's game—it just won't work, and it may leave you far worse off than when you started because of losses that can result from speculating. It is much more prudent to begin building retirement wealth earlier in your life (even if it means making small investments), to allow time and patient compounding to work to one's benefit. But if you can't begin saving and investing early on, then the best thing to do is to stay with sound investments that will produce realistic returns. This is the only wise choice if you find yourself in the unenviable position of not being prepared for retirement. Remember, most full-time investment professionals don't earn above-average returns, so why do you think you can?

Judging from an historic perspective, even waiting until the retirement window to begin generating cash can be dangerous. Since 1926, there have been seven five-year periods when stock market losses have occurred, with the worst loss for a five-year period being 11.2 percent of the value held at the beginning of the period. If you had had 3 percent per year inflation during that period (the historic average), your stock holdings would be worth a total of 27 percent less than they were at the start of a five-year retirement window.

A common misconception is the assumption that you can wait until you reach the retirement window to move aggressively and quickly to sell stocks to raise money to buy bonds that will generate income to pay retirement living expenses. But this is shortsighted and misguided. The demographic reality is that all too many Americans will be approaching retirement age during the first decade of the twenty-first century. With everyone heading for the doors at once, it may be virtually impossible to abruptly shift a portfolio out of long-term stock investments into income-producing investments or cash.

By waiting until you get to the retirement window to position your portfolio to generate more cash, you are assuming that stock market prices will be favorable when it comes time to sell some of your long-term equity holdings for cash to buy bonds that will generate a retirement income. If, when you get to retirement, the stock market is in a prolonged slump, you may be forced to take a loss in an effort to generate the cash you require. This loss of retirement capital could well be impossible to replace, and the only option left to the investor would be to accept a lower retirement lifestyle. Finally, adding insult to injury, when retirement capital is diminished, there is not only a smaller asset base to live on, but the potential for future compound gains and income is gone forever, as well.

While many people simply arrive at the retirement window without having prepared themselves for retirement, other people plan carefully. Many folks find this planning effort to be daunting enough to hire a professional financial advisor to guide them through the process. That process usually takes the following form:

- You and your financial advisor choose a target amount of retirement income. Most financial planners suggest using 65 percent to 80 percent of your working-age income, but the actual target will depend on the maintenance of a realistic standard of living, given your circumstances.

- You and your financial advisor calculate estimated annual income from defined-benefit retirement plans (if any) and from estimated Social Security payments. Estimated Social Security benefits are available from the Social Security Administration. It may be wise to reduce these estimates of annual benefits by at least 30 percent to 40 percent to account for the probable decrease that will occur.
- You and your financial advisor can calculate the number of years until you plan to retire and the number of years from this date to the end of your life expectancy. Take whatever retirement investments you now have and assume a rate of return between 6 percent and 10 percent per year, depending on the mixture of investments you have. Adjust both your investment portfolio and your targeted retirement income by your expectation of average annual inflation (somewhere between 4 percent and 7 percent per year seems reasonable).
- You and your financial advisor calculate how much you would need to save, on a tax-deferred basis, to make up for the expected shortfall between your present retirement investment portfolio and what you need to augment your other retirement income.

Upon doing these calculations, the average person often finds out that it is necessary to save between 15 percent and 25 percent of current income to achieve the retirement objectives. At the high end of this range, this is simply more money than most people are able to devote to retirement, underscoring the need to begin saving and investing for retirement early.

But important as this planning process may be, it does not provide a disciplined and consistent method for attainment of your desired goal. This conventional method of planning helps define your destination and tells you how much you might have to save and invest to get there. However, there are a number of other important things it does not cover. It does not tell you how to define the retirement problem or how to structure your retirement account to properly use the capital markets to your advantage. It does not tell you how to adjust your investing to match your life-cycle requirements. To understand what a fully defined and structured approach looks like or where to begin, one must understand the underlying first principles of retirement investing itself.

THREE

An Introduction to the Capital Market Tools Used in Life-Cycle Retirement Investing

FIRST PRINCIPLES

The investment world probably has a greater number of specialties than even the medical world. Each specialty has proponents and detractors who debate narrowly framed issues of risk and return. This means that the specialist in, say, a small biotechnology company has hardly anything at all in common with the expert who specializes in European bond futures. This specialization has led to the decline of the generalist who draws lessons from many different corners of the investment world. A parallel development to the decline of the generalist is a decline in the appreciation and understanding of what might best be called *the first principles of investing*.

A first principle is an idea that serves as a foundation for other ideas. First principles are basic truths. Any disciplined and sober retirement investing process must be built around what might be considered as the first principles of retirement investing. The most important first principle of investing is that the investor's human financial objective must be served by the investment operation. A human financial objective is always expressed in human terms, not financial terms. For example, saving and investing to finance your retirement at age 65 is a human financial objective. Seeking to generate an 11 percent total return from investing in domestic stocks is a capital markets financial objective. This distinction is important because only human financial objectives give meaningful purpose to an investment operation. This means that what is important in retirement investing is defining the problem and solving it in human terms. The retirement investing universe must be centered on human beings and not solely on the capital markets or on higher returns.

By *investment operation,* we mean the entire process of investing. This process is what must serve the investor's human financial objective. Simply generating a higher rate of return, for example, may or may not serve the objective of the exercise. Simply doing better than the markets or better than other investors does not necessarily mean that you are doing things in a way that will ultimately get you where you want to go. At heart, every investment objective depends on when you need to use the invested money or the income from it and the consequences for not having the required money or income when it is needed.

The first principles of retirement investing provide the rationale for the selection of stocks and bonds, the proper assessment and management of risk, and the appropriate allocation of assets. These first principles involve elements of time, the ability to save and invest, the ability to take on risk, the imposition of an organized and disciplined process to achieve the desired result, and the importance of tax deferment. The desired result is to try to build and protect retirement wealth when younger and then to preserve that wealth while simultaneously generating retirement income when retired. These five first principles are interrelated. Each one conditions the retirement investing process. Let's consider these principles one by one.

Time

Time is the single most important element involved in retirement investing. It imposes itself on all investment decisions. Some of the time-related issues you should consider are:

- How old are you? How much time do you have before you will retire?
- What age will you be when you retire? How long do you estimate that you will need to rely on your sources of retirement income?
- How much is invested in your retirement portfolio and when did you invest these monies?
- How much time does your investment portfolio have to compound itself and grow?
- If you lose principal, income, or purchasing power during any part of your retirement investing process, how much time will it take to make up for those investment losses?

Ability to Save and Invest

Where are you in your life cycle? If you are young, you may have more time, but you may not have the ability to generate a lot of money for investment. If you are older, you may have more savings capability, but you have less time before your retirement. If you are already retired, how do you avoid outliving your retirement portfolio while managing the risks associated with not having regular income from employment?

Risk

Risk involves loss and the consequence of loss. Loss comes in three varieties: loss of income, loss of principal, and loss of purchasing power from inflation. The questions retirement investors face concern how risk is manifested at each point in their life cycles and how they actually deal with it.

A Disciplined Process

An organized and disciplined process is important in building a solid retirement investing program. "Make sure you arrive alive" might be a good guide to follow. This requires a steady and patient outlook. A consistent, disciplined effort will yield better results than chasing after every rainbow. Fads, hot tips, market timing, and running with the crowd are all contrary to the organized and disciplined process required for good results. Slow, patient compounding is more valuable than all the brilliant market analysts in the world. Remember who won the race between the tortoise and the hare.

The Impact of Taxes

No discussion of the first principles of retirement investing would be complete without a mention of taxes. Next to inflation, taxes are the largest single obstacle to a successful long-term investing program. Most retirement accounts have a special tax-deferred status that allows investment income and gains to compound tax-free until they are withdrawn.

This tax-deferred status provides a huge benefit to the retirement investor. Consider the illustration shown in Figure 3.1. Suppose starting at age 25 you invest $1,000 every January 1 in an account that earned an 8 percent total rate of return, which was taxed at a 31 percent rate. Next, suppose you invested in the same account on a tax-deferred basis.

Figure 3.1 demonstrates what an enormous benefit the tax-deferred account would have over the taxable account by the time you reach the age of 65. Put into plain dollar terms, the tax-deferred account is almost double the value of the taxable account. This means that, whenever possible, you should take the fullest advantage of tax-deferred retirement investment programs. This is true regardless of whether you invest before-tax money or after-tax money.

THE TWO PRINCIPAL ASSET CLASSES AND THEIR HISTORICAL RETURNS

The other morning we had to take the New Jersey Transit train to New York City. We usually drive to Trenton from Pennsylvania to get

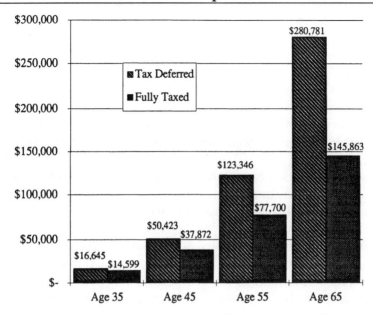

Figure 3.1 Taxable retirement account versus tax-deferred retirement account.

into the city at a reasonable hour. The 6:15 from Trenton never ceases to amaze us. The typical commuting grunt has an executive lunch box (briefcase), a small cup of coffee to ease the pain of the early hour, a bagel, and a newspaper to help shut out the world. These rail jockeys just want to get where they are going and get there as undisturbed as possible.

As any commuter sooner or later finds out, sometimes a person who wants to talk sits next to you. These people can't stand to ride in silence; the temptation to talk is just too great. Well, it was our lucky day. There we were, in the seats that go three across, when a young man in a power tie sat down. Yup, we now had the great good fortune to be stuck next to Pete "the power broker" Hobbs. As it turns out, Pete is the consummate securities salesperson. The guy lives by the "three foot rule"—anybody within three feet gets a pitch. Mr. Hobbs proceeded to brighten up our day by commenting on the weather and then introducing himself.

"Hi guys, I'm Pete Hobbs with First Brokerage."

Now, we understand the rules of the game in the securities sales business. Every salesperson has to have something to sell. And securities salespeople are always selling the next big thing. Knowing full well that it would be like throwing meat to the hungry lion, we said the magic words, "So, Pete, what are you selling these days that's hot?"

Pete was off and running. "Well guys, you just don't know from day to day. But the market seems to have been rolling through various sectors over the last few years. And, to really make money, you have to be in the right place at the right time. You do this by getting into stock groups that will derive value from the next market trend. This way the market can produce outstanding returns for you. Our research group has done some innovative work in coming up with a method to identify the groups that will next benefit from market movements. This idea is simple, but it works."

Next, like any good salesperson, Pete tried a trial close on us. "So you guys look like you play the market. Can I call you with some specific recommendations?"

The rest of this vignette isn't worth discussing, but later we reflected on this little chat with Pete Hobbs. What was bothering us was the idea that markets "produce" returns for investors. Somehow, this didn't quite make sense. How can markets produce returns? They don't make anything. Markets merely provide a forum where value can be exchanged. That's all. The notion that markets produce returns is simply foolish.

Later, while back in our offices, a research report on a certain biotech company happened to arrive. As fate would have it, this report came on the same day the newspaper was reporting the failure of the company's flagship product to generate clinically significant results. The stock was valued at $15 per share before the announcement and at $5 afterward. The funny thing is that the reality of the company's clinical trials hadn't changed. What had changed was the perception that the trials would succeed or fail. It wasn't the market that produced the perception of value, it was the market reflecting the reality of the clinical trials. This is an easy concept to forget when you are involved in the securities business. The market itself seems to produce gains and losses. But it doesn't. The real value that gives meaning to Wall Street's gains and losses is generated outside Wall Street.

Yes, there are traders, arbitrageurs, and derivatives wonks who feed solely upon the market. But they, too, are entirely dependent on the real world outside the securities markets. The world where goods and services are delivered to people. The world where companies must sell those goods and services for more than it costs to deliver them to the customer. The world where companies must eventually pay dividends to their shareholders to maintain their loyalty. It is true that, in the short run, both individual stocks and entire markets go up and down for reasons related to psychology and emotion. In the long run, however, markets must revolve on a wobbly orbit around the real world and not the other way around.

Try telling this to Pete Hobbs. To him and the legions of like-minded market addicts, the market is the mysterious beast that delivers a reward or refuses to do so. Nonsense, we say. Markets are made up of people who are interested in buying or selling something. The ultimate value of that something resides elsewhere. It is true that the market is the final arbiter of the price obtained in each sale. But don't confuse the true locus of value.

Alright, you say, what's an investor to do about this? The best remedy is not to worship the market itself. Don't get hung up on the popular idea that it is the market mechanism itself that adds the most significant value to securities. However important the price-setting and liquidity-giving features of the market may be, it is merely a collection of human beings buying and selling pieces of debt and ownership—nothing more, nothing less.

Financial markets are notoriously unpredictable, especially in the short run. Over the long term, however, buyers and sellers of securities have experienced average financial returns related to the fundamental characteristics of the securities bought and sold. Financial historians have long noted that different types of securities have distinctly different investment characteristics, on average and over the long haul. But averages hide unsettling periods of ups and downs that can last for years. Given these uncertainties, it is important to understand which are the right kind of securities to achieve the desired result in a retirement investment portfolio and when to use them.

Figure 3.2 shows average returns from the five fundamental classes of securities during the period from 1926 to 1994.[1] However, the illustration of total annual compound returns illustrated in Figure 3.2 does not even begin to tell the whole story. Each type of security has its own special characteristics, especially with respect to the risk of loss.

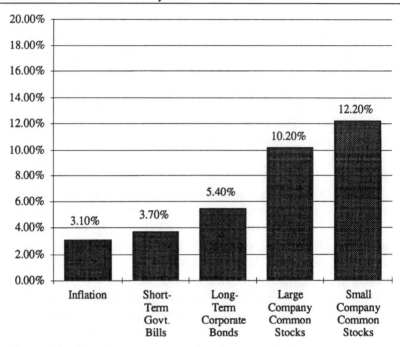

Figure 3.2 Historic average annual total returns, 1926 to 1994. (SOURCE: Ibbotson Associates, Inc.)

To understand the implications of Figure 3.2, we must first understand the basics of stocks and bonds. Ownership is sometimes called *equity* or, simply, *stock.* Broadly speaking, there are two kinds of stock: common stock and preferred stock. When people speak of stock, they are usually referring to common stock. As a group, common stockholders own the corporation that issued the stock.

Most common stock that is traded in the stock market was first sold by an issuing corporation sometime in the past. Corporations sell stock to the public to raise capital and to provide liquidity for their shareholders. However, once shares of stock are issued by the corporation and registered with the regulators, they become available to be bought and sold by third-party investors in the marketplace.

The stock market itself consists of a number of physical locations known as *exchanges,* as well as several computer networks operated to serve as electronic markets. The New York Stock Exchange and the American Stock Exchange are the largest and most important of the exchanges, although there are other, smaller regional exchanges located in cities such as Boston, Chicago, Philadelphia, and Los Angeles. These exchanges are places where buyers and sellers come together to trade stocks through intermediaries who work on the trading floor of the exchange. The stocks traded on these exchanges are said to be *listed* stocks and must meet minimum qualifying standards to be eligible to be traded.

The largest electronic market is known as the NASDAQ system, an acronym for the National Association of Securities Dealers Automated Quotation. This network provides securities brokers and dealers with price quotations both for certain listed securities as well as for the so-called over-the-counter, or OTC, stocks. OTC stocks are those that are not traded on the exchanges. Historically, OTC stocks were of smaller companies that did not meet the listing requirements of the exchanges. Today, however, OTC stocks traded on the NASDAQ systems are often of very large corporations that have chosen not to be listed on the exchanges.

Daily quotations for the stock market are often provided on the evening news or in the morning newspaper. Most commonly, this daily quotation cites the value derived from a calculation involving stocks of the Dow Jones Industrial Average. This index tracks the ups and downs of share prices of 30 large American corporations. It is too small to be truly representative of the market for domestic stocks in general, so the more widely used measurement of share prices for American corporations is found in the Standard and Poor's 500 Index (sometimes known as the S&P 500). This index is calculated by the Standard and Poor's Corporation, from which it derives its name. The S&P 500 Index is not based on the 500 largest companies in the country. It is not even made up entirely of domestic companies because it includes a small number of foreign firms. Instead, it is based on the 500 mostly large companies deemed by Standard & Poor's to be most representative of publicly traded domestic equities. There are numerous other indexes that track many other segments of the stock market.

Debt is sometimes called *fixed income* or simply known as *bonds*. Bonds represent the contractual promise to repay a loan made by a bondholder, usually to a corporation or a governmental entity. Most of these loans mature in a period that ranges from 1 to 30 years.

Debt is bought and sold after being issued by the debtor. Unlike the stock market, though, there is no organized exchange or single computer system where bond buyers and sellers can readily obtain pricing information on an entire universe of qualifying securities. Instead, the bond market consists largely of bond dealers who buy bonds for their own inventory and sell them out of their inventory to customers. Despite the lack of market information about bonds, indexes have also been constructed to track representative average bond price and yield movements for given types of bonds.

Debt securities also include very short term obligations that mature in days, weeks, or, at most, a few months. These short-term investments are sometimes called *money market securities*. Money market securities are traded like bonds and do not have an organized exchange or computer system as such. Often, U.S. Treasury bills that mature in 30 days are used to track average money market returns.

FUNDAMENTAL DIFFERENCES IN THE PATTERN OF RETURNS OF STOCKS AND BONDS

Asset allocation is how you divide up your money among investment alternatives. As previously discussed, these investment alternatives involve two broad classes of investments: ownership and debt. Ownership in corporations is bought and sold in the form of shares of stock. Debt issued by corporations and governments is bought and sold in the form of bonds. There are many subspecies of these two main types of assets, but they are all based on either ownership, debt, or a combination of the two.

There is unanimity among investment professionals that the most important financial decision you can make as an investor is how your money is split up between stocks and bonds. Studies have suggested that 91.5 percent of all return in a diversified portfolio of securities will be determined by the asset allocation, while only 8.5 percent will be due to the selection of individual stocks or bonds.[2] Put another way, picking the best stocks and bonds is not as critical as picking the right proportion of stocks and bonds in your investment portfolio.

Historically, stocks have outperformed bonds. From time to time, though, you can lose a lot of money in the stock market, because it is susceptible to unpredictable ups and downs. And some categories of stocks are riskier than other categories. In general, larger companies with solid histories of paying consistent dividends are less risky than smaller, non-dividend-paying stocks. That's because cash dividends act as a cushion to falling prices. But, regardless of whether there is a dividend, all stocks are subject to decreases in price and to periods of no appreciable increases. What's more, these price decreases and flat periods can last for years and years. Figure 3.3 compares the maximum positive and negative ranges of total returns for stocks over holding periods of varying length from 1926 through 1994. This chart shows that, at least from an historic perspective, for the domestic large-capitalization stocks that make up the S&P 500 Index, there have been certain 10-year periods of losses in the stock market, but no such 15-year periods.

Since record keeping began in 1926, there has never been a 15-year-long period where stocks produced a cumulative negative total return. During shorter periods of time, though, losses in the market value of stocks can be substantial. During one particularly bad year,

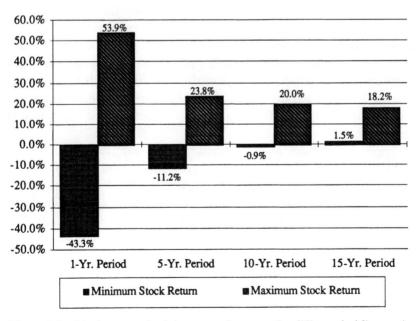

Figure 3.3 Maximum and minimum stock returns for different holding periods, 1926 to 1994.

the stock market lost 43.3 percent of its value. The worst loss during a five-year holding period was 11.22 percent.

We must keep two factors in mind when considering the analysis of historic market returns. First, one cannot overemphasize the devastating impact of stock market losses experienced from 1929 through 1932. These four years of losses reduced overall values of stocks by a total of 64 percent and thus shaped the historic data significantly. Following this period, Congress passed a number of laws designed to prevent a recurrence of the capital market problems of this era. To date, there have been no similarly deep losses experienced by stock market investors. There have been other painful periods, however. The five-year prewar period of 1937 through 1941 reduced stock values by 32 percent, and the two-year period of 1973 and 1974 saw a reduction of value of 37 percent. So losses in the stock market can be painful. And almost as painful as an outright loss is a pattern of returns that delivers a rate of return far below one's expectations. For example, during the ten-year period from 1969 through 1978, you would have made a paltry 3.16 percent by investing in the S&P 500, and earning even this small return would have been a wild ride.

We must remember that nobody can predict the future course of the stock market. We cannot be certain that market forces won't once again plunge stock valuations into negative territory for an extended period of time. Merely because we have seen only three negative one-year periods during the last 20 years is no guarantee that we will not experience a multiple-year decline of major proportions in the future. It has happened before and it could happen again.

Figure 3.4 illustrates the comparison of the maximum positive and negative ranges of total returns for bonds over holding periods of varying length from 1926 through 1994. It shows that, at least from an historic perspective, for domestic high-quality corporate bonds that make up the Salomon Long-Term Corporate Bond Index, there have been five-year periods of negative returns but no such ten-year periods.

The market value of bonds fluctuates in accordance with interest rate movements. Thus, in periods of rising interest rates, bond investing can also produce losses in the value of your investment. Prices of long-term bonds fluctuate more than the prices of short-

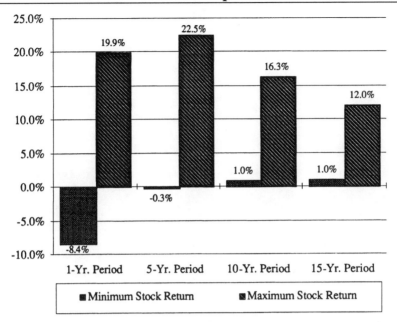

Figure 3.4 Maximum and minimum bond returns for different holding periods, 1926 to 1994.

term bonds. And, just as with stocks, the total return from bonds can be negative for years at a time. However, even though bonds can produce negative returns for prolonged periods, when they do drop in value, they do not tend to go down as far, or for as long, as stocks.

59

FOUR

Capital Market Tools Used in Life-Cycle Retirement Investing—Stock Investing

WHAT WE WON'T DO for our kids. One recent weekend, we spent uncounted hours at a two-day swim meet watching young swimmers compete in an invitational tournament. Saturday and Sunday morning consisted of multiple preliminary heats in each event, with the evenings reserved for the finals. For those swimmers who qualified for the finals, this arrangement makes for a long day. The parents spend the time in between their children's events in various pursuits. Some read. Some try to catch up on office work. Some volunteer to work the meet. Others are engaged in taking care of nonswimming children. We read, worked, and volunteered.

Our reading material was about Benjamin Graham, the well-known father of securities analysis and value investing. It seems that

Graham was quite the financial sleuth. During the 1920s, financial information about publicly traded companies was not always readily available. This was an age that saw the first wave of federal laws and regulations governing the timeliness, scope, and accuracy of financial information provided to investors. In general, financial information moved slowly, if at all.

Interestingly, in the absence of a Securities and Exchange Commission, accurate financial information about railroads and oil pipelines was available only from the Interstate Commerce Commission. By studying documents available from the ICC, Graham peered into the balance sheets of an oil pipeline company in an in-depth fashion not otherwise possible. Graham saw that this firm was dramatically overreserved for obligations due on its outstanding bonds, having enough marketable securities on hand to cover interest and principal payments ten times over.

To Ben Graham, these excess reserves represented a unique investment opportunity. After loading up on shares of the stock in question, Graham began agitating the pipeline company to pay out its excess hoard of cash as a special dividend. The company resisted the efforts of Graham, who was viewed with suspicion as a meddler. Ultimately, after a two-year fight, Graham won two seats on the company's board and from that vantage point persuaded the company to pay out a special dividend to its shareholders.

In Graham's day, information was not as readily available as it is today, to put it mildly. Now, we not only have a regulatory apparatus that demands full disclosure of material financial information concerning publicly traded companies, we also have technologies that spit out information across the globe at the speed of light. Talk about a big change from the days of yore!

After we read about Ben Graham and his use of ICC financial information, it was time to go to work on the main deck of the pool. It's incredible how even small regional meets are held in pools with computerized timing. The starter will start each race with an electronic tone and a simultaneous flash from a strobe. There are touch pads on the wall at the end of each lane. At the finish of every race, a swimmer hits the touch pad and stops the clock. Each lane has three backup timers, as well as two finish judges who write down the order of finish as they see it. However, because of the computerized timing devices, both finish judges and lane timers are redundant. They are there solely to back up the computer, which, on balance, is a very good thing. These races are often decided in terms of mere hundredths of a second, too short an interval for any human judge to accurately assess.

Instantly following each heat, time and place information is displayed on a large electronic board. Everyone knows what happened right away. These computer-timed meets are a far cry from the days when runners had to pick up time sheets from each lane, give these slips to a scoring table, and then wait for the judges to average the times and determine the winner. The old system not only took longer, it was not as accurate. Human timers, no matter how experienced, have to see the finish in their lane, process the information in their brains, and then send a message to their stopwatch finger to depress the button. And, even though digital stopwatches are far more accurate than their mechanical predecessors, the human element can add to or subtract from a swimmer's time as much as a half of a second. This can mean the difference between winning and losing.

There are other big changes in the sport of swimming besides the widespread use of computerized timing. Swimmers train harder than they used to. Just look at the times recorded for each event. They continue to go down year after year. But—and this is important—the times do not usually come down by more than a few tenths of a second for each new world record established. In fact, it's far more common to see a record beaten by a few hundredths of a second than by a few tenths of a second. This means that not only is the information about each race getting more and more accurate, but swimmers are getting more and more competitive. Swimming strokes are becoming more refined all the time, and training methods continue to improve. If you think this sounds a lot like what is happening in the capital markets, you're right.

In Benjamin Graham's day, opportunities to take advantage of distortions in the capital markets were far more abundant than they are today. Graham could take advantage of these situations for two reasons. First, fundamental corporate and capital market information was not only disseminated slowly, it was often either incomplete, inaccurate, or both. And second, there were far fewer people who spent their time poring over these matters, panning for gold. Thus, when effort and insight were applied diligently, an intelligent investor could exploit investment opportunities far more readily than is the case today.

Consider that, of the 383 general stock mutual funds with ten-year records, only 79 outperformed the S&P 500 Index.[1] This reflects the widespread data that show most professional money managers fail to beat the market averages. That these professionals do not beat the market is not because they are lazy or uninformed. In fact, there are probably more bright and hardworking professionals in the money management business than ever, and they clearly have command over better and faster information sources all the time. Yet it has not measurably improved their ability to beat the averages. There are probably several reasons for this, some of them structural and some of them emotional.

On the structural side, we have to consider the fact that conventional securities analysis has come up on pretty much of a dead end in the average analyst's ability to take consistent long-term advantage of distortions in market pricing of securities. Information is not evenly distributed, but it is generally evenly available. Thus, it is less and less possible for someone to consistently "discover" undervalued securities, in the traditional sense of the phrase. There is simply too much competition and too much available information about companies and their securities to obtain a distinct informational advantage.

Graham published his book, *Security Analysis,* in 1934. Forty-two years later in 1976, he was giving a seminar on investing and talked about having revised his opinions. He said, "I am no longer an advocate of elaborate techniques of security analysis in order to find superior investment opportunities. This was a rewarding activity, say, forty years ago, when our textbook Graham and Dodd was published: but the situation has changed a good deal since then. In the old days, any well-trained security analyst could do a good professional job of selecting undervalued issues through detailed studies; but in light of the enormous amount of research now being carried on, I doubt whether in most cases such extensive efforts will generate sufficiently superior selections to justify their cost."[2]

On the emotional side, we find professionals and amateurs alike ride an emotional roller coaster when it comes to managing their investments. This is because most investors lack investing patience. Investors don't understand that returns are built slowly over time, just as companies are. Today, many investors are like children. They can't wait for what they want. They must have it now. This is the perfect recipe for emotional investing. Furthermore, most investors do not have a sound investing discipline. They wander from investing idea to investing idea, relying on their intuition. They have placed so much of themselves into each investing decision they make that they have trouble applying consistent and unemotional judgment to the process.

This is not to say that one cannot make money exploiting informational distortions in the current investment era. People do it all the time. It's just that it is nowhere near as easy as it used to be when information was less evenly distributed, less fully disclosed, and used by far fewer people. However, when you listen to the professionals, all you hear is about how great and wonderful their investment returns are. How does this happen? How is it that eight out of ten money managers do not beat the averages, yet they all claim to have special power and insight to select winning investments?

We have a friend who has spent some 31 years in the financial industry. He owns and operates a Florida-based brokerage firm that services both institutional customers and wealthy individuals. The hallmark of his firm is execution management. This is the little-known science of how to protect customers' rear ends when they place orders to buy or sell securities. This winter, our friend invited us to go fishing in Florida. And, since it was so darn awful cold, we left in quite a hurry.

This guy has a nice place in Palm City. His house sits against one of those waterways that lead to "Bass Heaven." All you have to do is walk out the back door and climb in the boat. It's that easy. So, bright and early one morning, we all headed out to fish. Of the three of us, only our friend is a truly experienced fisherman, but even he is partial to using a fish finder, a sonar device used to locate fish. After all, he reminded us, if you don't have fish in the water under your boat, the only thing you'll catch is sunburn.

Fishing takes patience. You have to wait for the fish to bite. During these lulls, the talk turns to sports, women, and finally business (usually in that order). We had just gotten onto the subject of business when our broker friend popped off with a classic. "You know guys," he said, "fish finders are a lot like stock pickers." Now that's the kind of comment that caught our attention. "Look," he said, "fish finders scan the water for fish. Stock pickers try to find stocks that beat the market. Trouble is, just because you're positive you see a lunker on the screen doesn't mean you're going to be able to catch him." We thought about that for a while, and the more we considered the matter, the better this analogy sounded. Anglers can't look at the fish finder screen and say, "That's the one I'm going to catch." Similarly, just because stock pickers have a bunch of stocks on their screens doesn't mean they will be able to land only big ones either. The truth is that, while stock pickers like to brag about their stock-picking prowess as if they had pinpoint accuracy, they're really fishing with a relatively small net that picks up all manner of sea life, including—they hope—a few big ones. It seems that stock pickers are no more able to pinpoint the big fish under their boats than anglers can catch only the big fish by using fish finders.

There are a lot of investors who are mesmerized by the great mutual fund stock picker's self-proclaimed prowess. We are told they have great fish finders to track down and spear their wily prey. But, deny it though they may, they fish with nets, not with spear guns. So, when your favorite big-cheese stock picker proudly displays his or her bucket of big ones, just remember that another 10 or 11 buckets were probably left at home holding all dinkers, crabs, and seaweed.

However, if money managers don't usually beat the market and if classical investment methodology has squeezed about as much as possible from Benjamin Graham's methods of fundamental analysis, how does one go about investing in stocks?

In our view, stock investing is merely part of a larger tapestry of investing activity. While there is nothing inherently wrong with trying to improve investment returns, this pursuit should not be separated from the purpose for which the activity is being undertaken. In the context of getting the job done, every investment operation must be undertaken with the full understanding of the impact of time, the ability to generate dollars for investment, and the nature of one's assets and liabilities. This is the natural course for the evolution of investing: defining the problem so it can be solved and then solving it. Benjamin Graham's methods are still correct, and his time-tested principles live on. They are just as valid today as when he formulated them 60 years ago. But the world has changed. Today, circumstances force investors to search for a larger purpose than simply hunting up undervalued securities. Modern investing must incorporate the boundaries of its purpose. To do otherwise is not only futile, but leads nowhere in particular (except, perhaps, to getting lost). If we do not invest with a purpose, we are on a relativistic and unconnected search for returns where one can only hope it will all work out in the end.

So how can we begin to understand how stock investing fits into the overall picture? First we have to go back to the fundamentals. We have to delve into that which is true about stocks. We have to strip them down to their basic components and ask the hard questions.

Over the last 70 years, the total returns from stocks (the return coming both from share price increases and dividend income) have been higher than the total returns from bonds. But—and this is important—stock prices have been known to be flat for years, and to decline precipitously from time to time. It is the unpredictability of stock price movements that makes equity securities hard to understand and at times difficult to deal with. It's not surprising that the stock market seems mysterious to many people. When you own a share of stock, you own a small piece of a company. But in and of itself, why would somebody want to own a small piece of a company? What is it about a stock that gives it value? This is the most fundamental—but rarely asked—question about stock investing.

COMPONENTS OF STOCK VALUE—WHAT DO YOU HAVE TO SHOW FOR YOUR MONEY?

The question most investors ask is, "What do I buy?" If you don't believe us, go to an investment seminar sometime. What you will see at these seminars are investors trying to figure out what to do with their money. Audience members will listen politely and then ask the presenter, "OK. I understand what you are saying. So what should I buy?" This suggests that investment education and information may not be what the average person wants. But there is another problem with investment seminars. Too often they present product knowledge and market developments as investment wisdom. In reality, nothing could be further from the truth. Product knowledge and market predictions don't help average investors and may even leave them more confused.

So how does one gain access to investment wisdom? In our opinion, this type of understanding comes only by studying the first principles of stock investing: Why invest in common stock and what creates value in them? Now we freely admit that talk of first principles sounds a bit highfalutin. But it isn't. It's just good common sense to start at the beginning and work your way forward through a problem.

One of the jobs that face parents is teaching their children the value of money. Most parents give their kids a small allowance and assign chores to earn it. The object of this exercise is simple—money must be earned and spent wisely. Learning to spend money wisely is one of the most difficult tasks people face as they mature. Probably the biggest reason for this is that kids are great impulse buyers. They see it. They want it. There's not much a parent can do when a child spends his or her own money. We sort of have to step back and let them make their own mistakes. But most of us parents don't let things go at that—and we probably shouldn't. Nope, we feel compelled to deliver the cautionary warning, "So now that you purchased that new Laser-Guided Thunderbolt Monster Truck set, what have you got to show for your money?" Or there is the well-known parental strategy that goes like this: "If you hadn't spent all your money on that new Laser-Guided Thunderbolt Monster Truck set, you might have some left over. So what did you get for your money, anyway?" The key thing is to remind kids that some purchases have more merit than others. The hope is that by asking such a question the child can be taught to make this distinction.

Now that you are all grown up, you are probably the one delivering the message to your kids. But the question remains, "When you spend your money, what do you have to show for it?" This is an especially good question to ask when investing in common stocks, whether through a mutual fund or through buying shares of individual stocks. To answer the question of what you have to show for your money when you purchase stocks, we have to ask why you wanted to buy stocks in the first place.

The most common explanation is that the owner of a share of stock wants the price to go up. If that happens, the share can be sold for more money than its original purchase price. But why would a new purchaser of this share want to buy it for more money than the previous owner paid? Again, the usual answer is that the new owner expects the share to be worth even more in the future. If the share is worth more, then the new shareholder can, in turn, sell the share to yet another investor. While this process appears infinite, it begs the real question: What gives a share of stock more value in the future than it has today?

Most people say the reason for this apparently endless cycle of increasing share prices is that a variety of factors contributes to making the company more valuable to the shareholder. Earnings, return on equity, corporate cash flow, growth of sales revenues, increasing market share, new product offerings, and many other elements are all cited as contributing to the increase in value for shares of stock over time.

How important these various elements are relative to one another is a subject of much debate. That said, one factor has been anointed as the single most important in the determination of future shareholder value. That factor is earnings—more specifically, future earnings. The process of earnings estimation itself is worthy of examination because so much weight is placed on the activity. However, if you are buying the perception of future earnings, what are you really getting for your money?

Let's begin our examination by looking at the never ending fascination with earnings projections. These projections are the staple of Wall Street analysis, and there are literally armies of these people who try to predict whether a company will have $1.05 or $1.10 in earnings per share.

Almost all modern office buildings have sealed windows to control temperature and air flow. The other day we were totally absorbed in watching a fly trying to get out of one of these sealed windows. What attracted our attention was the gut-busting effort the fly was expending to get outside. Unfortunately, the window pane was an insurmountable barrier. Soon the little creature became exhausted and dropped to the window sill. As that happened, we asked ourselves, "Is there a lesson here?"

Isn't it obvious that hard work and effort don't always pay off or make a difference? Look at the effort this fly put out. The only thing that happened is that it became exhausted and will probably end up dead on the windowsill. There are parallel behaviors in people. Look at the hordes of financial analysts in the investment industry. These people spend countless hours poking and probing companies to derive earnings estimates stretching from next quarter to five or ten years into the future. The problem is that the overwhelming majority of these estimates are wrong. The poor investors who rely on these predictions are often left high and dry. Now, these financial analysts serve an important function, and they are well paid. But, as to the fruits of their labors—well, let's just say that, while analysts don't end up dead on the windowsill, they still engage in some pretty useless activity.

There are several important issues here. First, are earnings estimates important? Second, are they accurate? And finally, if in and of themselves they aren't particularly important or accurate, why does the game of earnings forecasting continue to attract such widespread attention?

Like moths drawn to light, most equity investors are entranced by corporate earnings. It's not surprising that this is the case. If a company is unprofitable, it cannot stay in business indefinitely. What's more, a record of increasing earnings is generally the sign of a healthy company, while declining earnings is correctly viewed as a very poor sign indeed. So far, so good. But how does an equity investor benefit directly from higher corporate earnings? The quick answer is that larger earnings may cause other investors to value the company more highly and thus be motivated to purchase the company's shares. This influx of new buyers tends to increase the price of the shares. If this increase takes place, earlier investors might experience a capital gain. So higher corporate earnings are important and desirable because investors believe them to be so. This is hardly a satisfactory explanation. However, adequate or not, this is the belief held by virtually all investors and it has now ascended to the pinnacle of financial dogma.

In and of itself, the flow of corporate earnings does not explain how a shareholder directly benefits from holding a share of stock. When a corporate entity is deemed to be more valuable than it used to be because of increased earnings, of what use are those increased earnings to the shareholder? It's true that the shareholder holds ownership rights to a share that is perceived to be increasingly valuable, but what good are these ownership rights? What tangible benefit do they offer the shareholder?

The more complete explanation for the importance of higher earnings has to go one more step to become fully rational. If earnings are the contemporary Holy Grail of investing, then surely dividends constitute the sacred wine. Dividends come from earnings. Indeed, dividends give meaning to earnings. Without present and future dividends, earnings are trapped inside a company forever. Earnings are important, but they ultimately derive their importance by being the source of dividends. While it is true that changes in earnings do compel investors to place varying values on shares of stock that are bought and sold, to declare that undistributed earnings have value in and of themselves is to deny common sense.

Thus, the only answer that makes any meaningful sense is dividends. Dividends are that part of the company's profits that are paid to shareholders. And if you are not being paid for holding a piece of paper, then why would you hold it in the first place? It is the present and the expected future dividends that stock investors must ultimately seek. To be sure, dividends do not usually provide as much income per dollar invested than does the yield from bonds. But at maturity, a bond can pay only 100 cents on the dollar, whereas the dividends and market values of stocks can increase in value for decades.

And yet, even though the lowly stock dividend yield (dividend yield is the price per share divided by the dividend per share, expressed as a percentage) is not usually as high as interest on a bond, the data show that over the long term, about half of all total return in stocks is provided by dividends and their reinvestment.[3] Moreover, it is both the expected dividend and the expected growth in dividends (however far into the future that growth may be) that must ultimately drive the other half of stock returns. Without dividends, the ownership of a share of stock is based on nothing more than the expectation of a tangible reward that never arrives.

This brings us to the other question. Are earnings estimates accurate? The data show overwhelmingly that earnings estimates are notoriously inaccurate. Professional investor David Dreman has done a significant amount of work on this subject and, after both original research as well as a thorough review of the literature, he has come to two major conclusions. Dreman explains how the consensus of earnings estimates is significantly wrong time and time again, regardless of which analysts were making the forecasts or which industry they followed. Dreman notes that ". . . *most analysts' estimates were simply linear extrapolations of current trends, and that the correlations between the actual and the predicted earnings turned out to be very low.*"[4] Dreman has also analyzed the accuracy of earnings forecasts during the period from 1973 through 1990. He studied 67,375 quarterly earnings estimates made by groups of six or more analysts and found that only a little more than half hit their target by plus or minus 15 percent and only about a quarter of the estimates were within plus or minus 5 percent of the actual earnings figure.[5]

Don't get us wrong. We are delighted that analysts spend so much time paying attention to earnings estimates. The activity is valuable largely because it serves as a check and discipline on corporate management. Without analysts, information would be less readily available and probably less accurate. Just don't go out and buy stocks on the basis of their predictions, because they are wrong more often than they are right.

What are the financial analysts' responses to the manifest inaccuracies of earnings forecasting? They keep banging their heads against the window and try to gather more data faster in the belief that this will always result in better forecasting. Unfortunately, the world does not work that way—instead, it is notoriously nonlinear. Each event leads to an outcome that conditions the beginning of the next event. This is why forecasting of this sort is doomed. It is not a lack of insight, intelligence, or data that leads to bad predicting. It is simply the nature of things.

If, in and of themselves, earnings are not as important as they are perceived to be and if the prediction of future earnings estimates is a fool's game, then why do people place so much stock in such things? There are several reasons. Earnings are the source of dividends. This makes them intrinsically valuable. Earnings are the lifeblood of a corporation. But earnings have the most certain impact on a shareholder in either one of two ways. When earnings are distributed in the form of dividends, the shareholder gets a direct benefit in the form of a check. Alternatively, if a shareholder sells shares that have increased in price due to an improvement in earnings, they can lock in a direct and certain benefit. Earnings increases that are neither distributed nor result in gains after the sale of shares do not necessarily benefit the shareholder. If not distributed, earnings are reinvested in the business. However, for a wide variety of reasons, reinvested earnings do not always result in permanently enhanced shareholder value.

People pay more attention to earnings forecasts than to dividends for several reasons. Earnings fluctuate much more than dividends. In a sense, earnings forecasts are about an unknown and possibly exciting future. Dividend investing is about a dull quarterly check that shareholders regularly receive in the mail. Then, too, not all companies are mature enough to pay dividends. Even though dividend-paying companies are usually profitable, not all profitable companies pay dividends. This means that a focus on earnings allows for a much larger universe of companies to analyze.

One well-known (but widely considered old-fashioned) theory for valuing common stocks is known as the *dividend discount model*. Valuing a stock this way requires the forecast of future dividends. Next, these estimated future dividends are discounted back to a present value.[6] While this dividend-driven description of what creates meaningful value in common stocks is not popular, it appears to be the only explanation that makes coherent sense. But one thing any investor knows is that the capital markets don't always make sense. The fact is that stock market investors seem to be motivated by something other than the usefulness of owning a common stock for its dividends. After all, the topic of present and future dividends is a small item in most discussions about common stocks, and stocks are regularly valued higher than the expected present value of their future dividends. So what is it about stocks that makes them valued by investors at prices higher than the calculated present value of an estimated future dividend flow?

In the first place, there is the same uncertainty surrounding the growth and continuity of dividend payments as there is about earnings estimates. This uncertainty exists even in the case of companies that have long and consistent records of paying regular dividends. Merely because a company paid dividends last quarter is no guarantee that it will continue to pay dividends this quarter or the next. For companies that do not yet pay a dividend, one question that arises is, when will they do so? And if a company begins paying a dividend, how large will it be? Uncertainty about the payment of dividends is accompanied by uncertainty about the future growth of dividend payments over time. When will a company boost its dividend? If so, by how much?

Uncertainties about future dividend-related growth probably cause some small measure of the differences of opinion about what a share of stock might be worth. Some investors will be optimistic, some pessimistic, and others neutral about the outlook for a company's dividend payments. But even though these multiple uncertainties about dividends can account for a small part of the value in excess of the present value of an estimated future dividend flow, they cannot account for all the excess value. Indeed, few investors and analysts seem to focus on dividends at all. So the question is what do investors focus on, and how does this focus relate to that portion of a stock's price that appears unrelated to dividends?

Most professionals who follow the stock market would answer that, over the long run, stock prices are determined by various fundamental characteristics of the companies that issued the shares.

What do we mean by the term *fundamental characteristics?* As noted above, the favorite fundamental characteristic is earnings. Most stock investors are mesmerized by the present and future earnings of a corporation. However, there are other fundamentals. Some investors also look at corporate cash flows. Some will look at the company's balance sheet to examine trends in the relationship between corporate assets and liabilities. Investors not only examine a company's financial statements, but they also look at a company's markets, products, management, customers, competition, and so forth. Taken together, all these items are supposed to serve as a rational basis for establishing the value of the price of a company's shares of stock.

It is not only those fundamentals directly related to a specific company that influence perceptions of stock values. Perceptions of fundamental forces in the business environment will also tend to move both groups of stocks, as well as the stock market in general. Movements of interest rates, money supply, overall economic growth, inflation rates, unemployment, and many other reported measurements will be assessed by stock market investors as having an effect on the overall climate for corporate prosperity. Similarly, to the degree that political issues are perceived to be positive or negative for business, they will tend to influence the overall climate for stock market investing. Finally, we cannot forget that emotion and psychology play a huge role in the general willingness to own stocks, a topic we will consider more fully later.

The importance of these fundamental characteristics should ultimately relate to one company's ability to generate present or future distributable cash to its shareholders versus another company's ability to do so. This ability to produce dividends is, in turn, related to a company's ability to deliver its goods or services to sufficient numbers of customers at high enough prices to cover the company's costs and expenses and still have some left over. This leftover money is profit. Profits can either be reinvested in the business or distributed to the shareholders as dividends.

Companies must strike a balance between reinvestment of profit back into the business and distribution of dividends to shareholders. Companies that pay out too much of their profit in dividends run two risks. First, they run the risk of having to cut their dividends should earnings drop precipitously. And, second, they run the risk of not reinvesting enough of their earnings back into the business and thus losing ground to competitors. Ultimately, if too little is reinvested, the company will lose the ability to sustain and increase dividends to shareholders.

As a matter of historic record, average dividends on large company stocks have been 4.6 percent, representing over 45 percent of average annual long-term total return. When you add in the reinvestment of dividends back into additional shares of stock, dividends account for 48 percent of long-term total return.[7] What's more, dividends have increased, on average, approximately 5 percent to 6 percent per year. To give you an idea of how growth can affect the value of a dividend, consider the following. Let's say a stock's price was $50 when you invested, and the yield on this stock was 4 percent, or $2.00 per year. Let's further assume that you held the share for ten years while the dividend increased by 5 percent per year, but the price of the stock did not increase at all. In this event, your $2.00 dividend would have grown to $3.26, resulting in a 6.5 percent yield on your original cost. Plus, you would have received a total of $26.41 over the ten-year period, a sum that could have been either spent or reinvested. If reinvested, the compound yield on this investment would have been even higher. Suffice it to say that dividends and dividend increases are meaningful to shareholders.

Companies that pay none of their earnings in dividends must be able to sustain a high rate of earnings growth through aggressive reinvestment into the business. Otherwise, shareholders will not continue to support high values for a company's stock. This is because, while dividends are the true long-term test of a company's worth to its shareholders, many investors look solely at earnings growth. Thus, it is the perception of both current and future earnings capacity that keeps company valuations high. If earnings growth slips, shareholders will lose interest in owning the company's shares and share prices will fall.

There is a dynamic marketplace that links dividends, dividend growth, and share prices to each other. For example, when dividends grow over time, real yields on the original cost of a stock will also go up. If you buy a share of stock for $40 that has a dividend of $1.00, the stock's yield is 2.5 percent immediately after purchase. If the dividend were to increase overnight to $2.00, then the yield would be 5 percent, as measured on the original purchase price of the stock. But, in the marketplace, this 5 percent yield would be compared to the current market prices paid for the stock of other similar companies. All things being equal, the market would tend to bid up the price of the $40 stock to $50, thus bringing the $2.00 yield back to the 2.5 percent level enjoyed by other similar companies' shares.

Returning for a moment to Ben Graham's work again, we find his introduction of a useful notion he called *intrinsic value*. To Graham, intrinsic value was a slippery concept, but an important one. Here's how he put it: ". . . intrinsic value is an elusive concept. In general terms it is understood to be that value which is justified by the facts, e.g., the assets, earnings, definite prospects, as distinct, let us say, from market quotations established by artificial manipulation or distorted by psychological excesses. But it is a great mistake to imagine that intrinsic value is as definite and determinable as is the market price. . . . Our notion of the intrinsic value may be more or less distinct, depending on the particular case. The degree of indistinctness may be expressed by a very hypothetical 'range of approximate value,' which would grow as the uncertainty of the picture increased."[8] This means that, if the market price of a security were to fall outside even these approximate bounds, Graham might consider it either over- or undervalued.

It may be helpful to split this concept of stock value into three components. One component consists of the present value of the dividend, the second consists of the company's other fundamental characteristics, and the third consists of that portion of the stock's price that is speculative or uncertain. We may refer to the price of a stock based on the present value of its projected dividend stream as the *tangible value* because, as long as the stock is held, only the dividend payout has direct and tangible usefulness to the stockholder. The stockholder must sell a stock to someone else at a higher price than he or she has paid to realize any more value from the investment other than the present value of the consistent flow of dividends paid by the issuing company. Investors regularly pay more (or less) for a stock than its tangible value. They will also regularly pay more (or less) for a stock than the stock's tangible value plus some rational assessment of its fundamental value. In effect, a premium or discount is paid that takes something completely subjective into account. The backbone of this subjective judgment is the promise and perpetual hope of every shareholder that his or her shares of stock will always go up in market price and create a capital gain.

This premium represents the *speculative value* of a common stock. It includes all the multiple uncertainties in a company's tangible and fundamental characteristics as well as all the emotional components embodied in investor fear and greed. That is, whatever value imparted to the price of a stock that is not represented by a tangible stream of consistent dividends or by a set of rationally determined fundamental characteristics is due to speculation about a company's future. Within certain bounds, common stock prices are often driven more by the widespread perceptions of value than by their ability to generate tangible value in the form of predictable, periodic cash flow in the form of distributed dividends paid to the shareholders. To the degree that this perception of value is related to subjective judgments, stock prices will tend to be more volatile. This is an issue investors must recognize and take into account when judging whether a stock is fairly priced.

The speculative component of the market price of a stock fluctuates with the ebb and flow of the prevailing opinions about the company's fortunes, as well as opinions about the stock market as a whole. Conversely, a discount is applied to the market value of a stock when there is fear that an investor may lose money if the price is either flat or expected to go down. Even subjectively perceived values have their limits. These limits are determined by those fundamental factors related to the present and future earnings capacity of a given business. So, while investor perceptions may inflate common stock prices beyond the level of the present value of any foreseeable dividend payouts, that potential inflation of price is not infinite. Given the subjectivity of stock price inflation, investors should always act with prudence and caution when investing in stocks.

If two hypothetical companies have identical fundamental values but one pays a dividend and the other does not, the stock of the company that has consistently paid dividends has a more solid component making up at least a part of its price than the stock of the company whose future dividend-paying ability is unknown. This conceptual composition of the share prices of identically priced stocks of two different companies is shown in Figure 4.1. On the left, we see the components of share price of a company with solid fundamentals, but which has never paid dividends. On the right, we have a company with "identically" solid fundamentals, but also with a long history of consistent dividend payments.

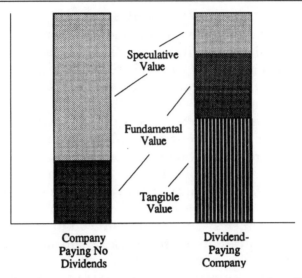

Speculative
Value

Fundamental
Value

Tangible
Value

Company
Paying No
Dividends

Dividend-
Paying
Company

Figure 4.1 Conceptual components of share price of
dividend- versus non-dividend-paying companies.

The value of the shares of a non-dividend-paying company is
derived differently. Some portion of the share price of a small,
growing company that pays no dividends will be related to its current fundamental characteristics. Revenues, earnings, cash flows,
and balance sheet items can all be compared to those of similar
companies, and share prices will fall within a range that takes these
characteristics into account. However, some portion of a share price
is based on the expectation of future performance. It is this part of
the share price that may be considered speculative in nature. Plus,
shareholders do not know when, if ever, the company will actually
pay dividends. Thus, a greater proportion of share prices of non-
dividend-paying companies is based on guesswork about the company's future.

Companies that have a history of paying consistent dividends to
their shareholders are more likely to pay dividends during the next
calendar quarter than those companies that have never paid any
dividends. This fact makes stocks issued by dividend-paying companies more stable than the stocks of companies that do not pay
dividends. Most companies that pay consistent, growing dividends
are mature enterprises. These firms generally have well-established
positions within their markets, and a strong financial position that

gives them an ability to weather many types of calamities. A substantial portion of the value of these types of companies is represented tangibly every quarter when dividends are declared and paid.

As illustrated in Figure 4.1, from a purely conceptual perspective, when a stock's tangible value and its fundamental value are added to its speculative value we arrive at the *market value* for the stock. This market value represents the total value of a share of stock, in the eyes of the buyer and seller, at the moment they complete a transaction and shares of stock change hands.

Nobody has found a crystal ball that will tell us when the stock market will go up or down. Over the long term, history has shown that investing in common stocks has been a wise way to invest. This is because companies have the ability to grow over time and thus generate increasing dividends to their owners. But, for unpredictable periods that have been known to last for years, investing in stocks can lead to disappointing losses. All stock prices move up, down, and sideways (i.e., not at all). What's more, not only do individual stock prices fluctuate, but the overall level of stock market valuations moves up and down as well. In the short run, these upward and downward swings are not entirely predictable. In the long run, the relative performance of one stock to another stock must be driven by tangible and fundamental characteristics, even though emotion, fads, and market psychology all play a role in the shorter run.

No discussion of dividends would be complete without at least a passing reference to the tax policies of the United States. Dividends must be paid from after-tax profit. This means that a corporation subtracts its costs and expenses from its revenues to calculate its profit and then pays taxes on that profit.[9] Only after the taxes have been paid is a company's board of directors permitted to declare and pay a dividend. Moreover, once the dividend payment is made to a shareholder, the shareholder becomes liable for payment of another tax on the dividend income. This double taxation of dividends lowers the effective rate of return to the taxable shareholder. However, shareholders who own dividend-paying stocks within a tax-deferred retirement account do not have to worry about double taxation on a current basis because the taxes will not be due until retirement when they are presumably going to be in a lower tax bracket. Additionally, the retirement investor who invests in dividend-paying stocks has the benefit of the compounding effect generated by the reinvestment of dividends within the tax-advantaged retirement portfolio.

WILLING BUYERS AND SELLERS MAKE A MARKET

Sometimes we remind ourselves of the robot in the movie *Short Circuit* that keeps saying, "Input! I need input!" Like many people, we are omnivorous consumers of information. The other evening we were watching a late-night documentary that included an old 1950s training film. These films, you might remember, were used in instruction of employees, army recruits, and students in health class. The subject of this film centered on the effects of high-altitude oxygen deprivation on air force personnel. A pressure chamber had been designed to give recruits firsthand knowledge of the oxygen deprivation they may experience while flying at high altitudes. The reason for the exercise was simple: Experience is the best teacher.

The trainees were taken into the sealed chamber, instructed in the use of the oxygen masks, and told to sit down on the side wall benches so the test could begin. The instructor put on his oxygen mask and signaled the console operator to begin depressurizing the cabin. Gradually, the oxygen content began to drop. At first, the changes in pressure didn't have any effect on participants and the trainees were able to perform assigned tasks without difficulty. But as the oxygen levels declined, funny things began to happen. The trainees began to lose motor skills as well as the ability to concentrate and think. Finally, there came a point in the test when the trainees became downright goofy, and were told to put on their oxygen masks while the test was brought to a halt.

Having pondered yet another fascinating tidbit of trivia, we wondered if it had any significance at all to the subject of investing in common stocks. Then we hit upon it. Look at the relationship between the changes in simulated altitude and the actions of the people in the pressure cabin. The higher the altitude, the goofier they acted. People get goofy in high altitudes and investors can get careless in high markets.

It is no secret in investing that everything is just hunky-dory until the moment that it isn't. Put in a more formal way, nobody has yet been able to predict the top (or the bottom) of a market movement. There are many examples of investing excess, particularly in times when everybody seems to be doing well. In the current environment, for example, stocks issued by those companies that seek to capitalize on the Internet have gone way past the boundaries of any reasonable measure of intrinsic value. At the end of 1995, for example, shares of six of the most prominent Internet companies' stocks were selling at an average of 329 times their per-share earnings.[10] Compare this to the historic average of the price-to-earnings ratio of the S&P 500 Index of about 15.5 times. Investors who were buying into the Internet companies at the end of 1995 were clearly getting woozy from not having had enough oxygen to breathe. But the fact remains that, at least for a short while, willing buyers and sellers were buying and selling at inflated prices on both sides of the trading in these shares.

So, what is the oxygen that drives stock valuations? Part of the answer lies in what Ben Graham called intrinsic value. When the range of market valuations rises beyond a reasonable approximation of intrinsic value, the market can be said to be overpriced. But making this statement does not necessarily help matters for the average investor, particularly when there are sharp disagreements about what constitutes a reasonable level of intrinsic value. The most tangible and easily quantified answer to the question of intrinsic value is dividends, both current payments and those expected in the future. That this is so seems almost quaint in the modern era of "sophisticated" finance. But a piece of ownership of a company does no good whatsoever to its owner until that person either sells the stock or receives dividends from it.

Although long-run logic supports dividends as the source of real value, you would be hard-pressed to find a clear and direct short-run connection between the two. While earnings are the most important factor in the perception of value, there are many other factors that drive stock valuations in the shorter run. Some of these factors are emotional and some are market-related. Market factors are those that have to do with the operation of the market mechanism itself— that is, the activity in which buyers and sellers exchange cash for securities and securities for cash. In a free, fair, and deep market, this is not a very complicated process. When there are more buyers than sellers, prices increase. When there are more sellers than buyers, prices decrease. Market factors operate on the level of an individual security (the stock of a single company), groups of securities (the stocks of an industry group), and for entire categories of securities (large company stocks or Treasury bonds, for example).

On the level of an individual security, daily events motivate people to buy or sell a specific stock. If a company reports news that people interpret positively, buyers are often attracted. Conversely, if a company posts bad news, some shareholders may be prompted to sell. Industry groups share characteristics that tend to cause them to be bought and sold more or less in tandem with each other. If a specific event or set of events is perceived to be positive or negative for a particular industry, shares of companies within that industry will tend to rise and fall as buyers buy and sellers sell.

The market mechanism becomes more complicated when we consider variables of a larger magnitude, particularly the political climate for corporate earnings and the economic variables of inflation and interest rates. Sharp and persistent increases or decreases in the market value of securities can change the public perceptions of the securities marketplace. The stock market crash of 1929 conditioned many people to avoid stock investing altogether. In fact, if you had invested in the stocks that made up the S&P 500 Index at the beginning of 1929 and kept reinvesting all your dividends back into the stocks in the index during the entire period, it would have taken you a full 15 years to achieve a lasting breakeven point compared to where you were at the end of 1928. This memory died hard in people's minds—and rightly so.

It is estimated that, at the time of the crash of 1929, no more than 28 percent of households were stock investors. However, due in part to promotional work undertaken by Charles Merrill (founder of Merrill Lynch) and the New York Stock Exchange, the number of securities-investing households increased to an estimated 42 percent by 1965. Perceptions of the overall market for securities are influenced by a wide variety of unpredictable events operating in conjunction with each other. For example, the rapid increase in oil prices in the early seventies seemed to serve as an inflationary catalyst for a number of subsequent events. In 1973, the S&P 500 Index lost 15 percent of its value, followed in 1974 by the loss of an additional 26.5 percent of its value. By 1980, the number of households owning stocks, bonds, or mutual funds had decreased to an estimated 21 percent.[11] Of course, with money market funds sporting yields of nearly 15 percent in 1981, while inflation for the same year was only about 9 percent, it is not surprising that many avoided the stock market.

Today it is a different story. Americans began to increase their stock holdings in the mid-1980s, so that by the end of 1995, it was estimated that 37 percent of American households would own stocks, bonds, or mutual funds.[12] Helping to propel this newfound enthusiasm for the stock and bond markets is a body of statistical research first published in 1977 by Roger Ibbotson and Rex Sinquefield.[13] These two men compiled a set of consistent measurements of the rates of return for domestic stocks, bonds, cash, and inflation. This research is updated and published as an annual yearbook. The result of this scholarship has been to establish the commonly received wisdom that over long periods of time, stocks will outperform bonds, and bonds will outperform cash. Regardless of the prospective truth of these findings, having been influenced by favorable markets and armed with this research, many stock investors have become more complacent than ever about the perils of stock market investing. More important, by shifting the focus of stock investing away from the companies that produce the returns, the Ibbotson-Sinquefield research has changed the debate into one of statistics and not of the intrinsic value of companies. The importance of this shift is critical to every investor's understanding of the contemporary capital markets.

Quite apart from factors such as inflation, interest rates, or fad investing is another issue that has driven the behavior of buyers and sellers. If you will recall, Figure 2.4 depicted in graphic form the different rates of saving that are exhibited at different times during a person's life. Next, Figure 2.5 showed a picture of a typical retirement savings account as tracked throughout the life of a single individual. If we could summarize these two charts, we might say that most people go through several distinct phases in their ability to save and invest for retirement. When they are young, they have few expenses and low incomes. As people have children, while their incomes tend to rise, their expenses rise even faster. Then, once people reach their late 40s, their savings ability increases as child-related expenses wane and incomes generally rise. Finally, in their late 60s, people retire and begin to use their savings to support themselves during retirement when they are no longer able to work as vigorously.

The phenomenon of the baby boom has been well documented. This is a phrase that refers to the approximately 76 million people born in the United States between 1946 and 1964. The baby-boom group constitutes almost 30 percent of the current population. However, it is not the absolute size of the group that makes it so important; it is that the group is so large in comparison to the other age groups in the United States. The interesting thing about the baby-boom generation is that it has defined much of what has happened in American society over the last 50 years.

Consider, the revolutionary time of the 1960s. Many of the phenomena of that decade can be explained by reference to the baby-boom generation. During the 1960s, the leading edge of the baby-boom generation moved through adolescence to young adulthood. Much of the social upheaval of the time might well be traced directly to the restlessness of adolescent youth. In a similar fashion, the increasing conservatism of the country that has taken place during the 1980s and 1990s could quite possibly be explained by reference to the increasing numbers of baby-boom Americans who have reached adulthood, now have children, and are seeking the stability of midlife. We hasten to add that there is much that cannot be explained by reference to demographics. Demographic analysis is, at best, an ax rather than a scalpel when it comes to dissecting social trends. But dispassionate observers ignore demographics at their own peril. This is particularly true for the recent history of the stock market and perhaps for the market's future as well.

In Figure 4.2, we have constructed an interesting chart that compares the total returns from the S&P 500 (adjusted for inflation) to the number of Americans having their 45th birthdays, and then to the number of Americans having their 65th birthdays. We selected the 80-year period from 1954 through 2034 as the period that best tracks the impact of the baby boom.

As you can see in Figure 4.2, there are three lines plotted in the chart. The line that tracks the S&P 500, as adjusted for inflation, is plotted on the right vertical axis. It shows the value of a dollar invested in 1954. A second line tracks the number of people having their 45th birthdays, and a third line tracks the number of people having their 65th birthdays. These latter two lines were plotted on the left scale, which shows the number of Americans having birthdays in any given year.

Because 1954 was a terrific year for the S&P 500, you would have had $1.53 for each dollar invested at the beginning of the year. Thus, the line that tracks the S&P 500 starts at the $1.53 mark as measured on the right-hand vertical axis. By the time the end of

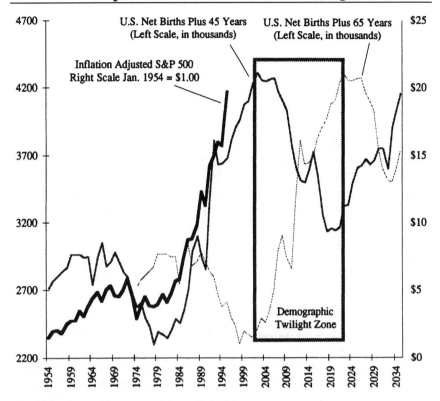

Figure 4.2 The Demographic Twilight Zone.

1954 had rolled around, a total of 2,718,000 people had their 45th birthdays. If you move along the horizontal axis, you will find that, by 1974, those same people who were 45 years old in 1954, had aged 20 years, and thus turned 65.

Looking carefully at the chart, we can see that the S&P 500 has tended to track the number of people reaching their 45th birthdays. Not to put too fine a point on this, but the latter half of one's fourth decade is when the ability to save and invest begins to emerge most strongly. From 1970 to 1982, the number of new 45-year-olds in the population fell from an annual rate of 2.9 million to 2.4 million. This decrease in new 45-year-olds correlates to the anemic 6.9 percent total return experienced by the S&P 500 during the 12-year period.

From 1987 to the present, an interesting picture emerges. During this period, not only does the number of new 45-year-olds begin to take off, but the number of new 65-year-olds simultaneously begins to drop off. This means that, in the big picture, there are many more people entering their primary savings years than entering their retirement years. Not surprisingly, this pattern has been mirrored by a steep rise in the S&P 500. Since 1987, the S&P 500 has increased at an annual compound rate of over 14 percent per year.

Now for the $64,000 question. If demographics can help explain what has been happening to the market for domestic stocks, can it help us understand a bit about what might happen in the future? Who knows? It's worth considering, though. Returning again to Figure 4.2, we can see that the number of new 45-year-olds increases until the year 2006, while the number of new 65-year-olds continues to decline until 2002. In 2006, the number of new 45-year-olds begins to drop. In 2002, the number of new 65-year-olds will begin to increase. This powerful demographic trend will continue for many years. The number of new 45-year-olds does not begin to increase again until the year 2021, and the number of new 65-year-olds does not begin to drop until 2023.

What are we to conclude about these data? Again, an important caveat. Demographic trends are not the only factor in determining market movements. They are, at best, just one in a whole soup of variables. That said, there does seem to be a powerful trend at work. Absent other factors, the period from 1996 through 2002 should continue to be a great time for the stock market. The baby boom is investing for retirement, and these folks will continue to invest in 401(k) plans, IRAs, and other retirement savings accounts. Meanwhile, the number of new potential retirees continues to drop during this period. Taken alone, these two factors would make for more buyers than sellers and drive stock prices upward.

Sometime from 2006 onward, however, the demographic trends do not look good for the stock market. Every year, there will be fewer buyers and more sellers as increasing numbers of the baby-boom generation retire and begin to use their portfolios to generate cash for retirement expenses. What's more, this period could last until the early 2020s, spanning almost two decades.

We call these two decades the Demographic Twilight Zone. Who the heck knows what will happen? One thing seems certain, though: Those folks who are not sticking to their fundamentals are more likely to get hurt than those who throw caution to the winds. What do you do to protect yourself? Again, who can tell? Our best advice is contained in the pages of this book, so continue reading.

FIVE

Stock Investing Styles

A GREAT DEAL OF TIME and attention is spent searching for the "right" stocks to invest in. As with so much of investment practice, a wide range of categories has been created to classify stocks that appear to share one or more attributes. For example, some of the more common terms we hear about stocks include:

- *Blue-Chip Stocks.* The so-called blue-chip stocks are issued by large, well-recognized companies. There is no clear and consistent list of which stocks are blue chip and which are not.
- *Growth Stocks.* These are stocks issued by companies that are growing more quickly than other companies. They usually pay little dividends. Technology companies' stocks are often cited as growth stocks.
- *Income Stocks.* These are stocks known for paying relatively high dividends. Utilities are often included in this group.
- *Defensive Stocks.* These are stocks issued by companies that provide basic goods and services such as food or electricity.
- *Cyclical Stocks.* These are stocks issued by companies whose earnings fall in recessions and rise during expansions.
- *Seasonal Stocks.* These stocks are issued by companies whose earnings rise and fall with the seasons. For example, retailers tend to do well at Christmas.

Most of these categories have been created in the effort to organize the way in which a stock investor goes about making decisions regarding which stocks to invest in. It is not surprising that these categories often cloud the fundamental issues behind stock investing. As you can see, these categories leave a lot of room for confusion and overlap. There are examples of companies that are large and well recognized (a blue-chip stock), are growing faster than other companies in an industry (a growth stock), pay relatively high dividends (an income stock), and tend to slump somewhat during recessions (a cyclical stock). The fact is that these categories are relatively artificial and do little to help us understand the merits of various investing approaches.

Most would agree that the pure financial objective of stock investing (as opposed to a human financial objective) is to maximize shareholder long-term total return, that is, price changes plus dividends. Plus, we want to accomplish this with a minimum risk of loss and a maximum degree of certainty. The task of defining the best approach to investing in common stocks requires that we examine our financial objective and define the fundamental approaches that could be used to reach that objective. Then we must examine the data to see which approach has given the best results, and finally we must be able to plug that approach into the solution of the problem.

Since total return includes dividend income and price changes, we should focus on these elements, rather than on artificial distinctions that have no direct bearing on our objective. There are two ways to increase the dividend portion of total return: Either purchase stocks that pay a high dividend or purchase stocks that pay a relatively low dividend but have a history of dividend increases. Either way, this is known as *income investing*. There are two ways investors can make money from a price change. They can purchase a security that has already appreciated in price but may go up even further. This is known as *growth investing*. Alternatively, they can purchase a security that is depressed in price and hope that it recovers. This is known as *value investing*.

A great deal of the confusion about these contrasting styles has to do with the terminology used. Some folks hear the word *growth* and think, "That's for me because I want my investment to grow." *Value* investing does not really have much of an image. Others hear the word *income* and think, "This investment must have high income, and that's what I want." Some investors believe they have to invest in all the styles, lest they miss anything. Others prefer to rely on one type of investing or another. One thing seems certain: Adherents to each style have their own ways of looking at the world.

Remember the old Groucho Marx game show *You Bet Your Life?* It had a great gimmick. At the start of every show before the guests came on, a duck would come down from the ceiling holding a placard with a "magic word" on it. The object was for the host to get one of the guests to say the magic word. If a contestant did blurt it out, the duck would come down and the contestant would win. It was a great antic that allowed Groucho to have plenty of laughs at the contestant's expense. Here's what might happen if you applied the same format to a show about retirement investing.

"Ladies and gentlemen! Welcome to *You Bet Your Retirement!*, the game show for stock investors. I'm Johnny B. and I'm here to introduce one heck of a nice guy. Heeeeeere he is, the host of our show, the one, the only, the incomparable Buffalo Bob! So let's give a great good welcome to the funny man of the mutual fund, the hero of stock men and women the world over, here he is . . . The Bobster of Bison!"

"Thank you! Thank you! Please, no, thank you. Hey, hey, hey! Greetings gang! What a crowd we have here tonight! I'll just bet you folks are itching to play our game, the only show for investment-savvy people in the know! My name is Buffalo Bob, and this is the only game that lets you be an investment guru just like those high-paid money men. But before we introduce our first guests, let's dial up the duck to see what tonight's magic word is. Here we go."

There is a short pause. Then the duck drops out of the curtain as if laden with buckshot. It has a placard dangling around its neck with the words "CASH INCOME" written on it.

Then Bob barks out, "Let's meet our contestants. Our first guest is Richard "Scrappy" Morrison, a P.E. teacher from Bangor, Maine, who describes himself as a real investment weenie. Our second guest is Buzz Bixby, an accountant by day and an ace stock picker by night. Our third guest is Winky Kreider, a retired purchasing manager from Evansville, Indiana, and our fourth and final contestant is Martha Mums, the founder of an investment club in Hibbing, Minnesota. Let's give our four contestants a big welcome!"

"So tell me, Scrappy, what kind of stock pickers do you like out there? Got any five-star winners for us?" asks Buffalo Bob.

"You bet!" replies Morrison. "Why, I got 'em all! There isn't a style I don't subscribe to. Why, I've got managers who are short, tall, skinny, and fat, 'cause diversity is my middle name. Why I betcha I have one of just about everything—that's how I push the frontiers of diversity to make 'em as efficient as I can. I got myself small companies and big companies. I got value and I got growth. I got domestic and got international. That's my whole financial strategy, if you don't mind me saying so. It goes sort of like this. If I have one of everything, then I'm portfolio correlated, as the pros say. It's a bit too complicated to explain here, but this means that when one thing's up, something else is sure to be down. It's sort of like working your offense and your defense on a ball team. You've got to have some guys doing push-ups while others do the log rolls. That way you get all the guys working different muscles in a correlated way. It's the same with investing. If all my managers are negatively and positively coordinated, I know I'm definitely on an even keel. This way I can eliminate the roller-coaster ride of the market. Know what I mean, Bob?"

"Thanks, Scrappy, I think we get the picture. But if we don't, I'm sure you can blow your whistle and clue us in," said Buffalo Bob, raising his eyebrows a couple of times for emphasis. He then turns to Buzz Bixby.

"So Buzz, what kind of stocks are you into these days?"

"Well Bob, I'm a bottoms-up and top-down kind of a guy, myself. I like to work on both ends. Bottoms up, I'm looking for hot companies. I invest in companies with technology of all sorts. I start at the bottom with the company itself and work up. That's why I call it bottoms up. I'm one of those guys who believes the future is now."

"Well, Buzz, if the future is now, then what comes tomorrow?" asks the host.

"That's exactly what I mean, Bob. I look in my crystal ball to tell what's going up fastest of all. No matter whether it's biotech, chips, or new restaurant themes, I also play the top-down momentum game on the aggressive growth side. That's where the big money is. I call it top down 'cause I predict what'll happen with the company by what's happening in that big, bad world out there."

"Tell us a little more about the top-down momentum game, Buzz. How do you know the momentum is going to go in your direction?"

"Well, it's not easy, I'll tell you. I figure out what's going to go up from what's already going up. That way, I never buy what's about to go down. You really have to keep on your toes to do this momentum stuff. So, just to make sure I have covered all my bases, I spend a lot of time trying to do the bottoms-up work so that I know what each company will do in the future in the way of earnings. Course, a company doesn't have to have earnings for me to like its story. Lots of good companies don't have earnings, you know. Look at the biotechs, for example. I'm big right now into auto-immunovirus replacement gene therapy companies. I'll tell you, Bob, there's going to be a lot of action in this area, just you watch."

"OK, Buzz, I'm sure we'll all be watching. Hey, Winky, you're up! What's the good word? It says here you're a value man. Just what does that mean?"

"Well Bob, if there is one thing I learned in all my years as a purchasing guy, you have to buy cheap if you expect to do well. So that's what I do. I like looking at balance sheets to discover assets that other folks miss. And I won't ever buy a stock unless I can buy it cheap. After all, everybody knows three nickels are better than a dime."

"Isn't that the truth, Winky. So, tell us how you avoid getting depressed buying these cheap stocks? I mean, you're zigging when the whole world is zagging. So what's that all about?"

"Well, I guess you could say I have the courage of my convictions. I don't much care what the market does on a day-to-day basis. Since I'm in it for the long haul, I can afford to wait for other people to come around to my way of thinking."

"If you say so, Winky. So, Martha, what's doing in Hibbing? What's hot and what's not? Actually, I guess if you're from Hibbing there's not much hot, way up in the north country, is there?"

"Well, Bob, the winters are long, if that's what you mean. But our club doesn't do things like the way Buzz does. He seems to be looking for the big winners all day every day. We just don't spend our time looking for hot stocks. And, as far as the other gentlemen's methods go, we don't subscribe to that stuff about correlating investments with statistics or looking for underpriced bargains. We feel we're better off having all of our investments produce cash and give us a margin of safety to boot. I guess we are kind of stick-in-the-mud folks who believe in getting as much cash flow from high-quality stocks as we can."

"Is dividend investing all you folks do, Martha? Because if it is, then you folks are probably leaving a lot of capital gains on the table. Everyone knows you can't have dividends and capital gains."

"Well, Bob, I'm not sure who 'everyone' is, but we found that, by looking after the dividends, we seem to be able to spot stocks that will produce higher capital gains. So we can have our cake and eat it, too. Nope, we just stick to our knitting and don't invest in stocks that don't have a high dividend paid by a healthy company."

"But Martha," said Bob, "How can you possibly have a modern portfolio if you don't have a little of this and a little of that? Don't you people know that you have to have a little of everything to be well diversified? What have you got against growth investing, anyway?"

"Well, shucks, call us old-fashioned, if you like, but we are just uncomfortable buying into all those so-called growth assets. We just can't get over the fact that those types of stocks are so unproductive. I guess if there is one word that describes our style of stock investing it's that we try to buy securities that create productive value for us. What we have found is that by focusing on the dividend, the capital gains seem to more than take care of themselves. We not only get more income from our productive assets, we also get more capital gains. And, since we only invest in really high quality companies, we can afford to wait for our capital gains because we get paid to wait by companies who pay out cash dividends to their shareholders every quarter without fail. If you had to ask me what our secret is, I'd have to say it's our focus on regular cash income." And, as soon as Martha says the word, down comes the duck and applause fills the air.

"Hey hey hey!" says Bob. "Martha has just said our magic word. So Johnny B, let's tell her what she has won."

"Martha, you and your investment club have just won steady cash flows with high capital gains. Yes, you and your fellow club members will join other dividend-oriented investors who demand that their investments be built on more than a hope and a promise of great markets and greater fools."

It's true. We plead guilty. We do feel strongly that the magic word in long-term total returns from stock investing is *cash income.* However, while we have discussed the important fundamental underpinnings for this viewpoint in our discussion of the dividend or tangible component of stock investing, there are alternate philosophies. As mentioned above, these alternate philosophies are known as investment "styles," and fall into three main categories broadly known as growth, value, and income.

Before we get into an overview of each style, it is important to note that the concepts of growth, value, and income investing are rarely applied consistently over time. Most fund managers place at least a few stocks into their portfolios that do not fit the criteria for which the manager is best known. Thus, so-called value or income investors often place growth stocks into their portfolios, and so-called growth investors often place value or income stocks into their portfolios. This makes consistent analysis of management styles difficult at best and practically impossible at worst.

For example, growth and income mutual funds are supposed to be a combination of the two stock investing disciplines. These funds are supposed to invest in a certain number of companies that produce dividend income and a certain number of companies that are expected to produce gains from share price growth fueled by reinvested earnings. Yet of the 406 growth and income funds tracked by the mutual fund rating firm, Morningstar, only 19 percent paid out dividends yielding more than the S&P 500 Index as a whole for the 12-month period ending February 1995. The other 81 percent of the income and growth funds did not beat the yield of the S&P Index as a whole, with 33 of these funds yielding practically no income at all.[1]

Underlying much of this question of investment style are certain widespread notions about which kind provides the best total return (i.e., the capital appreciation plus the dividend income achieved over a certain period of time, usually a year).

GROWTH STOCK INVESTING

The growth investor is everywhere. The combination of greed and optimism seems irresistible. We go to the Y to work out. It's not fancy, and there aren't any spandex-clad personal trainers, but there are a lot of regular folks just trying to stay fit. After going to the same weight room for a while, you begin to get to know the regulars. They include cops, truck drivers, barbers, and even an aluminum siding salesperson. The free weight room is in the basement, situated among insulation-clad steam pipes. With a couple of stinky wrestling mats on the floor and a rough-welded weight rack, it is the perfect environment to struggle against the iron.

Two of the regulars, Jim and Frank, are always trading stock tips as they work out. Each one has hot tips to give to the other. The thing is, they never talk about their losers. No, it's always the winners that get discussed, and the bigger the better. The way these guys approach it, to outwit everyone you only need to be ready for the next hot tip.

The hot tip takes two to tango. Tipsters usually want to prove that they are in the know. That way they just might be able to get regular tips in return. The person who gets the tip is often driven by greed and just wants to make a killing by getting in before the crowd, riding the darn thing to the moon, and then getting off at the top. The trouble with the hot tip is that almost none of the desired events take place. Most hot tips don't result in a killing. Most of those who play the tip don't get in before the crowd. That's because these people *are* the crowd, but don't know it. Besides, even if they are lucky enough to catch the wave, these investors have another problem. It is virtually impossible to know where the top is, much less to have the discipline to get off there. But guys like Jim and Frank are always willing to try, eager for that next bit of exciting information that will make all their past disappointments nothing but bad memories.

Most of the time, a hot tip will have to do with some little company that's about to hit it big by doing a deal with some large company, or they have some new process that does this or that and is just about to break out of the pack. The hot tip usually involves some little-known but significant event that is going to happen in the future. The situation is usually characterized as urgent (that's why you have to act fast) and the information is supposed to be known only by a few. Tomorrow, everybody will have discovered the "truth," the stock may have gone up, and you will have missed the boat. Oh, and one more thing, hot tips almost never make money.

There is a remarkable similarity between the hot-tip mentality of the small-time stock picker and the growth-investing mentality of the professional. Professional growth stock managers work on their share of hot tips, as well. No, most of them do not get inside information. Neither do they rely on their buddies at the Y for stock picks. Instead, they apply themselves to forecasting the future. They root around so-called research reports looking for insights about which company is going to be the next big winner. They spend most of their time trying to divine the future by looking at earnings trends, revenue projections, market analyses, and so forth.

Growth investors seek to purchase shares of companies that they think are going to grow rapidly in the future. They are typically not concerned with buying stocks that are priced inexpensively today compared to the fundamental ratios. Instead, most growth investors try to identify companies in which there is high projected growth in earnings and cash flow. Some growth investors attempt to identify companies whose share price has been surging because of a dynamic story about the company's ability to grow rapidly. These folks are unusually skittish and try to identify the next fad or wave of stock investing that will provide momentum to the share prices of certain companies. This latter type of growth investor is sometimes called a *momentum* player. Other growth investors try hard to shoot the moon with each and every stock they pick. These folks are sometimes referred to as *aggressive* growth managers. Typically, growth investors do not pay much attention to dividend yields. Their companies are reinvesting earnings to further fuel additional growth.

VALUE STOCK INVESTING

Those familiar with Wall Street might also be familiar with another type of stock investing known as *value investing*. Value stock investors typically search out companies with share prices that are perceived to be valued less than the company's intrinsic value. Value investors believe that if they purchase a stock for less than its intrinsic value, the marketplace will ultimately recognize that value and reward the investor accordingly. This can be a dicey game, though, because it is extremely difficult to determine the appropriate range for a company's intrinsic value. True value investors are the bottom feeders of the stock market world. They scrounge around the junkyard looking for treasures that others do not see.

Not too long ago we decided to have a garage sale ourselves. The basement and the closets were scoured for items that we didn't want or need any longer but didn't have the heart to throw away. Our junk included toys the kids had outgrown, a broken table that had been sitting in the basement, a piece of exercise equipment we no longer used, and lots of assorted things we no longer needed. We advertised in the local paper, put up posterboard signs, and started filling the garage up with all the stuff we were going to sell. The event was to take place Saturday morning, so Friday night, we put price labels on all the items for sale. We didn't have any idea of what prices to charge, but we understood that many potential buyers would try to negotiate. Most of the time, the pricing was easy.

What's an old jigsaw puzzle featuring the Teenage Mutant Ninja Turtles worth? About 50 cents. How about paperback books? A quarter apiece, five for a dollar. The broken table? Maybe $50 negotiable. And on it went into the night, getting ready for the next day's sale.

Everyone has heard of the saying that one person's junk is another person's treasure. Boy, is that true. At about 7 A.M., the cars started to line up down the street. We went out to post the signs at 7:15, and found seven or eight cars already parked, waiting for the garage door to open. As we came back into the house, one scrounger stepped out of a van and asked if we had any old golf clubs. As it turned out, we did have a number of old golf clubs, and said so. Once we opened the garage door, the man looking for golf clubs came and immediately paid full price for all the clubs we had. Hmmm. Maybe they were underpriced. No time to worry, we had junk to sell! By midafternoon, the garage was virtually empty.

Some of the stuff we sold didn't work or was broken. But everyone who goes to garage sales knows that they have to be careful, and our customers were no different. No doubt that bargains were had. Maybe those old golf clubs were worth $50 each to the knowledgeable buyer, but much of the stuff was low-priced junk.

Loosely put, value managers like to go to flea markets and junk sales. They believe themselves to be able to discover bargains where others have overlooked them. One principal problem with this approach is that if you go to flea markets and junk sales, you just might go home with fleas and junk. Not always, of course. From time to time, value investors discover the stock market equivalent of an original copy of the Declaration of Independence. More often, though, they get at least a few stocks that end up like a worn out vacuum cleaner that took two marbles to its plastic heart and died on the spot.

Value investors use a number of financial tools to judge the intrinsic value of the shares of a company. Primary among these tools are certain ratios that compare a certain fundamental characteristic such as book value, cash flow, or earnings.[2] These fundamentals are expressed in dollar-per-share terms and then compared to the price per share. So, for example, a company that sells at a market price–to–book ratio of 2 to 1 would have $2.00 of book value for every $1.00 in the market price for each share. In general, value investors seek companies whose shares are selling cheaply when compared to their fundamentals. Finally, value stocks often have higher-than-average dividend yields because they are earning and paying out more dividends relative to their share price than other stocks. This is true even if the value investor's primary objective is seeking undervalued securities as opposed to securities that pay high and growing dividends.

INCOME STOCK INVESTING

The third type of stock investor is the income investor. To this investor, the dividend is the single most important factor in determining which stocks to purchase. Dividend investing may include elements of value investing, but they are used not so much to identify undervalued securities as to measure the sustainability of the dividend. In a similar way, income investors may pay attention to certain characteristics of the growth style of investing, particularly as they relate to the growth of the dividend. Income investors are often thought of as being the most conservative type of stock investor, because a larger proportion of their returns come from dividends rather than price increases. Dividends are a known quantity, while share price increases are much more difficult to predict, and thus less reliable. By reducing the proportion of total return that must come from price changes, income stock portfolios can generate smaller capital gains and still outperform portfolios that do not earn dividend income.

In market downturns, a dividend payment can cushion the investor against a measure of loss at least equal to the dividend. Additionally, dividends can be reinvested and compounded, adding further to their positive impact on total return. Then, too, companies that pay dividends are usually more mature than those that do not. Mature companies are correctly perceived as less risky than immature companies.

Income investing may be more conservative than either value investing or growth investing, but our research shows that it is not necessarily less rewarding. This is because when stocks with high dividend yields are carefully screened for quality, the result is a portfolio of modestly underpriced, yet high-quality, dividend-paying stocks. In essence, you get paid to wait for the stock price to recover.

MARKET CAPITALIZATION

The three basic stock investing styles are applied to different-size companies, ranked according to the size of what is known as the *market capitalization* or *market cap*. The market capitalization of a company is its share price multiplied by the number of total shares outstanding. The figure equals the value of all of a company's shares to all of its shareholders at any given time. On this basis, stocks are loosely described as *micro-cap, small-cap, mid-cap,* and *large-cap*. As with many areas of investing, the rules are not applied consistently as to what constitutes one size market cap or another.

Sometimes the capitalization size range of a given group of stocks is defined by taking all the companies listed on a given exchange and arbitrarily defining companies that fall into one size group or another as small-, mid-, or large-cap companies. For example, one such method ranks companies listed on the New York Stock Exchange by market capitalization and then divides them into groups, with an equal number of companies in each group. Different market cap labels are then assigned to the various size groupings.

Generally speaking, micro-cap companies can range in market capitalization from about $10 million all the way to perhaps $100 million in size. Companies with market capitalizations between $100 million and $250 million are sometimes referred to as small-cap companies. Companies with a market capitalization greater than $250 million but less than, say, $750 million are usually referred to as mid-cap companies. And companies over approximately $750 million in market capitalization are usually referred to as large-cap. As a point of reference, as of the end of 1995, the smallest market capitalization within the S&P 500 was about $200 million and the largest was $98 billion.

There are a number of specialized listings of stocks that have been constructed to form indexes based on the market cap of the underlying companies. We briefly discussed the S&P 500 Index as the most widely used broad-based index of domestic equities. There are other indexes consisting strictly of large-cap stocks. Most people have heard of the Dow Jones Industrial Average. It is an index of 30 large-cap companies that are supposed to be representative of industrial American stocks. While too small to be truly representative of large-cap stocks, the DJIA is the most widely followed domestic stock index. Another example is the Russell 1000 Index of large-cap domestic equities, published by Frank Russell Company. Russell also publishes the Russell 2000 Index of small-cap companies, as well as the Russell 3000 Index, which is a combination of all the large- and small-cap companies in both the Russell 1000 and the Russell 2000.

PASSIVE VERSUS ACTIVE MANAGEMENT

By definition, passive investment managers do not attempt to beat the averages. Instead, passive managers try to mirror an average. To perform this task, they do not exercise any judgment about which stocks should be in their portfolios. Active managers, on the other hand, strive to outperform the average. That is their objective. They attempt to do this through a reliance on an ongoing analysis of each stock in the portfolio in an effort to decide whether to buy, sell, or hold. Despite all their attempts to do so, active professional money managers rarely beat the market averages on a consistent basis. As we wrote in our first book:

> This fact has often been associated with a view of the capital markets known as the "efficient markets hypothesis." Sometimes, proponents of this hypothesis liken investing in the stock market to "a random walk down Wall Street."
>
> The underlying principle of the efficient markets hypothesis is that prices in liquid markets such as the New York Stock Exchange pretty much reflect the true value of those stocks, because all available knowledge about those stocks is in the hands of the buyers and sellers as they decide to buy and sell. As a consequence, the hypothesis goes, bad news is discounted quickly and good news assimilated just as fast. Money managers who select individual stocks because they believe them to be good investments do not talk much about the efficient markets hypothesis because it contends that all the energy and money spent in the quest for bargain-priced stocks is wasted. Discomforting reports indicating that the majority of professional money managers fail to outperform the indices only seem to confirm the hypothesis. [Remember, as we noted above, that of the 383 general stock mutual funds with ten-year records, only 79 outperformed the S&P 500 Index.]

It is interesting to contemplate the notion that the market *is* actually random in nature, either because of the efficient markets hypothesis or for any other reason. Here's why. Let's assume that the largest component of a manager's investment performance is knowing whether, in general, the market will go up or down. This knowledge allows the manager to be more or less fully invested, depending on the coming swing in the market. Now, if market movements were truly random, let us ask the question: What is the probability that the direction of the market's movements is possible by sheer chance alone? Looking at a simplified example will clarify this problem. Let's ignore the magnitude of the market's movements and focus only on whether the market (however defined) is up or down at each year's end. If we make these admittedly simplistic assumptions and examine a seven-year period, what are the chances that an equity manager will have predicted each year's market movement accurately for all of the seven years? As it turns out, without the application of any skill whatsoever, the chance that a manager would predict the market seven years out of seven is about eight in a thousand. If there are 2,500 active equity managers in our example, about 20 of them would accurately predict the turns in the market for all seven years, by simple chance alone. Granted, the world is much more complex than this example, but the business of stock market prediction is nevertheless fraught with problems, regardless of whether the efficient markets hypothesis is true.

But, in fact, when examining the stock market, we can see at least two apparent trends that seem to dispute the efficient market hypothesis. These are what are known as persistence and reversion to the mean. Now these may seem like pretty fancy-sounding concepts, but they really aren't very hard to understand. When the stock market moves up one day, it is more likely to move up the very next day. This is what is called persistence. When the stock market moves up sharply over one or more months, the following period will probably underperform the historic averages during the next period of comparable length. While these tendencies do not form the basis for accurate predictions, they are quantifiable observations that appear to contradict the random walk or efficient markets hypothesis.

Yet these observable phenomena do not seem to be based on the market values of equities grounded in the fundamentals surrounding each issuing company. Instead, these trends seem to be based on the psychology of crowd behavior, or what is sometimes referred to as investor sentiment. Is investor sentiment predictable? Nobody knows for sure, but, to date, it does not seem to have yielded its secrets in a systematically predictable way.

But that the efficient market hypothesis is almost certainly invalid in certain specific circumstances does not mean that it has had a negligible impact on the behavior of investors. One principal reaction of many investors has been to throw up their hands in dismay and not worry about the selection of specific stocks on the basis of fundamental value or the perception of future growth. As a result, many investors have turned to strategies which seek only to mirror the performance of an index and do not rely on managers to exercise judgment in the more tedious process of selecting individual securities. This practice is known as *indexing* or *passive management,* whereas managers who select specific securities are known as *active* managers.[3]

Index managers do not manage stocks in any traditional sense of the word. Instead, they have a truly passive approach to the problem. An indexed portfolio operates by buying and holding all the stocks in a target index (e.g., S&P 500 Index). Many indexes are *market-cap weighted.* This means that each stock is held in the index in direct proportion to the weight that its market capitalization has in relation to all the stocks in the index. To understand indexing better, let's see how it would work with a hypothetical market-cap-weighted index consisting of only four stocks.

Table 5.1 illustrates certain facts about index construction that deserve comment. Most indexes try to replicate a specific segment of the capital markets. This is why they are market-cap weighted. That is, the stocks in the indexed portfolio are held in exact proportion that their market capitalization has to the sum of all the market capitalizations in the index. Thus, Stock A is worth half of the index's total market cap, while Stock D has only 5 percent of the index's total market cap. This means that the holding in Stock A will be exactly ten times more important than the holding in Stock D. Notice that the price per share in and of itself is important only

Table 5.1 Hypothetical Index with Four Stocks

Name of Stock	Number of Shares of Stock Each Company Has Outstanding	Price Per Share	Market Capitalization	% of Total Capitalization	Dollars Per Stock in a $20,000 Indexed Portfolio
Stock A	200	$25	$5,000	50	$10,000
Stock B	200	$15	3,000	30	6,000
Stock C	150	$10	1,500	15	3,000
Stock D	10	$50	500	5	1,000
Totals			$10,000	100	$20,000

when compared to the total number of shares outstanding. This is how the $50-per-share stock is only 10 percent of the index, while the $25 stock is 50 percent of the index.

Indexing is cheap to manage. You need only a computer and enough money to buy the required stocks. Indexing is intended never to outperform the index it is tied to, and, under many conditions, indexing does outperform most active management.

Every index is constructed with a certain objective in mind. In the case of the S&P 500, the objective is to replicate the universe of large-capitalization domestic American stocks. That replication implies a preference for the largest-cap stocks over the smaller-cap stocks within the index and makes the implicit assumption that, since most managers cannot beat the index, why even bother?

Indexed investing is a fascinating strategy. When compared to much of the active investing performed in the world of professional money management, it does have a certain attraction. But before we abandon the effort to make reasoned judgments about the management of a stock portfolio, let's put the discussion into context and look at the conventional wisdom about the matter of active investment management styles.

CONVENTIONAL WISDOM

Shown in Table 5.2 are the commonly held ideas about the relative returns and risks of various equity investment styles. It is interesting to note that the facts as set forth by financial researchers do not support all of these commonly held ideas equally well. Thus, we will explore the facts as they relate to each of these style notions.

WHAT THE DATA SHOW

Powerful as conventional wisdom is, sometimes it doesn't square with the facts. Charles Kettering, a famous scientist who worked for General Motors, knew this phenomenon well. Some of the ideas he developed were the automotive starter motor and the process for spray painting cars. What made Kettering a great practical scientist was that he took nothing for granted unless it was proven. This

Table 5.2   Commonly Held Notions of the Risk
and Reward Potential of Stock Investing Styles

(Ranked from lowest return and
lowest risk to highest return and highest risk)

Investment Style	Purported Characteristics
Large company income	High dividend income with modest capital gains potential
Large company value	Moderate dividend income with high capital gains potential
Large company growth and income	Moderate income with moderate potential for capital gains
Large company growth	Little or no income with potential for high and sustained capital gains
Large company aggressive growth	No income but large potential for high and sustained capital gains
Small company value	Moderate dividend income with high capital gains potential
Small company growth and income	Moderate income with moderate potential for capital gains
Small company growth	Little or no income with high potential for sustained capital gains
Small company aggressive growth	No income with highest potential for high and sustained capital gains

meant Kettering never blindly accepted any statement that said something was true or false, which requires an unusually open and objective mind, because often things are not as they are portrayed. Kettering knew to look before he leaped. That's how he protected himself from folly. As Kettering observed, people get strange notions in their heads and believe them to be true, regardless of what the evidence shows. Kettering likened the human mind to flypaper: Once an idea got stuck in it, the mind didn't want to let it go, regardless of whether it was right or wrong. Most people know plenty of things that are just not so. None of us are immune from this problem. Just think of all the opinions you have heard that were presented as fact. Now, some of those opinions were actually facts—but others were not.

For example, up until several hundred years ago, people were convinced that the earth stood still and the planets and stars (including the sun) revolved around it. Then the astronomer Copernicus visualized the sun at the center of the universe and began a revolution in astronomical thought. By supporting this new idea, Galileo found himself in big trouble with the Church. There were numerous other astronomers who refined the Copernican view of things, but it remained for Sir Isaac Newton to arrive on the scene and describe how gravity and planetary motion both operated on the same set of principles. Years passed, and conventional wisdom was not seriously challenged until Albert Einstein came along to describe the special relationships that arise when dealing with celestial measurements of space and time. Theoretical physics has now passed into the weird realm of quantum mechanics and string theory, where uncertainty reigns, and truth is much stranger than fiction. Theories of the commonplace change as we learn more about the world.

Our perception of the reality of planetary motion is grounded in the very language we use to express our observations. Despite data that show otherwise, we still speak of the sun as rising in the east and setting in the west. Upon examination of the data, we will show how the reality of stock investing is different from conventional wisdom. However, even when the data show differently, the labels used in stock investing sometimes only reinforce widely accepted conventions.

It is widely assumed that the hierarchy of returns begins with the lowly income investor, who is outperformed by the value investor, who is outperformed by the growth investor who, in turn, is outperformed by the highest-returning style of all: the aggressive growth investor. In point of fact, numerous studies show that this hierarchy is exactly backward. The facts support the reverse.

But conventional wisdom is not always wrong—not by a long shot—for common wisdom also has it that small-cap stocks outperform large-cap stocks, and this does, in fact, appear to be the case. However, as we will see, some data indicate that the investing style may have a lot more to do with high returns than market cap size. Finally, the data support the common notion that growth stock investing and small-cap stock investing are usually riskier than income and value investing.

GROWTH AND VALUE

Let's examine the case for the growth versus value versus income styles of investing. Consider information taken from studies performed by Professors Josef Lakonishok of the University of Illinois, Andrei Shleifer of Harvard University, and Robert Vishny of the University of Chicago.[4] These three studied S&P 500 returns from April 1963 through April 1990. They found that low price-to-book stocks, low price–to–cash flow stocks, and low price-to-earnings stocks all outperformed those stocks with high ratios. It wasn't even close. Put in another way, the data show that value stocks outperformed growth stocks for the 27-year period from 1963 through 1990. Table 5.3 shows data based on average annual rates of return with linked annual buy and hold periods.

So what does conventional wisdom say about these results? Simple—conventional wisdom says that higher returns must be offset by more risk as measured by volatility. Well, is this what happens in the real world? Nope. As it turns out, the professors found ". . . little if any support for the view that value strategies have been fundamentally riskier."[5]

One thing is true about the question of value versus growth styles of investing. During certain periods, one style will do better than the other. This is as true of growth investing as it is of value investing. But—and this is important—over the long-term periods, when selected in a disciplined and consistent fashion, the value stocks tend to outperform the growth stocks. The three professors in the study cited above tried to identify why value investing outperforms growth investing but couldn't come to any demonstrable conclu-

Table 5.3 Value Stocks versus Growth Stocks, 1963–1990

Ratio	Annual Returns for Stocks with Lower Ratios (%)	Annual Returns for Stocks with Higher Ratios (%)
Market price to book value	19.8	9.3
Market price to earnings	19.0	11.4
Market price to cash flow	20.10	9.10

S&P 500 Index Total Return 1963–1990 = 10.73%

sions. However, no matter which way they sliced the data, the results were the same. For example, companies with high growth rates in sales revenues were outdone by those with low growth rates. Other combinations made the same point. Portfolios of companies with, say, high growth in sales and high price–to–cash flow ratios, tended to underperform those with slower sales growth rates and low price-to-book ratios.

So what is one to make of this? Does the old saying about figures lying and liars figuring ring true here? Probably not. When consistent and rigidly quantitative methods are applied to stock investing, it is clear that over the longer term, value investing is a superior strategy to growth investing. Let's take another example from the quantitatively oriented investment research firm, BARRA.

In May 1992, BARRA introduced its S&P/BARRA Value Index. This index was constructed by ranking the 500 companies that make up the S&P 500 Index by the single fundamental characteristic of the market price–to–book value ratio. After ranking companies by their market price–to–book ratios, BARRA then selected those companies that make up half of the market capitalization of the S&P 500 Index with the lowest price-to-book ratios. (Remember, the market capitalization of a company is the number of shares it has outstanding multiplied by the market price per share.) The resulting group of companies constitutes the S&P/BARRA Value Index. Holdings of stocks composing this index are weighted within it according to their market capitalizations. Every six months, the S&P/BARRA Value Index is rebalanced to bring it into line with the set of market and book value data prevailing at the time of the rebalancing. For the period from January 1975 through November 1994, the S&P/BARRA Value Index had a substantial 1.45 percent per year compound annual premium when compared to the S&P 500 Index on a stand-alone basis, as shown in Figure 5.1.

A premium of 1.45 percent per year might not sound like a lot. However, if the Value Index outperformed the whole S&P 500 Index by 1.45 percent per year, then one would have been substantially better off for the entire period in question from 1975 to 1994. Table 5.4 illustrates this difference in terms of a $1,000 investment made at the beginning of the period, with all dividends reinvested.

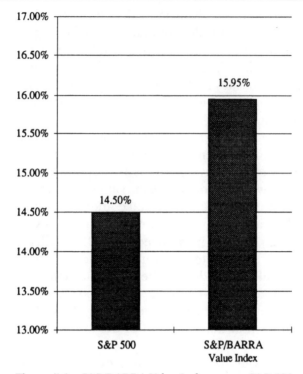

Figure 5.1 S&P/BARRA Value Index versus S&P 500, 1975 to 1994.

GROWTH, VALUE, AND INCOME

Not surprisingly, other researchers have found the same result when value stock selection is compared to growth stock selection. When applied in a consistent and disciplined way, the value style outperforms the growth style on a consistent basis, particularly when focused on the price-to-book ratios of the two contrasting styles. As we will discover later, though, there are some substantial discrepancies between the discipline of the research and the actual results posted by real-life value investors when compared to real-life growth investors. But before we tackle that question, let's look at income stock investing, for this is perhaps the most rewarding area for examination.

While the S&P/BARRA Value Index ranks and discriminates the S&P 500 on the basis of price-to-book ratios, this method also

Table 5.4   Value of $1,000 Invested in the
S&P/BARRA Value Index versus S&P 500, 1975–1994

Index Used	Annual Rate of Return (%)	Value of $1,000 Invested 1/75 to 11/94
S&P/BARRA Value	15.95	$19,057
S&P 500 Index	14.83	14,832

results in the selection of a portfolio of higher-yielding stocks than the S&P 500 Index taken on a stand-alone basis. The reason for this is that companies with low price-to-book ratios have typically had relatively low share prices at the time that the price-to-book ratio is calculated. Thus, dividend yields on the stocks within the S&P/ BARRA Value Index also tend to be higher than their growth stock counterparts. Thus, by categorizing stocks with a low price-to-book ratio, we end up with a portfolio of stocks that have higher dividends.

One study performed by professional investor David Dreman confirms the importance of the income style of stock management. Mr. Dreman is known for his focus on stocks with low price-to-earnings ratios. Yet when he examined the dividend component of a number of portfolios ranked from the highest price-to-earnings ratios to the lowest, he found that the dividend income component strongly correlated with higher total returns.[6] Table 5.5 shows the dividend yields and total returns for portfolios of 1,251 of the largest publicly traded stocks selected on the basis of their price-to-earnings ratios from August 1968 through August 1977.

Table 5.5 shows a high correlation between low price-to-earnings ratio, high income, and high total return. Interestingly, the nine-year period in question was an awful time for the stock market in general. The S&P 500 posted an average compound annual return of only 3.79 percent for the entire period, far below its 69-year average return of 10.2 percent per year. Finally, it appears as though when the portfolio was regularly rescreened according to the price-to-earnings decile, total returns tended to go up. Thus, the three-month interval for rescreening outperformed the nine-year holding period, while the one-year and the three-year screening intervals fell in between the three-month and the nine-year periods.

Table 5.5 Low Price-to-Earnings Ratios and High Dividends, 1968–1977

P/E Ratio Decile 1—highest 10—lowest	Rescreening after 3 Months		Rescreening after Each Year		Rescreening after 3 Years		Holding for All 9 Years	
	Yield	Total Return	Yield	Total Return	Yield	Total Return	Yield	Total Return
1	1.17	-2.64	1.15	-1.13	1.22	-1.43	1.17	0.33
2	1.76	0.92	-1.70	0.56	2.28	-.028	2.96	1.27
3	2.17	0.51	2.21	1.63	2.25	0.85	2.32	3.30
4	0.94	3.06	2.78	3.31	2.95	4.87	2.89	3.36
5	3.21	2.19	3.21	2.93	3.31	5.02	3.00	3.72
6	3.65	4.84	3.67	6.70	3.43	4.82	3.39	4.52
7	4.00	7.90	4.06	6.85	3.93	5.89	3.82	6.08
8	4.19	8.83	4.18	8.56	4.05	7.78	4.44	6.35
9	4.28	11.85	4.22	6.08	4.27	7.73	4.21	6.40
10	4.26	14.00	4.06	10.26	4.26	10.89	4.83	7.89

Average Annual Total Return for Sample = 4.75%
Average Annual Total Return for S&P = 3.79%

The fact is that most value portfolios are also high-dividend portfolios. But which is the best or most reliable determinant of greater total return? Is it a fundamental value-oriented criterion such as price-to-book ratios? Or is it the dividend? There is no doubt that there is a high correlation between the two investing styles, but which is truly the most important factor?

Taking the debate one step further, in late 1994, BARRA released the BARRA Equity Income Index, which uses the same methodology as the S&P/BARRA Value Index, but uses dividend yields to identify the half of the S&P 500 market capitalization with the highest income instead of with the lowest price-to-book.[7] The annualized compound results of the S&P 500, the S&P/BARRA Value Index, and the BARRA Equity Income Index for the period from January 1975 through November 1994 are shown in Figure 5.2.

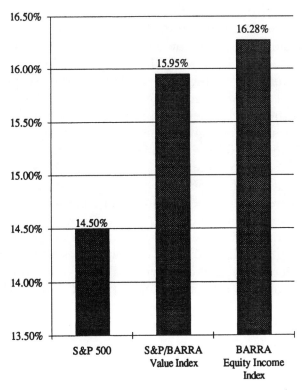

Figure 5.2 Value versus income versus S&P 500, 1975 to 1994.

As Figure 5.2 demonstrates, for the period in question, there was an additional one-third of a percentage point per year premium earned by directly focusing on the highest-yielding stocks within the S&P 500 Index instead of focusing merely on price-to-book data as does the S&P/BARRA Value Index. Intuitively, this would seem especially true in the case of retirement accounts, where taxes on dividend income can be deferred until retirement, allowing dividend payments to be reinvested and compounded on a pretax basis. And while these results do not factor in the transaction costs or other expenses of rebalancing these indexes twice a year, they are accurate in the sense that they were derived quantitatively, and thus there was no active involvement that would have injected extraneous factors into the analysis.

Let's consider another quantitatively oriented method of income stock selection, but one that includes far fewer stocks. This method of stock portfolio management is sometimes called "The Dow Dogs." It is derived by selecting, at the beginning of each year, the ten stocks in the Dow Jones Industrial Average (DJIA) that have the largest dividend yields. At the end of the year, the investor again determines the ten highest-yielding stocks in the DJIA and sells those held during the previous year that do not now qualify, while buying those that do. Annualized compound returns from this method for the ten-year period from January 1975 through December 1994 are shown in Figure 5.3.

A Dow Dogs portfolio has too few stocks in it to be considered well diversified from a statistical point of view. However, since the DJIA is composed of the 30 stocks that Dow Jones & Company considers most representative of industrial America, the Dow Dogs method confers some benefits not automatically available to other poorly diversified stock portfolios. By confining the portfolio to a relatively high quality universe of companies while picking the ones that have the highest dividend yield and lowest relative prices, the portfolio makes up in quality what it may lack in diversification. This allows the Dow Dogs investor to generate high compoundable income, as well as price increases, should the fundamental and tangible prospects for the company appear to be improved.

The importance of quality in income investing is interesting and significant. However, before we delve into additional research in this area, let's consider a few other pieces to this puzzle.

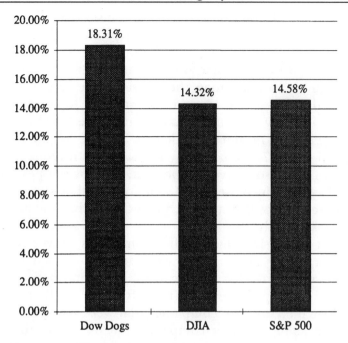

Figure 5.3 The Dow Dogs, 1975 to 1994.

THE SMALL-CAP EFFECT

Historically, the stocks of smaller companies tend to outperform the stocks of large companies. Using the most widely cited data from Ibbotson Associates, Inc., Figure 3.2 showed the comparison between the total return for small-cap stocks (12.2 percent) and that for large-cap stocks (10.2 percent) during the 69-year period from 1926 through 1994. According to these widely circulated statistics, the difference between the two was a whopping 2 percent per year of compound annual return.[8] Since this comparison seems pretty clear, then one should always invest in small company stocks, right? Well, not exactly.

To properly understand the small-cap effect, we have to consider how corporations are started, grow, and mature. At inception, a corporation may not have much intrinsic value. Its revenues are small, its products are unknown, and it is usually not profitable. However, as the successful company grows, its growth rate will usually start out very high and slow down over time. Consider Table 5.6, tracking the historic growth of revenues and profits at Microsoft, the computer software giant, from 1985 through 1995.

As Table 5.6 shows, Microsoft grew much more rapidly when the company was small than they have in the recent past and, although they are likely to continue growing for some time to come, it is unlikely to continue at the rate posted during many of its earlier years. Consider the following. For the 12-month period from 1986 to 1987, the company increased its revenues by $149 million, an increase of over 75 percent, and for the period from 1994 to 1995, the increase was $1.2 billion. Yet that makes for only a 27.7 percent growth rate. The plain fact is that the arithmetic always works like this.

It is not surprising that smaller companies grow faster than larger companies. Their growth rates are tied to their size. Neither is it surprising that smaller companies are more prone to failure and mishap. For every Microsoft, there are literally thousands of smaller software companies that were started and failed during the 1980s. Smaller companies not only have the potential to grow faster, they also have a heightened potential for failure.

Table 5.6 Historic Growth of Microsoft, 1985–1995

12 Months Ending June 30	Revenues ($ millions)	Revenue Growth Rate (%)	Net Income ($ millions)	Income Growth Rate (%)
1985	140		24	
1986	197	40.7	39	62.5
1987	346	75.6	72	84.6
1988	591	70.8	124	72.2
1989	804	36.0	171	37.9
1990	1183	47.1	279	63.2
1991	1843	55.8	463	65.9
1992	2759	49.7	708	52.9
1993	3753	36.0	953	34.6
1994	4649	23.9	1146	20.3
1995	5937	27.7	1453	26.8

Interestingly, though it is not generally recognized, all successful growth companies eventually become large dividend-paying companies over time. Think about it. Railroads were a hot growth industry in the 1800s. When electric utilities were in their infancy during the early 1900s, they were the growth industries of their time. IBM, now viewed as a large, somewhat stodgy technology company, epitomized the growth company of the 1960s.

But there is another aspect to smaller companies that makes them a problem for the retirement investor. Small companies are focused on growing the business. This means that all their profits are reinvested, no money is available for dividends, and the entire rate of return to the investor must come from share-price increases alone. Since share-price increases are much less reliable than dividends, retirement investors in small-cap companies are left with an additional exposure to the vagaries of the capital markets for their returns. For example, from 1926 through 1994, dividends on large-cap domestic stocks were 15 times more stable than large-cap stock prices were during the same period. When compared to small-cap returns, dividends on large-company stocks were over 26 times more stable. Shareholders of publicly traded smaller companies are therefore much more exposed to the uncertain movements of the capital markets than those with portfolios of large-cap, dividend-paying stocks. What this suggests is that retirement investors should focus on dividend-producing companies to build value in their retirement accounts first, and then possibly look at small-cap stocks later when they can better afford the risk.

Small-cap stocks by their very nature provide less liquidity than large-cap stocks. They have fewer shares outstanding, and the number of shares available for sale and purchase at any given time can be limited. This makes them more difficult to buy and sell, and makes their prices more volatile. Compounding this occasional lack of liquidity is the fact that there is some evidence that the principal market for small-cap stocks, the NASDAQ market, is more easily manipulated than is the principal market for large-cap stocks, the New York Stock Exchange.[9]

While it is undeniable that smaller-cap companies boast higher returns than large-cap companies, they also provide higher risks. This is a topic we will revisit later when we examine the subject of risk more thoroughly.

VALUE AND GROWTH, GIVEN DIFFERENT
MARKET CAP SIZES

This is a topic that produces more heat than light. As conventional wisdom would have it, if large-cap growth stocks outperform large-cap value stocks, then this phenomenon should be even more pronounced in small-cap stocks. Thus, it is widely believed that small-cap growth stocks will outperform small-cap value stocks. However, when pursued in a consistent and disciplined manner, nothing could be further from the truth.

Let's examine the data from Frank Russell Company. If you will recall, Russell compiles and publishes a number of indexes, including the Russell 3000 which represents some 98 percent of all the investable publicly traded stock on the U.S. market. Making up the Russell 3000 are two other indexes: the Russell 1000, the thousand largest publicly traded companies, and the Russell 2000, the 2000 smallest publicly traded companies.

The Russell 2000 is a good representation of the domestic small-cap market. In a way similar to the S&P/BARRA Growth and Value Indexes, the Russell Indexes have been split into value and growth components. These are known as the Russell 1000 Value and Growth and the Russell 2000 Value and Growth. The Russell Value Indexes are based on below-average price-to-book ratios and below-average rates of forecasted earnings growth. (When constructed in this way, the value indexes also end up with higher-than-average dividend yields and lower-than-average price-to-earnings ratios.) The Russell Growth Indexes contain those stocks with the opposite characteristics.

Figure 5.4 illustrates the value-versus-growth question in the context of market cap size. The figures are the total annual returns for the Russell Indexes shown for the 16-year period from 1979 through 1994.

As we can see, the large-cap value style outperformed the large-cap growth style by 1.15 percent per year of annual return. The difference between the small-cap value style and the small-cap growth style is even more pronounced. Value beats growth again, this time by 4.09 percent per year of annual return. Additionally, the small-cap growth style managed to underperform both the large-cap styles, lagging the large-cap value style by 2.52 percent per year, on average, for the 16-year period from 1979 through 1994.[10]

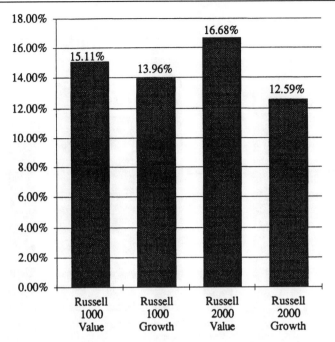

Figure 5.4 Russell Value versus Growth Indexes, 1979 to 1994. (SOURCE: Frank Russell Co.)

Another set of value and growth style indexes was developed by Wilshire Associates, an investment consulting firm. These indexes are constructed with three different sizes of market capitalizations: large-cap, medium-cap, and small-cap. The Wilshire value indexes are based not only on low price-to-book ratios, but also on low price-to-earnings ratios and high dividend yields. The growth indexes are constructed with companies that have high sales growth, high return on equity, and low dividend payout ratios. When we examine Wilshire's 15-year data for the period ending in February 1995, we see the same sort of results seen in our other examples, as shown in Figure 5.5.

Once again, the value-versus-growth issue seems to transcend different market capitalizations, from the largest to the smallest. And, while different periods and different indexes give different results, the fundamental trend seems self-evident: The value style of investing outperforms the growth style. Although it is less self-evident that the driving force behind the superior performance of

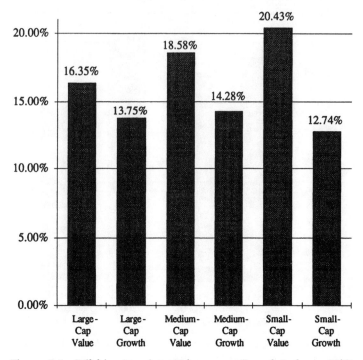

Figure 5.5 Wilshire Associates Value versus Growth Indexes, 1979 to 1995. (SOURCE: Wilshire Associates Incorporated.)

the value style of investing is dividends, a number of signs point in that direction.

VALUE AND GROWTH, GIVEN ACTIVE AND PASSIVE MANAGEMENT

Thus far, we have been talking about styles of equity selection. We have shown that, when selected on the basis of their numerical characteristics, the long-term total returns on indexes constructed of value stocks have outperformed the total returns on indexes constructed from growth stocks. These numeric characteristics have typically included price-to-book ratios, as well as measures of earnings and dividends. But, given the evidence that value investing outperforms growth investing, what happens when active professional managers attempt to apply these style disciplines to the management of an actual portfolio?

To test this proposition, the mutual fund rating service, Morningstar, Incorporated, tracked actual mutual fund performance by style for mutual funds that invest in large-, medium-, and small-cap stocks in either the value or growth styles using their own characterizations involving price-to-book ratios and price-to-earnings ratios. For 5-, 10-, and 15-year periods ending February 28, 1995, the total annualized returns are shown in Table 5.7.

Now this gets interesting. The quantitative value indexes all show that the value style of stock selection will outperform the growth style. Yet, in practice, Morningstar found that growth fund managers have outperformed the value fund managers. What's going on here?

To understand the nature of this quandary, we have to examine how active value managers actually make their investment decisions. More often than not, value management techniques consist of using classical securities analysis as set forth by Ben Graham. As we discussed earlier, the most important concept in Graham's methods is the notion of a reasonable range of intrinsic value for each stock. If an investment falls outside the upper end of this range, value investors will consider it overvalued. If an investment falls outside the lower end of this range, they consider it a bargain. Value managers want to purchase bargains. And when they do this,

Table 5.7 Growth Mutual Funds versus Value Mutual Funds

Period Ending Feb. 28, 1995		Large-Cap (%)	Medium-Cap (%)	Small-Cap (%)
5-year	Growth funds	11.58	12.36	14.84
	Value funds	9.94	10.05	11.69
	Growth funds premium	1.64	2.31	3.15
10-year	Growth funds	12.97	13.33	11.77
	Value funds	11.08	11.71	11.26
	Growth funds premium	1.89	1.62	0.51
15-year	Growth funds	13.21	13.84	11.55
	Value funds	12.60	13.59	12.57
	Growth funds premium	0.61	0.25	(1.02)

they fly in the face of the accepted valuation range for the stock as perceived by other participants in the market.

People who go to garage sales and flea markets regularly genuinely like the valuable bargains they collect. Sometimes their passion goes beyond the search for a good deal. They get sentimentally attached to the point where they and they alone know the value of that torn sweatshirt or the old bicycle that sits rusting in the barn. Active value investors are a lot like these people. They get attached to their stock picks. They believe that other people must inevitably come to value their junk as highly as they do themselves. Investing requires patience, to be sure, but the clock is an unmerciful taskmaster when it comes to calculating rates of return. We suspect that the psychology of many value investors works like that of junk sale aficionados. They like their junk, and the nuggets they are able to find motivate them to continue seeking the next great treasure that lies just around the bend.

The problem is that a lot of junk deserves to be junk. Other junk requires the passage of so much time to become valuable that one can never be sure when it passes from being junk to become an antique. Some low-priced stocks deserve to be low-priced stocks. If their low book values have resulted from years of losses or huge write-offs stemming from strategic failure, it is possible that the share prices of many companies with low price-to-book values will remain low. It doesn't take too many of these kinds of securities to seriously compromise a rate of return.

Making the value manager's problem even more difficult is the increasingly efficient nature of the stock selection process. As noted previously, the world has changed since Ben Graham's time. There are more analysts dealing with more information that comes more quickly than ever. This makes it harder and harder to separate the real bargains from the junk and the actuality of value from the perception of value.

Active growth managers, on the other hand, just might do better (yet still fail to beat the averages) because they tend to follow the crowd with respect to their stock picking. That is, when everyone thinks something is hot, they do, too. Growth investors are quick to spot a trend and even quicker to jump off the trend as soon as it appears to slow down. A good example of this happened in January 1996. The computer chip manufacturer, Intel, reported record 1995 fourth-quarter profits of $867 million. Although this was more than double the profit shown in the fourth quarter of 1994, it fell 13 cents per share short of analysts' expectations, and Intel's stock price fell 10.3 percent the day following the announcement. What's more, a record 68 million shares of Intel traded as hordes of growth investors all tried to get out at the same time.

Value investors will hold a low-priced stock darned near forever waiting for the market to agree that it should be valued more highly. Growth investors will jump like fleas on a hot griddle whenever they smell the slightest deviation from their expectations. Passive value investing, on the other hand, requires the purchase of a large number of low-priced stocks without regard to which stock is the better bargain. Passive growth investing requires purchase of a large number of high-priced stocks without regard to which stock may be overpriced. On average, a passive value investor will tend to do better because it is advantageous to pay too little for a basket of stocks than to pay too much.

We are left with a fundamental quandary. The quantitatively managed value portfolio outperforms the quantitatively managed growth portfolio. But the actively managed value portfolio underperforms its growth counterpart. The small-cap portfolio outperforms the large-cap portfolio. But the small-cap portfolio is going to give you a bumpy ride with indigestion along the way and offers almost no dividend income to boot. What is a retirement investor to do? If only there were a quantitative way to find value and income in the large-cap marketplace without buying your fair share of junk. We did some research to try and find a way to do it.

BOOK VALUE IS NOT THE BEST QUANTITATIVE STOCK-PICKING TOOL

Much of the academic research in the value-versus-growth debate has focused on price-to-book ratios. The book value of a company is what is left over after you subtract all of its liabilities from all of its assets. Increasingly, book value is difficult to calculate. Here's why. Certain liabilities may not even appear on the balance sheet but are still an obligation of the corporation. More important, assets on the balance sheet are harder than ever to value appropriately. What is a brand name worth? How about a logo? With the increasing prevalence of mass communication and mass marketing, these assets are more valuable than ever but devilishly difficult to put a price on. Then you have intellectual property related to technology. How can a software company value its software? What about a company that developed software, but only for its own internal use? To be sure, there are accounting rules that apply to these questions, but they leave a lot of room for interpretation. When you combine these valuation problems with the balance sheet write-offs that come from multiple waves of corporate restructurings, it is easy to see why book value has less meaning than it did only a few years ago.

A good test of using book value as the main ratio to boost total returns has come from those few mutual funds that have actually tried the theory out in practice. As it turns out, virtually all of them have done relatively poorly, according to the mutual fund rating company, Morningstar.[11] This is not to say that the price-to-book ratio is unimportant. Neither would we claim that value investors will continue to do poorly if they stick to their guns and invest strictly in those companies sporting low price-to-book ratios.

What we are saying is that there is something a lot more important to focus on when investing in stocks. Ideally, you want a tool that would help measure quality so as to find stocks that happen to be underpriced at the time they are purchased but are still fundamentally sound. We would also want a portfolio management tool that allowed us to know when to sell a stock because there was probably a better stock to own than the one we owned. As it turns out, evidence points strongly that the lowly dividend is just such a tool. And, provided you are not forced to sell shares at a loss, the dividend payment itself makes the ownership of a stock a productive proposition in and of itself, regardless of share price. Plus, an additional bonus is available to those who collect dividends from their stock portfolio. That is the compounding effect available from the steady reinvestment of dividends.

We have seen evidence (in David Dreman's work, in the BARRA Equity Income Index, the Dow Dogs investment method, and the Wilshire Indexes) that a focus on the dividend yield of stocks may yield higher total returns. However, our studies show that, if history is any guide, by focusing on the dividend, one may construct quantitatively managed stock portfolios that perform very well over all multiyear periods during the last 20 years. Why is the dividend so important?

When we were kids, somebody told us there was a pot of gold at the end of the rainbow. We can remember actually having climbed on our bikes to look for the gold. Shovel in hand, we pumped furiously toward the rainbow, only to have it recede into the distance. When you depend on the prediction of future events as the core of your analysis, you are bound to be wrong at least as often as you are right. When you chase the pot of gold at the end of the rainbow because somebody told you that it was there, you are going to be disappointed when you don't find any gold. Instead, you arrive where you thought the gold would be, tired and empty-handed.

Price to earnings, price to book value, return on equity, revenue growth rates, and all the other tools of stock analysis are informative and interesting. But, in comparison to dividends, they are just numbers. In and of themselves, they do not necessarily indicate anything. But when a company sends out checks to shareholders, that money is real. It is tangible. It is the payment made to the owners of a business for being the owners of the business. What's more, dividends, as noted earlier, are remarkably stable. Companies that pay dividends usually continue to pay dividends. Moreover, a stock portfolio constructed entirely from high-quality dividend stocks can be assured that, if history is any guide, the dividend payments will not only be stable, they will actually increase over time.

We spoke previously of the intimate connection between dividends and the price of a company's stock. The big difference between this relationship and other measures of stock valuation is that the dividend is real and the other numbers are just numbers. But there is more to this issue of the tangible reality of dividend payments. As it turns out, when properly viewed and managed, dividend yields are true north on a compass we can use in the search for capital gains.

Please be aware that the idea of producing superior capital gains *and* superior income is not conventional wisdom. It is widely assumed that you may have either income or capital gains, but you cannot have both. Our research tells a different story.

DIVIDEND INVESTING: CAN YOU HAVE YOUR CAKE AND EAT IT, TOO?

The focus of our research into dividend investing was simple. We wanted to create high cash income and high capital gains in a portfolio of first-rate, high-quality stocks. To accomplish this, we focused on the dividend as the arbiter of true value. We also knew that we wanted to develop a quantitative method for stock selection that would eliminate the emotional content of the stock selection process.

We employed computer screening of our own design using publicly available data. We started with 12 different screens for yield and quality and gradually narrowed our focus down to those 6 screens that had the largest demonstrated impact on long-term total return. Each screen was bound by quantitative factors. If a stock passed all six screens, it was automatically placed on the list. If it did not qualify, it was not on the list. The precise final design of each of the variables became subject to extensive testing over multiple historic periods using data that went back to 1975. The S&P 500 Index was selected as the universe to use in our research for a variety of reasons:

- The S&P 500 is perhaps the best-known broad-based index and represents approximately 80 percent of the value of the market capitalization of the New York Stock Exchange.[12]
- The S&P 500 is an index that attempts to include companies in each industry proportionally to their representation of the total market capitalization of all widely traded stocks.
- The S&P 500 includes mostly large-capitalization stocks but does include some medium-capitalization stocks, thus giving an exposure to a larger range of the publicly traded equity market than an index based solely on large-capitalization companies would give.
- The S&P 500 is made up entirely of domestic stocks, thus eliminating most of the international risks associated with foreign stocks.
- The companies in the S&P 500 are all widely held stocks that are relatively liquid; that is, trading in these stocks is sufficiently active to allow an investor to buy and sell as freely as possible without unduly influencing the price.

Following selection of the universe of stocks, we began our search for those disciplined quantitative tools that would tell us which were the highest-quality, highest-yielding stocks. The first five of these screening factors were used to weed out lower-quality stocks, while the last screen was simply to select the 40 highest-yielding stocks that remained after the first five screens. Through extensive testing, we found that the first five screens had to be designed to be as inclusive as possible within rather wide ranges, and then the final screen had to be more exclusive to construct the final portfolio. The six screens used are as follows:

- Growth in dividends
- Payout ratios
- Debt-to-equity ratios
- Price-to-earnings ratios
- Price-to-book ratios
- High dividend yields

Let's examine these screens one by one to analyze the thinking behind the construction of the research data.

Growth in Dividends

Yield alone does not tell us anything about the quality of a stock. Here's why. When a company has net profits, the company's board of directors must decide how much, if any, to pay to shareholders as dividends and how much to keep for reinvesting in the business. But once a board of directors begins paying dividends to shareholders, that dividend is cut only as a last resort. This is true even if the company is doing poorly from a financial perspective. If a company's operating earnings slip, the stock price will usually go down, but rarely is the dividend cut. Remember, if a stock's price goes down and its dividend stays the same, the dividend yield will increase. Thus, if we search solely for stocks that have a high yield, we are bound to end up with a fair number of disappointments by investing in companies whose stock deserves to be priced low.

When a company's earnings go up, its dividend is not always increased. Instead, the company's board increases dividends only when it feels that the increases are sustainable in future quarters. If earnings go up, but the company's board does not believe they will stay higher, then the board will not vote to increase the regular dividend payment. Thus, increases in dividends are a reasonably reliable sign that the company believes its earnings will be able to sustain future dividend payments at the new, higher level. Dividend increases are a good sign that a company is fundamentally healthy.

There are many companies whose dividend has increased regularly over many years. The stock prices of these companies are likely to have already been bid up as stockholders have a built-in preference for regularly increasing dividend payments. Due to their generally higher prices, these stocks are likely to have moderate yields with a history of steady dividend growth. However, we learned that because stocks with a long history (7 to 15 years) of dividend increases are usually already highly priced, then there is less of a chance for the capture of capital gains.

Given that the behaviors of investors and boards of directors lead to these results, we attempted to find a quantitative measure of dividend growth that would indicate a healthy company whose stock happened, for any number of reasons, to be temporarily depressed. Through quantitative research, we found that companies that had only a few years of dividend increases were fundamentally healthy but were not always valued as highly in the market as those companies that had had a longer record of increasing dividends.

Thus, the first screen for growing dividends excluded all those companies in the S&P 500 that do not pay a dividend or whose dividend has gone down or been flat for the past several years.

Payout Ratios

From the stocks that are left over after we finished our screening for dividend growth, we screened for payout ratios. The payout ratio is the amount of earnings a company pays out in dividends. If a company has $100 million in earnings and pays out $75 million in dividends, it has a 75 percent payout ratio. The higher the ratio, the greater the proportion of earnings that are paid out in dividends. The idea behind this screen was simple. Companies must not pay out too much of their earnings in dividends or they will not have any margin of safety to continue the dividend payment if their earnings go down. This screen was intended to eliminate those companies that are getting too close to the blades, without weeding out those fundamentally healthy companies whose earnings dip was purely temporary. Thus, we screened out all those companies whose payout ratios are too high.

Debt-to-Equity Ratios

The debt-to-equity ratio is the comparison between a company's debt and the value of its shareholders' net ownership in the business (or equity). If a company has equity of $100 million and debt of $50 million, then it has a 50 percent debt-to-equity ratio. The larger the ratio, the more debt a company has in comparison to shareholders' equity. The reason you don't want a company with too much debt is that if the company is faced with adverse conditions such as declining sales or increased expenses, it might have to pay creditors rather than paying dividends. Additionally, when debt levels are too high, companies may not have enough earnings to grow the company, pay the dividend, and service the debt. Again, we screened for debt levels that were extraordinarily high and thus were an indication that the company was overextended.

Price-to-Earnings Ratios

The price-to-earnings ratio is the comparison between a stock's market price per share and its earnings per share. If a company has earnings of $5.00 per share and a stock price of $50 per share, its stock will have a price-to-earnings ratio of 10—that is, the stock is selling for ten times its earnings. The larger the ratio, the higher the price as compared to the earnings. Some active value investors use the price-to-earnings ratio as the most important screen for the selection of undervalued stocks. However, we used it only to eliminate those stocks that had ratios that were way too high or were negative.[13] Thus, on either end of this spectrum of price-to-earnings ratios, we decided that higher-quality companies would be safer choices.

Market-to-Book Ratios

We have already discussed this ratio, as it has been used in numerous studies as the defining characteristic for the identification of value stocks. We did not use it as the most important variable, though. Instead, we used this ratio to eliminate only those stocks selling at extremely high values compared to their book values, as well as those stocks that were selling at negative book values.

Dividend Yields

After running the first five screens, we then ranked the stocks that remained by dividend yield and selected the 40 highest-yielding stocks. The selection of 40 stocks was made to ensure adequate diversification across industry categories and companies. No attempt was made to select or eliminate any given industry group from the list. When a stock passed all the screens, it was included.

The resulting portfolio was equal-weighted. This was done because, despite repeated testing, we could not find a more advantageous way to weight each holding. This means that the portfolio began each testing period with 2.5 percent of the total investable value in each of the 40 selected stocks. All dividends were considered reinvested as received. Repeated testing was performed to determine what the optimal period would be between screenings. A six-month rescreening period was selected, with the screens to be run based on financial information submitted to the Securities and Exchange Commission (SEC) as of the end of the March and September quarters. During each rescreening event, we applied the entire discipline to the S&P 500 Index and compared the resulting list of stocks with the list that had been in place during the preceding six months. On average, between 10 and 15 stocks were eliminated from the portfolio after rescreening and new stocks put into their place. Additionally, all positions were rebalanced to their 2.5 percent equal weighting, regardless of where the market prices had driven the prices and weightings since the prior rescreening.

The results of the research for the periods ending December 31, 1995, are summarized in Figure 5.6. As with the previously cited data, all returns shown in Figure 5.6 are gross of any expenses and expressed as annualized total returns, including all dividends and reinvested capital gains.

Interestingly, by focusing on high quality and high dividends, the quantitative methods used in this research performed better than the equity total returns generated in any of the other studies cited earlier.

That said, there are several other appropriate caveats about the results of this research. First, while the methods used in construc-

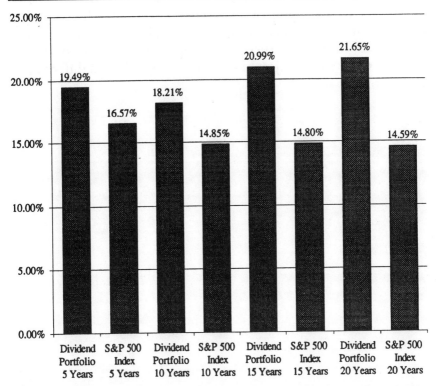

Figure 5.6 Dividend portfolio versus the S&P 500 for periods ending December 31, 1995. (SOURCE: Benson White & Company.)

tion of the dividend portfolio were strictly and quantitatively applied, it is impossible and unwise to extrapolate from these results into the future. Even though the methods are fundamentally sound, one can never be sure of what lies ahead. And, regardless of the equity investing style employed, the period studied, from 1975 through 1995, was a very good period for stocks. Second, there are a number of real-world problems that cannot be fully taken into account in performing this kind of research. The cost of trading (buying and selling the stocks), the exact date of trades, and the actual accuracy of the contemporary information compared to subsequently corrected but initially inaccurate data. Finally, we should note that, due to a lack of consistent research data from before 1975, the period in question does not include the absolutely terrible decade from 1965 through 1974 when the S&P 500 registered a paltry 1.2 percent per year average annual return.[14]

Criticism of this type of research is inevitable. But the fact remains that high dividends from high-quality companies appear to be the key to the construction of a superior retirement portfolio. Now let's turn to the subject of bond investing, where a different set of questions awaits.

SIX

Capital Market Tools Used in Life-Cycle Retirement Investing—Bond Investing

BROTHERS OFTEN FIGHT over property. We know of two kids who squabble all the time about one thing or another. It is a familiar pattern—one boy gets into the stuff of another and "borrows" it for a while.

When discovered, the borrower says, "Hey, you told me I could borrow that CD."

The "lender" will have none of this, "Yeah, I might have said you could borrow it, but not for three months! I've been looking everywhere for it and I want it back now."

"OK, OK. Here, take your CD," says the borrower.

"Next time you want to borrow my stuff, ask me if you can keep it. Don't just take it without returning it," complains the injured party.

"If you're so upset about me borrowing your CD, then you can borrow two of mine for as long as you want," the other one says.

"Maybe I will," the brother shoots back. "But I want three of your CDs for a month, it's only fair."

As Sydney Homer noted in his well-known book, *A History of Interest Rates,* when property is transferred to another owner without payment, it can be classified as a gift, a loan, or theft. "Loans occur even when not formally negotiated; credit can exist without being clearly defined. This ambiguity is not new." Credit has been with us before commerce. Farmers who borrowed seed until harvest time would be required to return more grain than they borrowed. Around 1800 B.C., the Babylonian Code of Hammurabi set forth elaborate rules governing lending, borrowing, and interest.[1] The practice of lending has been around for a long time.

Lending is not the same as ownership. Ownership implies discretion over property and the right to receive any benefits that the property might confer on its owner. In the case of a stock, the owner can benefit from the dividend income and from a possible increase in price. Since the company that issued the stock can grow distributable benefits to its owners, the potential for return is larger than the return available to a lender who agrees to lend money at a specific rate for a specific period of time.

In other words, stocks outperform bonds over the long term. This familiar refrain has been repeated so often that many people can't think of why anyone would own any bonds—ever. It's true that the total long-term returns from stocks are higher than the total returns from bonds. But so what? Stocks and bonds are fundamentally different. Saying that stocks have greater total returns than bonds is like saying that a bird can fly better than a dog. It's true, but it doesn't make a lot of sense to compare birds and dogs when it comes to flying. This fundamental fact is sometimes forgotten by those in the financial services industry. In the scramble for higher total returns, some investors begin to believe that dogs can fly—or that they ought to be able to.

A bond is the evidence of a loan. When people buy bonds, they are exchanging cash for a promise from a corporation or a government to repay the original loan amount plus a specified amount of interest to be paid at specific times. Bonds pay a rate of interest (known as the *coupon*) in accordance with their maturity, credit quality, and the prevailing conditions in the credit markets. Bonds with longer maturities usually pay higher interest rates. Conversely, bonds with shorter maturities usually pay lower interest rates. Long maturities usually pay more than short maturities because there are more unknowns in the distant future than there are in the near future, and a lender must be compensated for those unknown risks. High-quality bonds will tend to pay lower interest rates. Bad credit risks must pay more interest to attract lenders because the lenders are not as certain to be paid their interest and principal in full and in a timely manner.

For most high-quality bonds, a bondholder who buys a bond when it is issued will never lose money as long as the issuer remains solvent and the bondholder is willing to wait until all the interest and principal has been paid. The bondholder may make less money than possible elsewhere, but, unlike investing in stocks, if a bond-holder buys a bond at its issuance and is willing to wait for a bond to be paid off, no loss will occur.

Bond interest rates are made up of several components, which, when taken together, add up to the total interest rate paid. There is the real interest rate, a risk premium, and the expected (or implicit) inflation rate. The real interest rate involves the "rental" rate on the borrowed money. This is the bond investor's nominal return. The so-called risk premium is made up of several factors. There is credit risk, which involves the risk of nonpayment of interest or principal. There is interest rate risk, when the price of a bond changes because of shifts in interest rates. There is reinvestment rate risk, which involves the rate at which a bond buyer can reinvest his interest and principal as cash payments are received. Added to this is the expected inflation risk. Here, the purchasing power of the bond investor's capital will diminish unless adjusted to compensate for the expectation of inflation over the holding period of the bond.

Bond investing is about the generation of steady and predictable cash flows. As we will see, prevailing interest rates go up and down, changing the value of bonds that have already been issued and establishing the rate of interest to be paid when new bonds are issued. But the essence of any bond is that it will generate steady and predictable cash flows from interest paid on it as well as preserve the invested capital that is ultimately returned to the bondholder. These facts aside, there are many people who try to generate better returns from bonds. Some try to anticipate interest rates (an impossible task). Others sacrifice credit quality for higher coupons (a risky tactic). Still others invent creative ways to complicate what should be a relatively simple proposition between borrower and lender.

In early 1995, Orange County, California, was in the news for the sorry state of its finances. The epicenter of this financial earthquake was the investment office of Robert Citron, County Treasurer. It seems the treasurer was a victim of his own financial alchemy. With interest rates in decline for years, a securities salesperson helped the treasurer stumble onto an idea to increase his return on the debt securities (bonds) he managed on behalf of the county and other public entities. It was going to be real easy—like shooting fish in a barrel. We bet the good treasurer thought himself quite the clever financial wizard, especially compared to those unsophisticated boobs who called for caution. His scheme was simple. He could borrow money based on the value of his fund's securities at an interest cost that was less than the interest rate he could earn by investing the borrowed money. The net spread between the two rates was extra yield that increased returns. He then multiplied the spread with leverage—by borrowing more. Consequently, when the additional spread from leverage was added to existing interest earnings from the portfolio, the fund got a big boost in return. So it was not long before this gentleman put Orange County into the big-time spread business. However, the treasurer forgot that the trends change. From time to time, if you set out to hunt bear there are times when the bear ends up hunting you.

Walter Paluka was a football coach from Scranton, Pennsylvania. People often mistook Walter for Joe Palooka, the boxer. At 6 feet 4 inches and 235 pounds, Walter was chicken quick and bulldog mean. The coach had no problem getting his players' attention. All Paluka had to do was howl in your face and you knew you had screwed up.

One of Coach Paluka's teaching methods was to constantly drill the fundamentals into his players' heads by repeating his patented one-liners over and over until they became part of each player's subconscious. Of all the sound bites Walter had in his repertoire, one of the most memorable was, "You won't fumble the ball if you squeeze the bejeezus out of it." Most of Coach Paluka's players really didn't understand the simple but important meaning of these words until years later. It's pretty clear that Robert Citron never learned the fundamentals of investing from a Coach Paluka.

The Orange County treasurer is responsible for investing monies on behalf of a wide variety of municipalities, schools, and public entities. His job description is most accurately defined by the term *fiduciary*. A fiduciary holds assets in trust for a beneficiary. Most fiduciaries are governed by a standard known as the *prudent man rule*. The guidelines for prudent behavior are simple. Act with the same level of caution, discretion, and intelligence as a prudent person would act in pursuit of his or her own affairs. In investing, this means seeking reasonable income commensurate with the preservation of capital, while avoiding speculation. This is not an empty rule, and these are not idle words.

Before his world came crashing down on him, we bet that Robert Citron honestly believed he was acting in a prudent fashion. He was consumed by the arrogance of his position and convinced that he was smarter than everyone else. Otherwise, how could he have asserted, just a few weeks prior to the crisis, that everything was under control and that his political opponent was misinformed about the state of county finances. How could Mr. Citron have strayed so far?

For one thing, it seems certain that Mr. Citron never learned the most fundamental tenet that underpins all fiduciary behavior: The money a fiduciary controls is held in trust for beneficiaries. Put another way, it was not Robert Citron's money to begin with, and he had an obligation to defend the beneficiaries from the irresponsible. That this seems so obvious to us and was so mysterious to Mr. Citron is a function of how far some fiduciaries have strayed from the basics. Nobody ever told him that he had to squeeze the bejeezus out of the ball so as not to fumble.

Safety of the funds entrusted to Citron's care should have been his first concern. These monies were intended to be similar to an interest-bearing bank account that used short-term bonds to earn a little extra money for Orange County public entities. That meant that *preservation of capital was always more important than maximization of return*. Funds of this sort are not intended for speculative purposes. In the jargon of the money market mutual fund industry, Citron's main job was not to break a buck—that is, it was his job to make sure that each and every account was assured of being worth 100 cents on the dollar.

But instead of acting as though the safety of principal was paramount, Mr. Citron acted as though he had to compete with the sharpies down on Wall Street to squeeze out the highest return possible. Mr. Citron never understood that it wasn't his job to deliver the highest return possible. Indeed, at their very core, bonds are not the kind of investment with which you have the ability to earn the highest return possible. That is not what a bond is designed to do. In the investing world, bonds are designed to generate cash flow safely. Because bonds are not intended to be used to increase portfolio returns, bond investing must consist of avoiding fumbles. Put in another way, bond investing is about the proper management of risk so as to ensure the preservation of capital and an uninterrupted generation of cash flow to the investor. To properly understand the fundamentals of bond investing, you must focus more on the risk and less on the total return. Let's explore the risks of bond investing one by one.

CREDIT RISK

Between the time a bond is issued and the time it is completely repaid, many factors can influence its value. One such factor is *credit risk*—the risk that a bond's principal and interest will not be paid as promised. Corporate bonds carry varying credit risks, depending on the perceived ability of the corporation to pay the principal and interest on its bonds. Bondholders generally assume that bonds backed by the U.S. government carry no credit risk.

Bond obligations are only as good as the creditworthiness (the ability to pay interest and principal in full and on time) of the issuer. Creditworthiness is evaluated by several independent rating organizations such as Standard & Poor's, Moody's, Fitch, and Duff & Phelps. These organizations assign quality grades to each issuance of bonds and continue to monitor the bond issuer for creditworthiness on an ongoing basis. While each rating firm has its own rating system, in general an *investment-grade* bond will carry ratings that range from AAA to Baa. Lower-quality bonds from less creditworthy issuers will carry lower ratings.

When a bond issuer makes a promise to pay interest and fails to do so, the bondholder earns less than anticipated. When a bond issuer makes a promise to pay principal and fails to do so, the bondholder suffers a loss of that principal. Yet if the issuer of the bonds makes good on the promise to pay both interest and principal, the bond buyer who buys a newly issued bond and holds it to maturity will receive exactly what he has been promised—nothing more and nothing less.

Below-investment-grade debt securities are sometimes known as *junk bonds*. Junk bonds usually have much higher risks to go along with their generally higher yields. When one factors in defaults, wild swings in price, and periods of illiquidity, there is growing evidence that junk bonds do not produce higher long-term returns than investment-grade bonds, and they certainly don't produce high enough returns to compensate for the risks undertaken by investing in them.[2]

INTEREST RATE RISK

Another risk of bond investing is known as *interest rate risk*. If prevailing interest rates rise above the coupon paid on a bond, then the bond's market value will fall. After all, if someone can earn more money buying a newly issued bond at a new, higher prevailing interest rate, why would they want to give you as much money for a bond that pays interest at an older, lower rate? Given identical credit quality and maturity dates, nobody will pay the same price for a lower-coupon bond than a higher-coupon bond. Two identical bonds with different coupons must therefore always trade at a price that gives each bondholder an identical yield as calculated on the market price of each bond, respectively.

When rates rise, a bondholder who bought a bond at issuance will not suffer a loss unless forced to sell the bond at a depressed price. When prevailing interest rates go down, the prices of existing bonds go up. Since the existing bonds pay more interest than the newly issued bonds, investors are willing to pay more to own the older bonds as a result. Accordingly, the older bond appreciates in market value, even though its coupon remains the same as when it was issued. But—and this is important—bondholders have to sell their bonds and take the capital gains or slowly lose them as the bonds march to maturity.

Interest rate movements increase and decrease the market value of bond principal unevenly, depending on whether the bonds are short term or long term. Time creates an odd sort of leverage in bonds. The longer the maturity of a bond, the more its price will increase when interest rates fall. Conversely, bonds with a longer maturity will tend to decline more in market value when interest rates increase than bonds with a shorter maturity.

Figure 6.1, shows, for an interest rate change of 1 percent, the price changes in a $1,000 principal value bond paying 7 percent annual interest and maturing in 2 years and a $1,000 principal value bond paying 7 percent annual interest and maturing in 20 years. Obviously, given the same movement in prevailing interest rates, the 20-year bond increases and decreases in value significantly more than the 2-year bond. Thus, the value of a portfolio of long-maturity bonds will tend to be more volatile than a portfolio of short-term bonds. If you have to sell a long-term bond before its maturity date, there is more of a chance that you may take a loss than is the case with a short-term bond.

But regardless of whether interest rates go up or down, in the final analysis, a bond will repay only 100 percent of its principal and 100 percent of its interest due during its life. It will not pay any more or any less. This means that the price gains or losses of the bond are always temporary. Of course, if you sell a bond before it matures, you may end up with a profit or a loss on the principal amount.

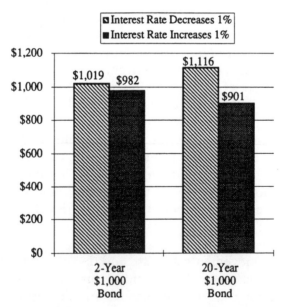

Figure 6.1 Price changes from 1 percent interest change in 2-year versus 20-year bonds.

REINVESTMENT RISK, CALL RISK, AND COUPON RISK

Bonds also have what is known as *reinvestment risk.* This is the risk associated with reinvesting the principal and the interest payments received from the bonds. Shorter-term bonds have a greater reinvestment rate risk than longer-term bonds because they mature faster, placing the reinvestment of the principal at a greater risk of earning a lower rate of return than it did while working within the bond itself.

Another type of reinvestment rate risk is known as *call risk.* Most corporate bond issuers reserve the right to call their bonds. This means that, after a preestablished period of time, the issuer can repay the bond principal, thus shortening the maturity of the bond. A corporation will do this only when prevailing interest rates have declined. Then they can issue new bonds at lower coupon rates to save money on interest expenses. Because bondholders will receive their money back when rates are lower, reinvestment of called bond principal amounts will almost certainly yield less than the original bond. Callable bonds can shortchange investors if they are not aware of the call provisions. Bonds issued by the U.S. Treasury are usually not callable.

While short-term bonds have less price risk during times of changing interest rates, they have more of another kind of risk not associated with long-term bonds. This risk is known as *coupon risk* and involves the increased volatility of the coupons on shorter-term bonds when compared to coupons on longer-term bonds. Thus, investment into short-term bonds will face less certainty of maintaining any given size of coupon than does investment into long-term bonds. When this investment is made with cash flows from other bonds, coupon risk becomes a special form of reinvestment risk. This can be a problem if an investor requires a certain level of income from his bonds.

Another special type of reinvestment risk is associated with mortgage-backed securities. Mortgage-backed securities are created from pools of specific residential mortgages. The least-complicated type of these bonds is sold on what is known as a pass-through basis. That is, the bond itself is not a direct obligation of the issuer. Instead, interest and principal payments remain the obligation of the homeowners while also being secured by an equity interest in the mortgaged properties. Interest payments, principal payments, and principal prepayments are all passed through to the mortgage-backed security holder. Several quasi-governmental agencies, such as the Government National Mortgage Association (known as "Ginnie Mae"), the Federal Home Loan Mortgage Corporation (known as "Freddie Mac"), and the Federal National Mortgage Association (known as "Fannie Mae"), intermediate this process, by serving as bond issuers and by providing various types of guarantees of timely and complete payment of interest and principal.

All mortgage securities carry inherent and unpredictable risks that must be controlled carefully. Most important of these risks is prepayment risk. Prepayment risk exists when interest rates fall and mortgage holders refinance their mortgages to take advantage of the lower rates. When a prepayment occurs, mortgage bondholders receive an acceleration of the maturity of their bonds, and get all of their principal back sooner than expected. Now, the bondholder must reinvest the prepaid principal at the very moment when that reinvestment can be accomplished only at lower rates of interest. During the last decade or so, average homeowners have become very efficient in this regard, often refinancing their mortgages more than once during a protracted downward trend in interest rates.

INFLATION RISK

Bond investing involves the risk that inflation will erode the value of each dollar that is invested in a bond. Because a bond will never pay more than its principal and interest, bondholders demand that bonds pay higher interest rates during times of high inflation to compensate for the loss of purchasing power over the life of the bond. Conversely, bondholders are willing to accept lower interest rates during times of lower inflation.

It is the perception of anticipated inflation that drives this area of bond investing. When bond investors expect high inflation, they will demand higher interest rates. When they expect low inflation, they will accept lower rates. These inflationary expectations have little long-term predictive ability, though, as investors will demand interest rates that turn out to be quite different from the inflation experienced during the life of a bond. Sometimes inflation is higher than the interest rate demanded. Sometimes it is lower. And sometimes, by happenstance, it is exactly the same. The message is clear: Both interest rate movements and inflation rates are impossible to predict. Figure 6.2 illustrates a few examples of the discrepancy between beginning-year yields on intermediate Treasury bonds and the average inflation rate experienced during the subsequent seven years. This demonstrates the inherent unpredictability of inflation as a component of interest rates.

Yet, unpredictable as both inflation and interest rates may be, changes in inflation inevitably have an impact on interest rates. If a bondholder purchases a bond yielding more than the rate of inflation at the time of purchase, and inflation rises, prevailing interest rates will rise and the value of existing bonds will go down to bring the yield into line with newly prevailing rates. But if this happens, the true yield on the bondholder's originally invested cost may now fall below the rate of inflation. Consequently, the bondholder can suffer a permanent loss unless interest rates (and thus inflation) fall

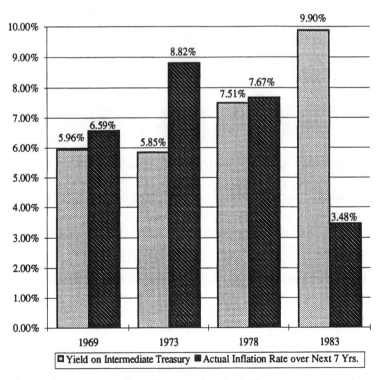

Figure 6.2 Intermediate Treasury bond yield versus actual subsequent seven-year inflation rate.

during the holding period. However, regardless of the prevailing rate of inflation, the after-inflation rates of return on bonds have been lower than the after-inflation rates of return on stocks. This means that real inflation protection is more likely to come from stocks than it is from bonds.

SEEKING CAPITAL GAINS FROM BONDS

As we can see, movements in interest rates drive movements in bond prices. One outgrowth of this fact is that most active bond managers attempt to predict interest rate movements in an effort to generate capital gains from bond holdings and avoid capital losses to improve the total return on their portfolios.

Noah benShea wrote an intriguing little book called *Jacob The Baker*. One interesting segment applies to all investments, and most particularly to bonds:

A student, clearly troubled by something Jacob had said, followed him as he left the bakery.

"Jacob, did you say that what is holy has no beginning or end?"

"Yes,"

"But that is not possible," said the student.

"That is because only the possible can be measured," said Jacob.

The student struggled to understand. "Jacob, you are not making sense."

Jacob nodded in agreement, then placed his hands in front of the student, covering her eyes.

"You see," said Jacob, "reason explains the darkness, but it is not a light."[3]

Only things with a beginning and an end can be measured. Even a seemingly continuous stream of information coming from, say, a speedometer, can be spoken of only in terms of the start and finish of a journey. Measurements are by necessity bound in time. It is no less true that investment performance measurements are bound in time. Let's look at bond return measurements as a good example of how a measurement caught in time can hinder understanding about investment performance.

Bonds have two return components: interest and the potential for capital gains or capital losses. Unlike a stock, though, bonds cannot increase in value over the entire time from issuance to maturity. Instead, they return interest plus repayment of principal. If you buy a bond on its date of initial issuance and hold it to maturity, you will experience no capital gain or loss. Of course, if you play the interest rate speculation game and sell a bond when it has appreciated in price, you can generate capital gains. Conversely, if you sell a bond prior to maturity when it has fallen in place, you will sustain a loss. While this may seem elementary, many people tend to get the next part mixed up.

Recently, we were talking to a person who seemed knowledgeable about retirement investing. We asked, "Why would anyone invest in bonds for capital gains unless they were prepared to sell the bond to capture the gain and put the proceeds into another investment?"

He replied with an exasperated tone as if the answer were so obvious that nobody in their right mind would even ask the question, "Because there are periods when bonds outperform equities on a total return basis."

And, you know what, he's right. There are periods when bonds outperform equities. But the questions remain: When and how you do you measure that total return, and what do you do with the measured returns generated by that performance? The answers to these questions are not as straightforward as they may appear. Remember, if you fail to realize gains, what were you really trying to measure anyway?

Measurement of total return in bonds is calculated as interest plus the change in price divided by the beginning price. Well, interest is easy enough to understand, and as long as any accrued but unpaid interest actually gets paid when due, we can all agree on the interest earned during the period. It is when we get to price changes that things get messy.

When you buy a bond at 100 percent of its principal value (par value) and interest rates go down, then the price of the bond is higher than par and, if sold, you will receive more than the principal amount in return. If interest rates go up, the price of the bond is lower than par and, if sold, you will receive less than the principal amount in return. If you hold a bond when interest rates go up or down, you won't get any more or less than par value when it matures.

If you buy a bond when prevailing interest rates are lower than the bond's coupon, you will pay more than par to acquire the bond. Conversely, when prevailing interest rates are higher than the bond's coupon, you will pay less than par to acquire the bond. During your holding period, the price of your bond will go either up or down, depending on interest rate movements, but you will still receive par value at maturity, with the entire premium you paid over par slowly amortized over the life of the bond. Conversely, if you buy a bond below its par value and hold it, again, you still receive only par value at maturity. The discount you got from par value is slowly written off (this is known as *accretion*) over the balance of the life of the bond. This means that, in the aggregate and in the long run, for every capital gain on a bond there is an exact corresponding capital loss (exclusive of trading costs). Stocks, on the other hand, represent ownership whose value increases or decreases over time, depending on the company and the market for its equity.

But things get interesting when we examine bond performance measurement. It should be obvious that we can generate capital gains (or capital losses) in our bond portfolio only if we sell bonds and apply the proceeds somewhere else. If, instead, we hold onto the bonds, the premiums amortize and the discounts accrete. If we sell the bonds and immediately return the proceeds (net of trading costs) back into new bonds of similar maturities, we have really just traded out of one position and into another with an identical set of dynamics. This is easy to understand because interest rates rise and fall all the time. Bonds are like boats that rise and fall with these movements. Some bond investors bet on future interest rate movements by taking a gain and buying bonds of longer or shorter maturity, trying to protect and enhance their gain. This is a game with few long-term winners because interest rate movements are impossible to predict with accuracy.

We won't go into all the many complex schemes bond managers have devised to try to outperform their brethren. Instead, we return to a basic question: Do conventional bond performance measurement techniques help us make decisions that further the objectives of our retirement investing program? Unless you can get a good answer about how to apply the proceeds from bond-related capital gains, be wary of performance measurement that presents an incomplete picture of your bond portfolio. The best explanation for the difficulties faced in predicting interest rate movements is the high number of variables involved. But this does not stop people from trying. Unfortunately, what investors fail to realize is that the portion of total return in a bond portfolio attributable to capital gains is either negligible or negative over the long term. For example, from 1926 through 1994, the total return from price changes in long-term government bonds was −0.45 percent.[4] Why was there this slight loss? The answer lies in trading costs. In the real world, there is always a cost to buying and selling, and, in this, bonds are no different than bananas. Given the negligible long-term opportunity for profiting from price changes in bonds, the message is clear: Realizable and sustainable gains in a bond portfolio are more fiction than reality.

LADDERED BOND PORTFOLIOS

So if interest rate anticipation is virtually impossible and if long-term gains from bonds always erode over time, how do you invest in bonds to your advantage? Just as investing in stocks should be done with an eye to the fundamentals, bond investing must stick to the basics as well. This means taking advantage of the opportunities in bonds while shunning the pitfalls.

People invest in bonds for stability of their principal value and consistent high relative income. Since stability and cash flow are the reasons for bond investing, it only makes sense that these first principles must be followed in the construction of a bond portfolio. Taking these two factors separately and despite all the risks outlined above, for all but the longest maturities, during bad respective markets for bonds and stocks, bond prices usually go down less than stock prices. For a wide variety of reasons, some stocks can go down from their purchase price and stay down forever. Given low credit risk, a bond will pay all principal back at maturity. That is the promise of the bond. There are no such promises in stock investing—only probabilities. Then, too, bond cash flows have proven to be more predictable than total returns from stocks. This means that you can be more assured of a steady stream of predictable income from a bond portfolio than from a stock portfolio.

By returning to these first principles of bond investing, we can construct a winning bond portfolio. Since bond investing provides lower total returns over the long term than stock investing, we must be especially careful to limit the risks in a bond portfolio. Put another way, since bonds should be prized for stability and cash flow, then we should make sure that these are the primary elements in bond investing. This means that risk management in bond investing is especially important. (Again, inflation risks as such can't be controlled using bonds, so you shouldn't even try to do so. History has thus far shown that, over the long haul, inflation risk is best managed through the judicious use of stocks, not bonds.)

Of the various risks of bond investing, only credit risks are almost completely under our own control. We can choose to invest in a portfolio of very high quality bonds, or we can sacrifice quality for yield. Since we invest in bonds for cash flow and stability and not primarily in the pursuit of the highest available total return, credit quality must not be compromised in the pursuit of higher yield. Thus, the first lesson in bond investing is to invest only in portfolios of high-quality bonds.

The next objective in a bond portfolio is the management of interest rate risk and reinvestment risk. Ideally, we would want to have a bond portfolio strategy that would consist completely of long-term bonds when interest rates are headed lower and short-term bonds when rates are headed up. However, since interest rate movements can't be predicted, we have to find another way to minimize their impact on the bond investor. There is a time-tested method known as bond *laddering* that can be put to good use in the construction of a bond portfolio optimized to take advantage of interest rate movements while minimizing their negative impact.

A bond ladder is built using bonds of different maturities, with each maturity forming a rung on the ladder of the portfolio and each bond being held to maturity. Interim trading is not done unless necessary to generate additional liquidity for the bond investor. While some laddered portfolios are constructed in the effort to anticipate interest rate movements, this is generally a useless exercise in which you will be right as often as you are wrong.

A simple example of a bond ladder would be a portfolio that consisted of bonds with maturities that fell due every six months for ten years. There would be 20 rungs to the ladder in this example, stretching from the maturity date of the first rung (six months from today), all the way out ten years into the future. If you equal-weight the money invested in each rung of the ladder, then you would spread the interest rate risk evenly throughout all the maturities of your portfolio. Since a ten-year bond will usually have a higher yield than a six-month bond, you will have 20 representative yields from 20 different maturities at all times, with the yields usually increasing from the shortest maturity to the longest. When the bonds on the first rung of the ladder mature, you would have 19 rungs left.

To maintain the ladder at its ten-year designed length, you would reinvest each bond's maturing proceeds to create a new 20th rung. As interest rates move up and down, you would be able to take advantage of higher rates through the reinvesting process, while keeping the value of your portfolio stable through the equally weighted mixture of maturities. Laddered bond portfolios provide the best combination of cash flows and stability under most conditions in the credit markets.

LADDERED BOND PORTFOLIOS IN RETIREMENT INVESTING

Bond investing has a vital role to play in retirement investing. When people are younger, the purpose of bond investing is to stabilize the value of the overall retirement account. When retired, the purpose is to create cash flows for retirement living expenses. In between, there are a number of uses for bonds, with the most prominent being to serve as a repository for assets converted from stocks over time. This conversion process will be described in greater detail later.

Laddered bond portfolios are the best way to preserve value and generate cash. However, the design and construction of the portfolio itself must take into account both the behavior of the credit markets and the needs of the retirement investor. Appropriate questions include:

- What types of bonds should be used?
- How many rungs should be on the ladder?
- What maturities should be used for each rung?
- How much of the portfolio should be invested in each rung?
- How should cash flows from the ladder be managed?

Let's take each question in turn to investigate the construction of bond ladders for retirement investing.

Types of Bonds Used in the Retirement Ladder

The watchword for bond selection is *quality*. Only the highest-quality bonds should be used in a retirement investing portfolio. The returns on bonds over time are too low to have to put up with any defaults on interest or principal payments. Bonds should never fall below an investment-grade rating by one of the major ratings services. This means that you should stay away from junk bonds in any form. Remember, controlling for credit quality does not prevent a bond from falling in value prior to maturity. It means only that the bond issuer has been judged by a rating agency on its ability to pay all principal and interest on a timely basis. But long-term bond returns are too low to sacrifice stability and certain cash flow for poor-quality securities.

Number of Rungs on the Ladder

This is a function of three elements: the historic yields for bonds of differing maturities, the need to control price instability, and the direction of interest rates. The more rungs on the ladder, the more opportunities there are to reinvest each maturing bond into the top rung of the ladder. This will favor ladders with more rungs in rising-interest-rate environments because you will be able to reinvest in higher-yielding bonds more frequently. The opposite can be said in declining-interest-rate environments. However, since interest rates cannot be predicted, it is safe to say that the number of rungs on the ladder should strike a balance between the two extremes.

Amount of the Portfolio to Be Invested in Each Rung

The weighting of the amounts invested in each rung of a bond ladder depends on the use to which the ladder will be put. In a bond ladder intended to service the needs of overall portfolio stability, more should be invested on the lower rungs of the ladder than the higher rungs. That's because the lower rungs of the ladder will tend to have fewer price movements than the higher rungs of the ladder. The opposite is true if the bond ladder is intended to service the cash flow needs of the investor. In this event, more should be invested in the longer maturities in the ladder to generate additional income.

Cash Management in Bond Ladders

A laddered bond portfolio whose first rung is always being reinvested to create a new last rung generates reasonably stable cash flows, depending on the direction and magnitude of the changes in interest rates. For the ultimate in stable cash flows, nothing beats a cash-matched bond ladder. This is a bond ladder constructed of bonds that generate a specific amount of cash in interest and principal payments on the day that those cash payments are needed to meet an obligation. Thus, a cash-matched portfolio "matches" the cash flows from the bonds to the cash obligations that must be served. A cash-matched portfolio of bonds is an excellent way to create a predictable flow of cash.

Alternatively, you can manage the bond ladder to allow for the interest to be used as cash to feed a retirement benefit, while the principal amounts would be reinvested back into the last rung of the ladder to perpetuate the portfolio. The main drawback to the construction of a bond ladder for individual retirement investing is the time and attention required for its maintenance. The ladder itself has to be constructed, and as each rung matures, new assets must be invested on the highest rung, or the ladder eventually exhausts itself when the final rung matures.

BOND LADDERS: WHAT THE RESEARCH SHOWS

We set out to determine the optimal laddering and bond selection techniques to use in the construction of the laddered bond portfolios that were well suited to retirement investing. We differentiated between two types of laddered bond portfolios. The first type is intended to bolster the stability of an overall retirement portfolio, with cash flow as an important but secondary objective (*the stability-oriented ladder*). The second type of portfolio is intended primarily to generate cash flow with stability as an important but secondary objective (*the income-oriented ladder*).

First and foremost, high-quality bonds should be used exclusively. Junk bonds are not suitable for a retirement portfolio. It should go without saying, but municipal bonds are also not suitable for retirement bond investing when they are placed in a tax-deferred retirement account. Interest from municipal bonds is usually exempt from federal taxes, as well as from many state and local taxes. This means that the interest paid on municipal bonds is lower than it would otherwise be if it were treated as taxable income to the bondholder. Thus, municipal bonds are a bad investment for tax-deferred retirement accounts, because you do not need the tax exemption in a retirement account and should not accept the lower interest rates as a consequence.

Federal obligations are excellent choices for bond ladders in retirement accounts. From the safest (and lowest-yielding) Treasury obligations, to the obligations of various federal agencies, federal obligations are presumed to have the lowest credit risk of any fixed-income security. Investment-grade corporate bonds are another good selection when there is a sufficient difference between the yield in corporate obligations and the yield in federal obligations of a similar maturity. If a Treasury obligation yields only slightly less than a corporate bond, you might as well buy the Treasury. On average, from 1926 through 1994, corporate bonds have had a 0.68 percent return advantage over Treasuries.[5] In general, then, you wouldn't want to place a corporate bond into your portfolio unless it has at least a 0.80 percent or 0.90 percent return advantage over comparable Treasury securities.

In the effort to increase cash flow for both types of retirement portfolios, it may be advantageous to include mortgage-backed securities in the portfolios (particularly if they are the conservative planned-amortization class type that decreases prepayment risk). Mortgage bonds usually have a return advantage of between 0.75 percent and 1.5 percent over Treasuries of comparable maturities. Mortgage-backed securities do have special risks associated with prepayments, so it is important not to have too many of these securities in a retirement portfolio. Remember, the guarantee provided by the issuers of these mortgages extends to payment of interest and principal, but this guarantee does not protect the investor from interest rate, prepayment, or reinvestment risks.

Foreign bonds that generate higher cash flows should be used sparingly (if at all) in the income-oriented portfolio because of the many unknowns involved in foreign debt investing. No foreign bonds should be in the stability-oriented portfolio. If foreign bonds are used, they should be the sovereign debt issued only by stable, developed nations such as Germany or Switzerland, or investment corporate debt issued by large multinational corporations domiciled abroad.

To sum up, a stability-oriented laddered bond portfolio should consist of Treasury, federal agency, and investment-grade corporate bonds. Tax-exempt municipal bonds, junk bonds, and foreign bonds have no place in this kind of a portfolio.

An income-oriented laddered bond portfolio should also be constructed with Treasury, federal agency, and investment-grade corporate bonds. However, in the effort to increase cash flows, it may be advantageous to include up to 30 percent of the portfolio in mortgage-backed securities. We performed numerous tests on historic bond data to determine the most advantageous structure for the two types of laddered bond portfolios to be used in retirement investing. Based on this research, we concluded that they should be constructed in accordance with the general guidelines shown in Table 6.1.

It should be noted that in actual practice, each bond ladder will vary from its theoretical design. There may be more than five rungs within the three- to seven-year maturity band. Additionally, weightings will fluctuate as income and principal is received, and the ladder is actively rebalanced.

Our research shows how bond ladders help to produce additional income and maintain the overall stability of the portfolio better than the relevant bond index comparisons. In the case of the stability portfolio, the additional income is a secondary concern, and the data confirm this. In the case of the income portfolio, the data show a considerable yield advantage for the ladder as compared to an indexed portfolio. The stability ladder was constructed entirely of Treasuries, and the income ladder was weighted 70 percent Treasuries and 30 percent mortgage-backed securities. Results of the research into total return of these bond portfolios for the 15 years ending in December 1994 is shown in Figure 6.3.

Obviously, the income ladder did not do much better than the comparative index. However, it was designed with stability in mind, so we have to illustrate how stable each of the portfolios was over the 15-year period in question. Figure 6.4 shows the price stability, or volatility, of each portfolio. The lower the percentage shown in Figure 6.4, the less chance the returns will be unstable. (See Chapter 8 for a further discussion of this concept of volatility.) As you can see, the stability portfolio has less variation in returns than any of the other portfolios studied. Additionally, it is interesting to note that neither ladder experienced a loss in any of the 15 years studied. The indexes suffered losses in 1980 and 1993.

Table 6.1 Laddered Bond Portfolio Construction

Portfolio Characteristic	Stability-Oriented Portfolio	Income-Oriented Portfolio
Type of bonds	At least 50% of the portfolio in Treasuries, agencies, and cash. No more than 50% in investment-grade corporates and mortgage-backed securities.	All bonds to be of investment grade. At least 25% of the portfolio in Treasuries and agencies. No more than 10% of high-quality investment-grade bonds of developed sovereign countries or multinational corporations.
Number of rungs	5 rungs (1 per year)	5 rungs (1 per year)
Minimum maturity	3 years	3 years
Maximum maturity	7 years	7 years
Rung 1	25%	15%
Rung 2	25%	15%
Rung 3	20%	20%
Rung 4	15%	25%
Rung 5	15%	25%
Cash flow management	Buy and hold—Reinvest cash flows to maintain rung weighting.	Buy and hold—Reinvest cash flows to maintain rung weighting.

SPECIAL CHARACTERISTICS OF BOND MUTUAL FUNDS

Owning shares of a bond mutual fund is different than owning individual bonds. When you own a bond, you establish a direct relationship between you and the bond issuer. This relationship is defined by the terms of the bond's issuance, establishing the rate and frequency of interest payments, the timing of principal repayments, the call provisions (if any), and all other legal features of the bond. Barring default, the bond issuer will pay you all interest when

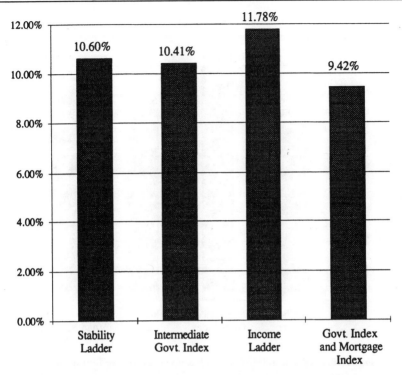

Figure 6.3 Laddered versus indexed bond portfolios, 1980 to 1994.

due and, upon maturity of the bond, the principal value will have been fully repaid.

Shareholders of open-end bond mutual funds face a different relationship between themselves and the bonds held in the mutual fund portfolio. This relationship is characterized by the fact that a bond mutual fund has a perpetual life. Unlike a bond, a mutual fund never matures. The underlying bonds in the portfolio may mature, but the mutual fund itself lives forever.

Shareholders in bond mutual funds have two advantages over investors who hold bonds outright. First, there is improved liquidity. Bond mutual fund shares may be sold conveniently and easily at the prevailing net asset value per share. Second, the diversity of the bonds held in a mutual fund portfolio will tend to spread the risks that might be associated with any given bond. Critical in the assessment of how this diversity will affect the shareholder is the average weighted maturity of the bonds in the mutual fund portfolio. The

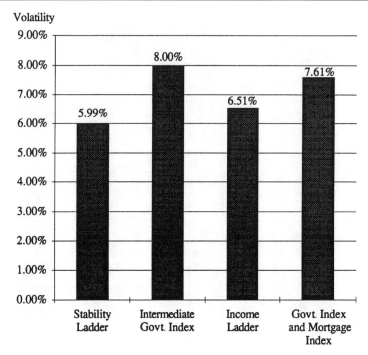

Volatility

Figure 6.4 Price stability of laddered versus indexed bond portfolios, 1980 to 1994.

longer the average weighted maturity, the more fluctuation will be experienced in the net asset value of the fund itself. On the other hand, the longer the average maturity, the larger the interest income that can be expected from the bond portfolio.

But because bond mutual funds have no single maturity date, they also present special characteristics to their shareholders. Bond mutual funds can be counted on to produce a source of steady income. If their average weighted maturities are not too long, they can also be counted on to preserve an investor's capital better than stocks. But, because bond mutual funds have no maturity, you cannot hold their shares until a specific date and always be assured of getting your principal back.

If interest rates rise, the net asset value of a bond mutual fund will fall. As the bond fund generates cash flow in the form of net new purchases, interest payments, and bond principal repayments, those cash flows will be reinvested by the bond mutual fund manager into bonds that will tend to have higher interest rates. If this process continues long enough, the bond mutual fund shareholder will end up recouping lost principal due to increasing interest rates in the form of increased income from those higher rates.

However, bond mutual fund shareholders cannot expect to use bond mutual funds to generate date-specific and dollar-specific cash flows. This can be accomplished only through ownership of bonds themselves.

What a mutual fund bondholder should be able to count on is relatively high income, moderately stable capital preservation, and an addition to the stability of a combined portfolio of stock and bond mutual funds. What's more, the use of well-constructed bond ladders inside a bond mutual fund will tend to enhance the probability of higher income and stability.

SEVEN

The Evil Twins: Emotions and Market Timing

EMOTIONS PLAY A ROLE in the determination of investment values. This is particularly true with common stocks where different people have different viewpoints about the worth of a company's stock. This means that buyers and sellers, each having their own perception of value, will place a speculative premium or discount on the price of a stock. This speculative component can be volatile. That's because life is uncertain and the future is unknowable. Uncertainty charges both sides of the market with emotion. On the sell side, there is pessimism and the fear that things will never get better. On the buy side is greed driven by the false sense that nothing will ever go wrong.

These emotions are familiar to anyone who has ever been an investor. Most people have a built-in level of greed and live in a more or less constant state of suspended fear. Even when we have more than we need, we still feel we need more than we have. The capacity for fear is also present in most people right from the outset of any investing activity. It comes from the fear of losing what you have. These emotions are amplified by changes in investment values and by the so-called contagion of crowds.

If an investment skyrockets in value, investors will be afraid that it might go down, all the while anticipating even further gains. Like a deer frozen in the middle of the road by the lights of an oncoming car, the investor can't decide what to do—sell or hold. Paradoxically, many investors forget that nobody ever went broke taking a profit. And, if that isn't bad enough, when an investment drops in value, the emotional trap is the fear that the investment's value will fall even further, along with the hope that it might rebound.

In the 1960s, the Beatles were big; Woodstock and free love were the rage. There were strobe lights, loud music, and The Doors, mixed together with heavy sweet-scented smoke. You didn't even have to partake to get high. All you had to do was walk in with a clear head and stumble out later, reeling from the fumes of the funny weed that were accidentally sucked in. Doing stupid things while in a crowd is part of growing up. History is full of examples of people who were reduced to the lowest common denominator of the crowd. In 1895, the French psychologist, Gustov LeBon, characterized crowds and their behavior with a series of stunning insights. He noted that crowds create a "mental unity" among their members. Crowd behavior is different from individual behavior in two important ways, LeBon noted. First, once in a crowd, a person's sense of individual responsibility disappears. Second, within a crowd, a person, "allows himself to be impressed by words and images—which would be entirely without action on each of the isolated individuals composing the crowd—and to be induced to commit acts contrary to his most obvious interests and his best-known habits." Crowd behavior is contagious, and will cause an individual to "sacrifice his personal interest to the collective interest."[1]

To enlarge on LeBon's observations, we might add that crowds have an almost magnetic effect on people, causing an individual's internal compass to go haywire. When this happens, the person has replaced individual judgment with that of the crowd. The mental unity of crowd behavior can transcend space and involve individuals who are widely separated, provided they fall under the influence of crowd contagion. This is an important phenomenon in the world of modern investing. It's easy to recognize a gang of thugs or a protest group acting like a crowd. But what about relatively isolated groups of people brought together through electronic information systems to buy and sell securities? Do these people act as if they were in a crowd? Not surprisingly, the answer is yes.

The contagion of crowds is an emotional amplifier. When "everybody" is saying that a certain investment is going through the roof, many investors suspend disbelief and plunge right in without hesitation. If everybody is saying that the sky is falling, it repels the average investor. Crowds are often spooked by an event or an opinion leader who sets off the crowd behavior. In the investment world, opinion leaders are a dime a dozen. Each and every one of them will claim to have the latest and greatest method of determining what will happen next in the capital markets. The problem is that most of these market seers are more often wrong than right. For example, according to the National Bureau of Economic Research in Cambridge, Massachusetts, only 25 percent of investment newsletters offer advice that would enable an investor to outperform the market averages.[2]

Individual investors who are honest with themselves will admit that they have been caught up in the contagion of a crowd and buffeted by the twin emotions of greed and fear. One important reason for this is that most of us are emotional by nature when it comes to matters involving our own money. Partially because of this emotional factor, many people have a hard time doing the right thing with their investments, even if they do know what the right thing might be.

The inability to impose a disciplined process on their investing has probably led more investors to "buy high and sell low" than any other single factor. Accordingly, it is important for investors to understand the inherent emotional pitfalls faced by virtually everyone who wishes to undertake a retirement investing program.

Even professional speculators have lost billions of dollars when their big bets went bad. During one period in early 1994, the well-known international investing superstar, George Soros, reported that he lost $600 million by betting the wrong way on the Japanese yen. Bankers Trust lost some $100 million in European bonds. Steinhardt Partners lost $650 million in bad bond bets. One might think that heads would roll on Wall Street after these people racked up such large losses. Not a chance. Listen carefully to the statement made to a *New York Times* reporter by a principal of a leading financial executive search firm: "Anyone lost their jobs? Not a single soul. This is a systemic problem, and no one individual can be faulted for their judgment when it is psychological and not fundamental factors that have caused the market to trade down."[3] If that's not blaming it on the crowd, then we don't know what is.

So what goes on in the mind of a professional portfolio manager when his or her fundamental judgment comes under attack by the contagion of the crowd? Well, it's not a pretty sight. A global bond manager for Chase Manhattan Private Bank put it this way: "I was fifty percent to seventy percent cash last summer, and I started to underperform, so I put half to work at the top of the market. I would have been on the cover of *BusinessWeek* but I buckled like a moron. . . ."[4]

Chasing relative performance is, by definition, chasing the crowd. Money managers are particularly susceptible to being pressured by the crowd because they know not to "fight the tape" (i.e., to buck a trend), even when the tape appears very wrong on a fundamental basis. The pressure to conform is tremendous. Consequently, many managers second-guess their better judgment to keep up with the crowd. If managers fall behind, they are replaced. This practice of periodically churning money managers tends to throw out the relatively poor performer just when things look the worst. Conversely, many managers are brought in at the top of their game and go downhill from there.

Emotional factors play a large role in any human endeavor, but investing is more of an emotionally driven pursuit than most. This is why it is especially important for individual retirement investors to make their decisions based on what's right for them. This takes common sense, caution, and the strict management of one's fear and greed.

THE IMPOSSIBILITY OF MARKET TIMING

The Magic 8 Ball is back! That's right, one of our favorite toys is once again being advertised and sold. Surely you remember the Magic 8 Ball—the toy that plays on our desire to know the future. Even though, as time passes, our memories seem to leak out unnoticed, we didn't prowl the toy store looking for the new Magic 8 Ball. That might have destroyed our pleasant memories of the original. So hearken back with us to the early 1960s when the Magic 8 Ball was at its zenith.

The plastic sphere had a little black pyramid suspended in a clear liquid inside the ball. On each facet of the pyramid was written one word or phrase. The Magic 8 Ball worked by shaking it and asking a question. The shaking caused the little black pyramid to tumble around and eventually float up to the small, flat, transparent view window on the surface of the ball. Whatever word or phrase was written on the facet facing the window was the answer to your question—brought to you by the fickle finger of fate. The fun of the game was seeing what answer would pop out of the ball in answer to your question.

Can you remember the original answers inside the Magic 8 Ball? Truthfully, we can't either. We seem to remember that one response was: "Answer unclear. Try again later." This reply was always unsatisfactory, so you had to shake it again to see if another answer could be coaxed out. Unfortunately, there was never a guarantee the next shake would produce any better answer than the first one. For instance, what help was an answer such as "Not likely" when you really wanted a positive response? Here's an example. Suppose you really wanted a Mr. Machine robot for your birthday. What good was a Magic 8 Ball that responded "Not likely" to your request? No good at all.

So most of the answers forced you to try another shake. Next time, if you were like us, you'd try a different strategy and really go for the gusto by shaking the 8 Ball hard to strong-arm a better answer. This didn't always work either because you were likely to get a coy "Maybe," leaving you empty-handed again. We remember rephrasing the question to get the desired answer. The old double negative worked well for this purpose—as in, "I won't get a Mr. Machine for my birthday, right?" Then you'd shake the Magic 8 Ball and it would come up . . . "Most definitely." You just couldn't win!

The allure of the Magic 8 Ball is the deeply ingrained desire to predict the future and thereby control it. Even when we know that prediction doesn't lead to mastery, humans gravitate toward gypsies, horoscopes, and Magic 8 Balls. The essence of the problem is the essential unknowability of the future. Why is the future unknowable?

Let's start in the capital markets. At heart, the capital markets are a human endeavor and subject to the vagaries of human behavior. Since human behavior is not always predictable, neither are the capital markets. But there is a more fundamental reason why capital market activity cannot be predicted. This has to do with the inherent complexity of capital market systems. Complex systems have a multitude of variables that must be factored into any forecast. The sheer number of variables that can influence an outcome means that the effect of any single variable has a potential for influence that ranges from the trivial to the profound—almost any size or type of event can be either meaningless or deeply significant, depending on the circumstances. This type of system is known as *nonlinear;* that is, future outcomes cannot be predicted by constructing a single line through all past data points out into the future. The reason complex systems do not behave in a way that would produce a straight line is because the outcome of any given event conditions the starting point for the next event. A good example of this type of system is the old verse about a nail:

> For want of a nail the shoe was lost,
> For want of a shoe, the horse was lost,
> For want of a horse the battle was lost,
> For want of a battle, the kingdom was lost.

The conclusion is inescapable: The kingdom was lost for want of a nail. This shows how small things can lead to a wholly unpredictable chain of events. Here's another example. Have you ever been in a car accident or known someone who has? If you had started out just a few seconds later (or earlier), would the accident have happened? In the world of the markets, there are so many events, large and small, that nobody can fathom how it will all work out. Think about it. There are a multitude of companies serving hundreds of millions of customers. There are millions of investors. Plus, there is the world of politics, of human society, of the natural world, and on and on. The big, complex systems in our world are nonlinear, so everything has the potential of having an impact on everything else.

We hasten to add that, within the boundaries of our perception, even nonlinear systems operate within limits. For example, generally speaking, the temperatures on our planet range between approximately −80°F and +140°F. While virtually all the highs and lows will fall within these two numbers, no meteorologist can tell us what the exact high and low temperature will be a few days from now. Examination and anticipation of the limits to nonlinear systems might be useful exercises, but trying to predict the next twist or turn in the capital markets is a fool's game.

Prediction is a mainstay of science and technology. The scientific method has worked magnificently in helping us control our environment. Here, we have endeavored to determine what causes what with so much success that we are able to duplicate causes to produce desired effects. This has led to a type of control over the future. We know that certain sequences of action will have wholly predictable consequences. A well-designed and tested disc brake is going to stop the car every time it is used. But successful techniques in one field of human effort do not automatically lead to success in other areas.

The scientific method has been so successful, though, that it has become an article of faith among many modern people that science is the answer to every human problem. Investing has not been immune from this disorder. In fact, the central theory of investing is singularly ill-suited as a predictive tool. And, make no mistake about it, that's what people lust after—the ability to predict and control. Investment theory takes that which is essentially unpredictable and tries to predict it anyway. The means by which control is attempted is through statistical interpretation of historic data. After all, if you observe that something has happened with a certain frequency, it's only a hop, skip, and jump to extrapolate from the past to project into the future.

Science works this way, too. But science goes one step further than investment statistics. Science is interested in knowing what causes what. That is, scientific inquiry is concerned with the mechanisms that underlie causality. Financial statisticians typically apply their knowledge of past events to the prediction of future events, but they fall far short of the mark when they attempt to explain why. Examination of first principles is rare in financial circles. This means that the effects of financial principles are studied with great intensity, while the causes remain largely unexplored.

Thus, even though equities have tended to produce higher returns over the long term than fixed income, the root cause of this phenomenon is rarely discussed. Similarly, while equities have tended to be more volatile than fixed income, the reasons for this are not discussed. The general unwillingness to establish a firm fundamental foundation for investment theory has led to all manner of foolishness. In many cases, what we see happening can best be likened to a vigorous shaking of the Magic 8 Ball until it yields an answer that coincides with the desires of the questioner.

Many investors are concerned with making the "right" decision about when to invest in the stock or bond markets. They realize that the market values of securities rise or fall, and they ideally do not want to purchase an investment just before it loses value or right after it has increased in value. In theory, this is an attractive strategy. In practice, it is virtually impossible to implement successfully over long periods of time.

Please be aware that the market movements we refer to are measurements of the *market as a whole,* however defined. Accurate prediction of movements in the value of any one of the broad-based indexes, for example, has never been conclusively demonstrated. However, efforts continue to try to time the market, regardless of the futility of the effort. Some stock investors will compare current valuations to historic averages and decide whether the stock market is valued too highly or not highly enough. Some try to anticipate broad stock market movements by identifying elements that seem to have been associated with prior movements, up or down. So-called market technicians use analyses that have rather mysterious names such as Fibonacci Cycles, Bolinger Bands, triple tops, and head-and-shoulders formations. Some bond investors will try to anticipate interest rate movements by looking at macroeconomic indicators such as inflation, employment, manufacturing capacity utilization, and so forth.

The problem is that none of these methods work reliably. Even the most seasoned and experienced professional investors fall prey to buying at the top of a market cycle or selling at the bottom. Part of the problem is that the markets do not move in smooth and predictable ways. If you miss the major but sporadic upward moves in market prices, you will miss most of the potential for appreciation. For example, during the 7,802 trading days during the 31-year period from January 1963 through December 31, 1993, domestic stocks rose an average of 11.83 percent per year. But if you missed only 90 of the best-performing days during this period, your return would have dropped to a paltry 3.28 percent. Figure 7.1 illustrates this phenomenon.[5]

Are there any demonstrated market-timing devices? The answer is no. There are certain phenomena that appear predictive in hindsight but fail to predict the future. For example, there is a concept in investing known as *regression to the mean.* This is the idea that, over time, rates of return for any given type of investment will tend

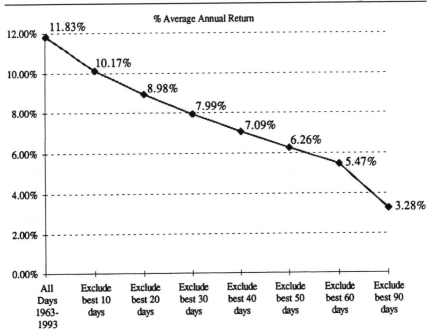

Figure 7.1   The cost of missing the best days in the stock market, 1963 to 1993.

to move toward the average return for that asset. For example, if stocks have had a higher-than-average return for a period, the tendency will be for stock rates of return to be lower than the average returns during a subsequent period. This is an interesting theory for which there is compelling evidence. The problem is that there is no way of telling whether or not it will continue to hold true in the future or when a period of high or low returns is likely to begin or end. This fact makes the concept of regression to the mean a poor predictive tool.

Then, too, periods of high returns are often (but not always) followed by periods of high losses, and periods of high losses are often (but not always) followed by periods of high returns. Accordingly, it may be in an investor's best interest to attempt to take incremental profits when high returns have been experienced and to reinvest those incremental profits when returns have been low. This incremental strategy is extremely difficult to do from a practical and emotional perspective, however, and most individuals will be unable to make consistent profit-taking decisions. Instead, a consistent and regular program of investing through thick and thin will usually serve the retirement investor better than flitting in and out of the market.

THE POWER OF DOLLAR-COST AVERAGING

There is another important benefit of investing on a consistent and regular basis. This is called *dollar-cost averaging,* and it is a time-tested and simple way of making variations in market prices work for you instead of against you. While principally thought of as a tool for stock investing, it also works well with mutual fund share purchases. Here's how.

Every month or every quarter, you invest the same amount of money. When valuations are down, you buy more shares because the price is lower. When valuations are up, you buy fewer shares because the price of each is higher. Over time, your average cost per share will be lower than the average market price per share over the same period. Table 7.1 shows an example of this method.

Table 7.1   Example of Dollar-Cost Averaging

Year Purchased	Month Purchased	Amount Invested	Price per Share	Number of Shares Purchased
Year 1	January	$300	$20.25	14.81
	March	300	18.00	16.67
	September	300	18.25	16.44
	December	300	18.00	16.67
Year 2	January	300	16.00	18.75
	March	300	14.75	20.34
	September	300	14.00	21.43
	December	300	12.00	25.00
Year 3	January	300	13.00	23.08
	March	300	16.00	18.75
	September	300	17.25	17.39
	December	300	18.00	16.67
		$3,600	16.29	225.99

Average market price per share	$16.29
Average cost per share	$15.93
Average savings per share	$0.36
Total savings	$81.74

As you can see in Table 7.1, the average cost per share in the example is 36 cents per share lower than the average market price for the shares. This method of investing can help smooth out the ups and downs of the markets. It should be noted, however, that dollar-cost averaging does not ensure either a profit or a loss. It simply makes timing of an investment less important and provides another benefit to the retirement investor who saves and invests regularly.

EIGHT

Fundamental Characteristics of Risk and Loss

MOST PEOPLE KNOW that risk is intimately associated with loss. Only finance statisticians think otherwise. The chance of losing either investment income or principal, with the attendant consequences of that loss, is at the heart of any understanding of risk. What is not as well understood, though, is the connection among time, savings, and investment purpose as they relate to a proper consideration of risk. While these three elements of risk are interrelated, each has its own characteristics as follows:

- *Time.* One effect of a loss depends on how much time an investor has before needing to use the money. This time factor is directly related to the ability to compound the principal remaining after a loss and the rate of return earned on that remaining principal. In general, the more time an investor has before needing to use the money for its intended purpose, the greater the risk of principal or income loss that can be afforded.

- *Available Savings.* The next effect of loss has to do with the ability of an investor to generate income to replace lost money. Losses are more keenly felt when there is an imbalance between the size of the loss and the investor's ability to replenish the investment account. An investor with few resources to replenish lost funds must be more careful than an investor whose ongoing earnings are extensive.
- *Investment Purpose and Resources.* There is a relationship between the size of the loss and the size of the need for the lost money. Put simply, any loss is more severe when a portfolio is small relative to the need for the money. If the portfolio is large relative to the need for the money, then the consequences of losses are not as severe.

TYPES OF INVESTMENT LOSS

Losses come in three general varieties: loss of principal, loss of income, or loss of purchasing power through inflation. Exposure to these three types of losses is different, depending on the type and mixture of securities in an investment portfolio.

Loss of principal can be either permanent or temporary. A permanent loss is taken when securities permanently lose value or when the investor is forced to sell securities and realize a loss. Losses are temporary if securities regain lost value and when the investor has the ability to wait until that value is restored. Of course, you never know whether a loss will be permanent or temporary until you have to sell the security or the issuing entity acts to make the loss permanent. Losses in large-capitalization stocks, for example, are much more likely to be temporary than losses in small-capitalization stocks. Losses in the principal value of most creditworthy bonds will be temporary if you can afford to hold the bond until its maturity. In general, the more speculative the investment, the more likely it is that losses will be permanent.

Losses in income not only mean that an investor has less cash flow originating from a portfolio, they also mean that cash flow income is not available for reinvestment, thus eliminating the chance for compound earnings on the lost income.

Inflation accounts for the final category of loss. Inflationary losses represent the decline of the purchasing power of money over time. This erosion of purchasing power is often so subtle that people don't realize its impact until they are on a fixed income during retirement. For the most part, some level of inflation will always be embedded in any economy where there is an expansion of credit. Notwithstanding this fact, there are periods when inflation is higher or lower than at other times. Inflation losses affect different securities to differing degrees, depending on the security's ability to produce total returns that are higher than inflation. Put another way, the higher the total return, the less of an impact inflation will have on the purchasing power that can be derived from an investment portfolio.

Losses due to inflation are hard to measure. When an investment loses value because of inflation, it is difficult to determine exactly how the loss will impact the investor. This is because inflation measurements do not ever reflect the exact purchases of any specific consumer. The Consumer Price Index, for example, has a housing component within it that takes into account the inflation in housing prices over a given period of time. But if you own your house free from a mortgage, then housing costs are not going to be as much of a factor in your own experience of inflation.

Average historic returns from the major classes of securities were described in Figure 3.2. However, as detailed in Figure 8.1, each security has distinct principal, income, and inflation risks associated with it.

We will take each of these securities classes in turn. Stocks usually carry higher principal risks than other securities. They make up for these risks by presenting a higher long-term rate of return than do the other categories of securities. For this reason, stocks have a relatively low inflationary risk. Income from stocks comes in the form of dividends. To the degree that a company (or a group of companies) pays regular dividends, the relative risk of losing those dividends is small. Companies that pay dividends do not like to disappoint their shareholders by cutting dividends unless it is deemed absolutely necessary by the company's board of directors. Dividend payments must come out of after-tax profits, so all of the company's other obligations must be fully paid before dividends can be distributed to the shareholders. Moreover, since dividends can grow indefinitely, ownership of dividend-paying common stocks can bring an increasing flow of income to the investor and provide a cash buffer against the erosion of inflation.

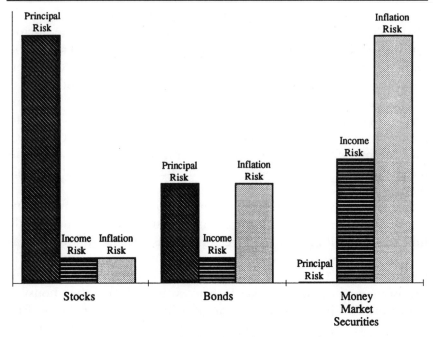

Figure 8.1 Relative risks of stocks, bonds, and money market securities.

It should be noted that not all stocks pay dividends. So-called growth stocks reinvest most or all of their earnings back into the company and do not distribute many cash dividends to shareholders. This makes growth stocks inherently riskier than dividend-paying stocks because more of the expected return must come from an increase in the market price of the stock itself.

Intermediate- and long-term bonds, ranging in maturity from 5 to 30 years, have a different set of risks. High-quality bonds issued by the U.S. Treasury would have no principal risk at all unless the bondholder must sell prior to maturity and interest rates have risen since the bond was purchased. Thus, Treasury bonds should be assigned a medium level of principal risk to reflect the occasional need to sell before maturity, thus losing principal permanently. Because high-quality intermediate- and long-term bonds carry their long-term return in the form of interest, the income risk of these securities is low.

Inflation risk is another matter. Even though bond coupons are usually higher than common stock dividends, intermediate- and long-term bonds do not have the potential for growing their coupons. The interest rate of a bond is fixed, so intermediate- and long-term bonds feel the squeeze of inflation more than stocks. Because intermediate- and long-term bond rates of return are lower than stock returns, the inflation risk of bonds is higher.

Short-term bonds from one to five years in maturity carry less principal risk than long-term or intermediate-term bonds because their prices fluctuate less prior to maturity. Short-term bonds also bear greater income risks and inflation risks than bonds with longer maturities. In general, the shorter the maturity, the more inflation and income risk, and the less the principal risk.

Money market securities have little place in the retirement portfolio itself. Instead, money market securities, like bank deposits, should be used as a place to hold cash, either for an emergency reserve or to be applied to anticipated expenses. These securities mature in less than a year and are generally very safe in terms of principal repayments, making their principal risks low. Because of the short maturity, high liquidity, and safe nature of these securities, however, they usually do not pay very much in income.

However, because money market securities mature quickly, investors face constant reinvestment risk, as a result of which their income is always in question. Money market securities have a moderately high income risk that tends to float along with the prevailing tides of interest rate movements. This makes them ill-suited to retirement income needs, where a more consistent level of cash flow is required. But it is in the context of inflation risk that these securities fare especially poorly. Money market securities barely beat inflation over time and, thus, do not usually yield much real return after inflation is taken into account.

ELEMENTS OF RISK

The fundamental nature of risk and loss as it relates to investing is clear—no matter what you do, your capital is always at risk. And while there is no completely safe haven for anyone's capital, some risk elements are more controllable than others. Capital market risk involves the risks of loss that are solely related to the vagaries of the stock and bond markets themselves. Security-specific risks relate to the circumstances of the issuing company and its industry grouping. International investing, derivatives, and mortgage-backed securities all have their own risk profiles. Let's examine each one of these risk factors individually.

UNPREDICTABLE CAPITAL MARKET RISKS

A certain amount of risk related to the capital markets is out of any investor's control. Stock markets have periods of high prices and low prices. Yet predicting when stock prices will rise or fall has proven virtually impossible to do consistently. To a large degree, this is a risk every stock investor must assume. Similarly, bond prices go up and down with the unpredictable changes in interest rates. Interest rate risk is inherent in the bond marketplace and will be borne by every bond investor.

The very unpredictability of movements in the capital markets frustrates even the most perceptive market gurus. Legions of very bright people have tried (and failed) to predict movements in the capital markets and thereby control capital market–related risk in their investment portfolios. These predictions are doomed to failure because of the complex nature of the markets themselves. It is a little like predicting the weather. There are simply too many variables to take into consideration, with each variable having an impact on the conditions that underlie the next variable.

It was this fundamental level of unpredictability that led to the application of probability theory (i.e., statistical analysis) to investing. This method of interpreting the capital markets, known as *modern portfolio theory,* has a great number of adherents. It is easy to see why. By using statistics, the hopeless task of predicting the next move in the market takes on the illusion of being solved. Statisticians can tell you with great precision what the averages are likely to be. They cannot, however, tell us what the next roll of the dice will bring. They can tell us only what the next thousand rolls of the dice are likely to produce.

The first application of statistics to the capital markets began with predictions of average returns likely to be produced by various types of investments. But things quickly became more complicated as probability theory was introduced as a way to measure risk in an investment. Using probability theory to measure risk gives the false appearance of solving a great many problems. For the first time, capital market theory took on a pseudoscientific patina. This led

174

people into the belief that finance theory could be carefully and scientifically researched to gain control over the unpredictable twists and turns of the capital markets. Unfortunately, this belief is an illusion. Let's see why.

The first step in the transformation of investing into a pseudoscience was to quantify risk and return. Quantification of returns is easy. The elements are all known before the exercise begins. You have a beginning value, intermediate cash flows, and an ending value. When the elapsed time between events is taken into consideration, a return calculation becomes self-evident. Risk is a different matter. Risk involves unknown future events. And, because of its unpredictability, capital market risk represented an area where probability theory could offer the impression of certainty in an all too uncertain world.

The first step was to define *risk* as the level of uncertainty of returns. Statistically speaking, the measurement of uncertainty requires the determination of the volatility of a group of observations. Average volatility is calculated using a measurement known as *standard deviation*. To illustrate standard deviation, consider that all investments of a certain type (each referred to as an *asset class*) don't produce identical returns. Examine the results from any asset class and we will see that, over any given number of observations, some investments within the class produce higher returns compared to others in the class, and some produce lower returns. In statistical parlance, we examine the distribution of the returns from the chosen asset class to see how the returns compare to each other.

Modern statistical methods don't just examine a distribution of returns, though. Instead, they examine what is called a *probability distribution* of returns. That is, statisticians look at a group of historic numbers and, if there are enough examples of those numbers, a judgment is made about the likelihood of future numbers being distributed in the same way as past numbers. This is an exceedingly important point in understanding this concept of risk, which uses standard deviation as a measurement of volatility.

Next, a statistician looks at the probability distribution to determine what proportion of the returns is unusually high and what proportion is unusually low; that is, how widely dispersed are the high and low returns from the average of all the returns. The more dispersed the returns are, the greater the probability that future returns will be less certain.

175

Standard deviation is a statistical tool used to measure dispersion. When an asset class has a high standard deviation of its returns, those returns are widely dispersed and said to be more volatile than returns that are less widely dispersed. That is, they can be either very high or very low, compared to each other on average. Nevertheless—and this is an important point—investors never know whether more volatile returns will be higher or lower than the average at any point in time. They just know that the returns are less likely to be clustered around the average.

In the calculation of volatility numbers, statisticians group a whole series of time-related observations together and tend to smooth out reality by sorting things out to make sense of the data. When these averages are used to try to predict which class of assets will be up when others are down, they may work in theory over the long term, but they do not always work in practice, especially over the shorter term.

The next step taken by finance statisticians involves applying standard deviation measurements to specific portfolios of assets, in the attempt to determine the level of certainty of future returns through the examination of historic returns. This is where the statistics weenies really start to have fun. They compare the standard deviation of one portfolio to another, then to that of the market and that of the asset class. They tease out ever more complex webs of statistical analysis, polishing the patina of scientific respectability with virtually indecipherable formulas. In this way, grand subtheories have been set forth as virtual fact. The problem is that these statistical analyses have only a limited application in the real world.

A central tenet of modern portfolio theory suggests that you should diversify a portfolio into types of securities that have not tended to go up or down at the same time in the past (known as minimizing cross-correlation volatility). This way, the hope is that gains in one security will make up for losses in another. The intention is to stabilize the overall value of a portfolio. These types of risk management rely on statistical examination of past patterns of return and loss. Then results obtained using historic data are extrapolated in an attempt to predict the future.

There are problems with the entire approach. It assumes that the past is always the prologue to the future, which may not be true. Examination of the historic patterns of return and loss do not enable an investor to predict the next twist or turn in the market. Reality does not proceed smoothly—it happens unpredictably, in fits and starts. So, while this type of analysis appears to work over longer periods of time, it cannot predict the next turn in the markets. This makes it an impractical method for controlling risk in a portfolio, particularly when investors require use of their money in the shorter term. This is because no investor can ever be sure assets will be fully intact when needed.

In the short run, any portfolio can go to hell in a handbasket. Over long periods of time, the historic fluctuations in the capital markets appear smoother than they are when an investor must live through them. Over shorter periods, market fluctuations are much more unpredictable. And since a retirement investor's time horizon is always growing shorter, whatever limited practical utility can be demonstrated by these statistical methods is always diminishing—eventually to the point of irrelevance.

The core reason that statistical methods of risk management are unworkable is related to the fact that investment objectives must always be defined in time-specific terms. Statistical analysis involves multiple observations that are collected from specific periods of time, yet are viewed as a timeless group. Statistics attempt to characterize groups of past events in an effort to generalize about the nature of future events. But a generalized analysis is not useful when the desired objective is specific and time-connected.

A generalized statistical analysis can be useful in trying to determine generalized historic characteristics of a given set of securities. That is, while statistics are not reliable enough to meet time-specific objectives, they can help establish the general tendencies of an investment portfolio. However, to have relevance to human needs, investment objectives must be connected to events that happen at specific points in time. Retirement investing has an objective related to producing sustainable cash flow during a specific individual's retirement. Thus, this type of statistical analysis is not particularly useful when investing for retirement.

Consider, for example, the charts shown in Figures 8.2 and 8.3, which illustrate the annual return patterns of stocks and bonds in the United States since 1926. Looking at Figures 8.2 and 8.3, it is easy to see that the 69-year average annual returns of 10.2 percent for stocks and 5.4 percent for bonds appear a whole lot more stable

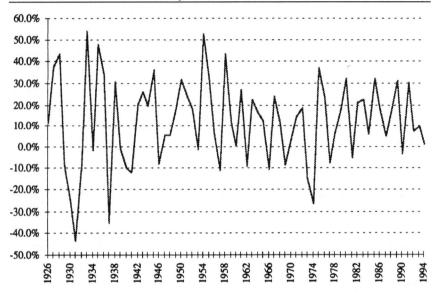

Figure 8.2   S&P 500 Annual returns, 1926 to 1994.

than the annual returns shown in the charts would suggest. Averages tend to smooth out investment performance and make it seem more predictable than it is in reality.

To illustrate this point, let's say you had a ten-year horizon, during which you would like to reach a specified financial goal. To establish your investment plan, you must know how much you will start with, what your dollar objective is, and what the required rate of return will be to reach that target. Here's an example:

- You start at 55 years old with $100,000 to invest on January 1, 1969. To make it simple, we are going to assume that no additional investments are made during the entire ten-year period.
- Assume you want to have $200,000 in ten years, a figure that will take an average compound annual rate of return of about 7.17 percent per year to attain. Considering that the S&P 500 has earned an average of over 10 percent per year, you figure that the 7.17 percent anticipated return is conservative.
- Now assume you invest all your retirement money in the S&P 500 Index.

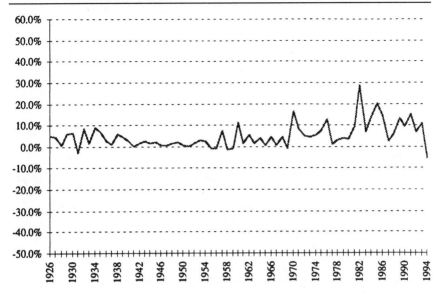

Figure 8.3 Intermediate government annual bond returns, 1926 to 1994.

At the end of the period, in 1978, you will not have come even close to your modest rate of 7.17 percent per year. In fact, you would have an account balance of only $136,497 by the end of 1978, an average annual return of only 3.16 percent. This circumstance is illustrated in Figure 8.4.

Now, Figure 8.4 doesn't present a pretty picture. And, to be sure, the period in question was a nasty time for stock investing. Just imagine how you would feel if, in 1974, you looked at your retirement portfolio and found that all you had to show for six years of being invested in the stock market was an $18,800 loss on your original investment of $100,000. It is a sobering illustration. In fact, if this had happened to you, you would probably have wanted to bail out and put your money in the bank. And that's exactly what happened. Many people did lose heart and bail out of the market in 1973 and 1974.

But some people are optimists. The thought would occur to these people that they might still have time to win the game. But in 1974, it would have taken a lot of courage to believe you could still win the game within a ten-year time frame because your principal losses would have increased the required rate of return beyond what is

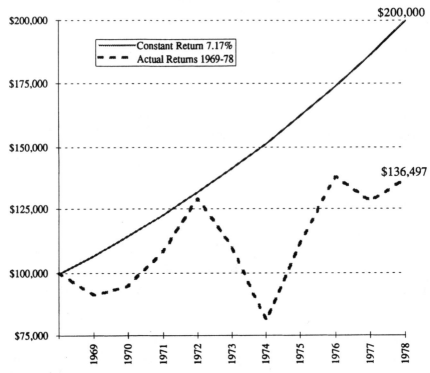

Figure 8.4   S&P 500 versus target 7.17 percent constant return, 1969 to 1978.

realistically achievable. Shown in Figure 8.5 is an illustration of how difficult it would be to play catch-up from the end of 1974. You would have to have earned a staggering average of 25.7 percent a year to end up with your originally projected $200,000 by the end of 1978. A four-year rate of return this high has happened only once in the 70 years of recorded history of the S&P Index, from 1933 through 1936.[1]

Figures 8.4 and 8.5 were selected purposely to show the effects of a bad market period on a retirement investment account. There is no doubt that, if you were young enough and had the time and the stomach to withstand a prolonged market downturn, you would be better off in the long run staying in the stock market. But here's the rub—nobody can predict when the stock market will do poorly. Worse yet, once the market goes into a prolonged period of poor and negative returns, there is no telling when it will recover. At times like these you will need a sound investment discipline to rely on.

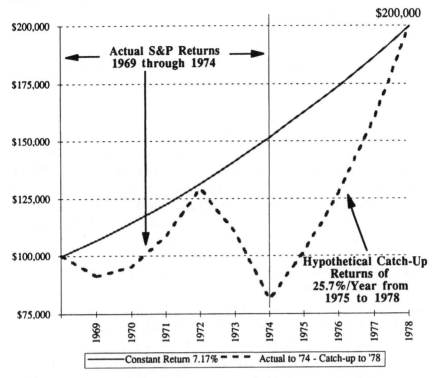

Figure 8.5   Playing catch-up after principal losses from 1969 to 1978.

This is the only thing that will keep you from acting foolishly, and things always feel worse when you are living through them than when you look back at them. However, if you reach 65 years old at the end of this ten-year period, and you wanted to retire, your ability to generate income to meet retirement expenses would be materially diminished. Moreover, if, out of desperation, you had invested more aggressively to play catch-up in 1974, you could have ended up even worse off.

DIVERSIFICATION BY FIRST PRINCIPLES

If using statistical averages won't always protect an investor, there are practical methods of portfolio construction that will tend to help. To fulfill its purpose, though, the portfolio must be constructed with a specific financial objective in mind. No single portfolio of investments will serve every investor's objectives. Thus, combining different types of securities to achieve a human financial objective is an important part of investing. However, the best way to take advantage of this type of portfolio diversification is to go back to the first principles that give value to each type of security in a portfolio. In this method, you can replace statistical nonsense with down-to-earth common sense.

For example, an investor who is saving money for the down payment on a house he or she intends to purchase in two years will not want to put those savings at any sort of risk of principal loss. It is far more preferable to accept less income and less return on this type of investment in return for ensuring the safety of one's capital. For this reason, a bank certificate of deposit or a money market mutual fund are both perfectly acceptable investments for this investor.

Other investors may be in a position where they desire a steady and predictable cash flow from a certain portfolio of investments but are not too concerned with the appreciation of capital. In this circumstance, a portfolio of bonds or a bond mutual fund might serve as the largest category of securities in a portfolio.

For investors who require appreciation of capital and are able, from time to time, to sustain the loss of income and principal, then equities are a suitable choice. However, as we noted earlier, there are differences among equities, ranging from high-quality, dividend-producing domestic stocks all the way to low-quality, small-capitalization foreign stocks. Generally, most investors will find themselves requiring more of the former and little or none of the latter.

The point is that different financial objectives will usually require different types of investments. Each type of investment has fundamental characteristics that can accomplish a specialized task. Most often, a portfolio involves a mixture of different investments as the best way to ensure a safe arrival at your financial destination, with each investment doing its part in helping you achieve your goals.

Much of risk is intimately tied to the fact that cash is what pays our expenses. The ultimate requirement of a retirement investing portfolio is that it generate cash for retirement expenses. A retirement investing portfolio can generate cash in two ways. Either the investments themselves produce cash in the form of dividends or interest income, or investments are sold to produce cash. Except for inflation-related risk, the riskiness of an investment portfolio can best be characterized by its ability to produce cash when and as required.

The phrase, "when and as required" is an important one. Much of the inherent riskiness of the capital markets takes place over periods that are too short for financial historians to worry about. But for ordinary human beings, the worry can be all too real.

There's a sad story that illustrates this. In 1968, after a lifetime of working and saving, Jim Iazzi retired with his wife. Jim was one of those guys who had played by the rules. He and his wife had had three children, and, although Jim never went to college himself, his two girls did, and both were now out on their own. The third child, a son, was drafted into the Army and died in Vietnam. Jim was born in 1903. The son of Italian immigrants, Jim had gone through the Depression when he was in his young adulthood. It is fair to say the experience left him wary and cautious. Consequently, he and his wife Edith scrimped and saved their entire working lives. Suffice it to say that Jim and Edith had known their share of heartaches, but both retained an unshakable optimism in the future. After the children were in their teens, Edith had gotten a job and the couple had managed to put money aside every month for their retirement.

In 1954, the stock market went wild. It gained over 50 percent for the entire year. Partway through the year, Jim and Edith were persuaded by a stockbroker to begin putting some of their savings into a number of stocks of large companies. It wasn't an easy step for them, but they gradually became patient and long-term stock market investors. They always invested in big companies and turned down a number of recommendations from their broker to invest in smaller and riskier companies. By 1968, Jim and Edith had a nest egg of just over $115,000. Now, neither Jim nor Edith had a tax-deferred account for any of their money; they paid the taxes on all their dividend income and then plowed the rest back into their stocks. They never panicked or sold, but it wasn't easy. In 1957, 1960, 1962, and 1966, they actually lost money, and Jim lay awake on more than one night wondering if he had done the right thing to trust the stock market.

But by 1968, on an after-tax basis, they had earned approximately a 12 percent compound rate of return net of taxes and were finally ready to retire. They had a small pension, their Social Security, and their nest egg of $115,000. Jim wasn't really worried about not having enough money for his retirement, because he had seen hard times before. But it did bother him that he had not been able to save and invest more through the years, and he was of the opinion that his nest egg was a little small. Jim had been listening to his broker talk about small stocks for years. The broker showed Jim that smaller stocks had done better than larger stocks and had racked up annual returns of about 20 percent, while Jim's portfolio had brought in only about 12 percent per year.

Plus, the broker was talking about the new concept of diversification, telling them that if they diversified their portfolio into smaller stocks as well as bonds, they would not only probably increase their returns, but they would also reduce their overall risk. The broker explained that this was true, even though Jim would have to sell some of his stocks and pay taxes to position himself to increase his return and get less risky. Jim knew that neither he nor Edith were going to be earning income except from their nest egg, and the broker's talk about increasing return and avoiding risk did make good sense. Jim decided to leave some of his money in stocks but also put some of it into government bonds and some into smaller companies' stocks. The government bonds were supposed to provide some risk protection even though they would earn less, and the smaller company stock was supposed to increase his returns, even though they were riskier.

To figure out how much money to put in which kind of investment, Jim, Edith, and their broker estimated what kind of a return might be produced by this newly diversified portfolio. Since Jim and Edith had earned about 12 percent on their big company stocks, they thought an expectation of about 9.5 percent was about right. And, although the small stocks had done over 20 percent per year over the past 15 years, they felt that they shouldn't count on more than about 12 percent a year from this part of their portfolio. The 1968 year-end intermediate bond yield was about 6 percent, so they thought they could count on a yield of about 5 percent. Finally, they hoped to earn about 3 percent on their cash. Then they split the portfolio up, as shown in Table 8.1, and tried to figure out what kind of an overall return they might expect. This estimated return was important, because they were planning on taking money out of the account to help pay retirement expenses. They had to pay about $15,000 in taxes on capital gains in their stocks to set up their newly diversified holdings, but they thought it would be worth it to get the

Table 8.1 Calculation of an Expected Portfolio Rate of Return

A	B	C	D	E
			Jim and Edith's Estimated	Jim and Edith's Estimated Annual Portfolio
Type of Investment	Dollars Invested	Percentage of Portfolio	Average Annual Return (%)	Return (C × D) (%)
Large-cap stocks	$45,000	45	9.5	4.275
Small-cap stocks	30,000	30	12	3.6
Intermediate govt. bonds	20,000	20	5.5	1.1
Govt. money market fund	5,000	5	3	0.15
Total invested	$100,000		Expected annual portfolio return	9.125

additional safety of the bonds and additional return from the small company stocks.

This expected return of 9.125 percent per year was well below the 12 percent return they had already earned, and they were comfortable that they could take out at least $9,125 a year, pay taxes due, and have enough left over to provide for their retirement without eating into their principal too much. They believed they were well diversified and could earn their way out of any minor downturn. In 1957, their stock portfolio had lost 16 percent, and they were able to hang tough at that time. They thought they could do so again, and if they just stayed on course they could ride out any downturns.

What happened to Jim and Edith during the next eight years was not a pretty sight. It's what you might call falling down the stairs. Figure 8.6 illustrates their predicament, showing the account balance, after taxes, at the end of each year.

Jim and Edith had set themselves up in retirement circumstances that would have been fine if their portfolio had only done what it was supposed to have done. But the markets were apparently not

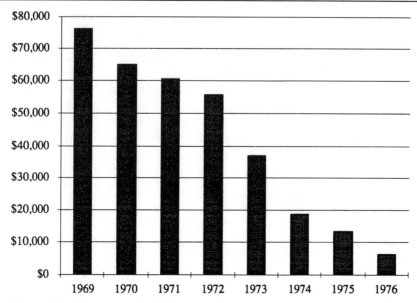

Figure 8.6 End-of-year balances in Jim and Edith's diversified retirement portfolio, 1969 to 1976.

listening to the averages. Unfortunately, because they needed the money and neither the markets nor the IRS was kind to them, they were left with only about $6,500 by 1976. Jim was 73 at the time, and his health was good. But they could no longer afford to live on their own and were forced to move in with one of their daughters. Needless to say, Jim and Edith had a severely reduced retirement lifestyle. Jim died in 1986, and Edith died shortly thereafter in 1987. They never did recover financially. The lesson to be taken from Jim and Edith's experience is not to avoid diversification. Instead, we must remember the following simple rules:

- No matter how we invest, our money is at risk. Thus, it always pays to be careful.
- Diversification can be useful, but it is not an automatic protection from loss.
- Loss is more keenly felt when you rely on your investments to pay for expenses during retirement.
- If you are retired, you have a limited ability to replenish principal losses from employment income.

Admittedly, Jim and Edith retired at the wrong time in the history of the domestic capital markets. But, if it happened once, it could happen again. A better way of organizing your retirement account is to focus both on what might happen, as well as on what you are going to do about what does happen. In Jim and Edith's case, this means that they should have configured their retirement portfolio more conservatively during retirement. It also means that they should not have continued to take out as much money from the account every year as the balance steadily lost ground.

While mere diversification can lull us into complacency about expecting to receive average returns from a diversified portfolio, it does have a place in retirement investing. Let's see how.

SECURITY-SPECIFIC RISK

We know of an English bulldog named Benson. The dog was received as a Christmas present, and by early January Benny stories started to come fast and furiously. Benny did this. Benny did that. What a great guy this Benny is. You get the picture. A bulldog is among the ugliest creatures to walk the face of the earth. They look like big, lumpy potatoes on legs. Plus, they drool and are uncommonly lazy. But perhaps the worst feature this dog possesses is that he passes the most noxious gas in the animal kingdom. Dogs are pack creatures. They relate to their owners as part of the pack and accept a subordinate role in the pack without question. Benny sleeps with his owners—the dog actually gets under the covers. Unfortunately, the creature is completely indiscreet. A few seconds after the event, the hardy gas works its way out from under the covers and stinks up the whole room. The dog's owner let us know that this is a sure sign that the dog has serious business to attend to outside. It is at this point that our friend begins to question the wisdom of owning a dog in the first place, especially on cold winter nights.

Believe it or not, companies can actually start to stink when things get bad. And if the smell coming from a company is none too savory, you'd better watch out, because you never know what might come next! A good example might be Johns Manville. This company used to be a thriving building materials firm. It had a first-rate line of fireproofed insulation for use in construction. Unfortunately, as Johns Manville shareholders came to find out, the insulation proved dangerous to all who worked with it, because it was made from asbestos. Once the connection was made between asbestos and the disease caused by asbestos (known as asbestosis), the lawsuits began to pile up. Eventually, the company was forced into bankruptcy and shareholders lost a bundle. If shares of Johns Manville had been your only investment, you would have taken an awful beating.

Portfolio diversification within any given asset class is essential to successful investing. It is a good idea to have a sufficient number of different individual securities so that bad results in any one security will not impair the portfolio as a whole. For example, if an investor holds a single stock and that stock drops in value by 25 percent, then the entire portfolio will drop in value by 25 percent. If an investor holds ten stocks and one of them drops in value by 25 percent, then the portfolio will have dropped in value by only 2.5 percent.

This principal must be applied carefully so that both company-specific and industry-specific risks can be minimized. If your stock portfolio contains 20 stocks, but they are all from one industry, then the portfolio as a whole will be much more subject to losses that arise from negative events that impact your chosen industry group.

In general, mutual fund investors in well-diversified mutual funds will find themselves with plenty of diversification. The exception might be the so-called sector funds that invest in only one type of company or industry. These funds will tend to whipsaw the investor with industry-specific risk that should be completely avoidable.

Research shows that individual investors who prefer to hold a portfolio of individual stocks had better be prepared to hold at least 40 different high-quality stocks from a variety of industries to be properly diversified from company-specific risk. In this way, we can diversify away some 97 percent to 99 percent of the risks associated with any single company.[2]

When we invest in stocks, we assume certain risks. But we also can participate in getting our share of a growing pie. What's more, common sense tells us that retirement investors are wiser to hold stocks that pay regular dividends. When dividend-paying stocks go up in price, some of that increase consists of growing cash flow paid out to shareholders in the form of dividends, and not on mere appreciation that must consist of at least some measure of speculation. After all, speculative values are based on subjective judgments, consisting of the collective opinions of the group of individuals who trade in the securities in question. This makes them more unpre-dictable than tangible or fundamental values. When stock prices go down, the payment of a dividend helps to cushion the shock of the downward price movement. And when stock prices do not go up or down much at all, the dividend payment will justify holding the asset while the shareholder is waiting for the share price to once again move upward. Thus, a diversified portfolio of high-quality dividend stocks offers the best protection from at least part of the principal risks associated with owning stocks.

You will recall that you can experience principal losses when own-ing bonds, too. This can happen if you are forced to sell before the bond matures and interest rates have risen since you invested in the bond. (Credit risks can also cause principal losses, but buying only high-quality bonds will minimize this possibility.) Well-constructed bond ladders help to manage the security-specific risks associated with bonds. Additionally, with the exception of Treasury obliga-tions, you must be wary of an overconcentration in the bonds of any single issuer.

QUALITY RISK

Another element of risk relates to the quality of the securities in your portfolio. Obviously, shares of stock issued by a company whose financial condition is fundamentally unsound carry more risk than companies that have solid fundamentals. By fundamen-tally unsound, we mean those companies whose financial or com-mercial condition is weak. Examples of corporate weakness include companies that have too much debt or too little profit (or losses), or whose success in the marketplace is uncertain. Many poor-quality securities are issued by companies that have not met the test of time. Initial public stock offerings of most companies fall into this category. You should avoid these poor-quality equities in favor of stock investments in those companies with a long-standing history of profitability and stable management.

In bond investing, so-called high-yielding bonds (sometimes known as junk bonds) issued by troubled governmental entities (both domestic and foreign) or by weak corporations, carry high risks of loss. Each of these different types of securities carries a differing pattern of risk and return. Junk bonds usually yield more than investment-grade bonds. These higher interest rates demanded by junk bond investors are compensation for the additional risk these bonds carry. Put another way, junk bonds are less likely than investment-grade bonds to pay interest and principal, in full and on time. Therefore, to attract investors to purchase these lower-quality bonds, junk bond issuers must pay higher interest rates. Additionally, as noted earlier, when we account for the long-term effect of defaults and illiquidity, junk bonds do not outperform investment-grade bonds.

SMALL-CAP RISKS

We like The Discovery Channel. The other day, it was doing a piece on several species of predatory plants, including the Venus flytrap, the sundew, and the pitcher plant. These plants are all carnivorous; they eat insects. For some reason, the pitcher plant captured our attention. The pitcher plant has an ingenious way of catching its prey. It has a pitcher-shaped vessel that holds a tantalizing liquid attractant. Unsuspecting six-leggers are literally drawn to it like flies to honey. Once perched on the lip of the vessel, the aroma of the juice emanating from the bottom of the well is overpowering. As an insect begins its descent into the pitcher plant, it finds that the inner walls of the vessel are so slick that there is no escape. But the liquid that smells so good from afar is really the pitcher plant's digestive juice. And once the little ol' bug is trapped in that juice, instead of having lunch, it becomes lunch.

There are a lot of pitcher plants on Wall Street. Typically, two attractant scents are used to lure the unsuspecting investor: the ever-popular Eau de Risk Control and our personal favorite, Parfum de Higher Total Returns. These fragrances can be found at all finer Wall Street shops and are available in many forms. Diversify! Control your risk, while pumping your returns! Go for small-cap stocks because that's where the big winners are! Our advice is not to get caught like a bug in this pitcher plant without being darned sure you know what you are doing.

As we have seen, small-cap stocks do seem to do better than large-cap stocks over time. But that is not to say that all small-cap stocks will do so. Small-cap stocks have a much more erratic record than large-cap stocks. In terms of long-term volatility, small-cap stocks have been shown to be 70 percent more volatile than large-cap stocks from 1926 through 1994. This means that the returns from small-cap stocks are considerably less reliable (on average) than the total returns from large-cap stocks.[3]

There are other issues with small-cap stocks. Small-cap stock total return includes a lower dividend component than large-cap total return. This exposes more of the total return to the vagaries of the capital markets, because dividends are much more reliable than stock prices. There are potential liquidity problems with small-cap stocks. Many small-cap stocks are not as widely traded as large-cap stocks. This means that there are fewer shares for sale on any given day. If you want to buy or sell these shares, you are more likely to pay a higher price or sell for a lower price than is possible for large-cap stocks. Small-cap stocks also have other trading problems, given the nature of the NASDAQ electronic market where most small-cap stocks are bought and sold. The nature of the NASDAQ system is that small-cap stocks are more subject to subtle price manipulation than the large-cap stocks traded on the New York Stock Exchange.

The sweet scent of the small-cap pitcher plant is not for the faint of heart. Its alluring attractiveness is heightened when folks don't have a clear understanding of their own financial objectives. Depending on your life circumstances, the risks may outweigh the benefits.

INTERNATIONAL INVESTING RISK

The idea of including international stocks and bonds in your port-folio is appealing, because some foreign securities seem to have attractive rates of return. The argument in favor of this type of investing usually takes three forms. First, supporters of international investing claim that foreign securities will have high expected returns because the economies of foreign countries are growing faster than the American economy. Next, they assert that international investments will not increase and decrease in value at the same time as domestic investments. If true, this would tend to smooth out variations in the overall value of your investment portfolio. Finally, there is the argument that the world economy is so internationalized that if you are not investing internationally, you are ignoring much of the investment opportunity available to you.

The evidence does not seem to support these claims. According to Rex Sinquefield, one of the most prominent figures in academic finance, large-cap international stocks had higher volatility with lower returns than the S&P 500. Mr. Sinquefield's research shows that international stocks produced a 10.52 percent compound annual return from 1970 through 1994, while the S&P 500 showed returns of 10.97 percent per year during the same period. In reality, it is only after you add in currency gains that international investing outperforms domestic investing for U.S. investors, because, while international stocks did worse than the S&P 500, domestic investors were able to increase their gains when converting foreign currencies back into dollars. As to the claim that you can diversify away the ups and downs in a portfolio by mixing international and domestic stocks, most of the time this is simply not what happens. In fact, 70 percent of the time, international stocks have tended to increase and decrease in value right along with the S&P 500.[4] And while it may be true that a strictly domestic investor ignores much of the world's investing opportunity, it is equally true that the domestic investor will also avoid much of the world's investing risk. Put another way, the more bells and whistles you hang onto your retirement investing portfolio, the more chance there is for something to go wrong.

Supporters of international investing do not usually speak at length about the risks of international investing. These risks are distinct from domestic investing and require careful examination by the retirement investor. International investing is broadly divided into two categories. There are the *global* markets of relatively developed nations, and there are the *emerging* markets of less-developed countries. Both of these categories carry unique risks when compared to domestic investing; however, the risks are especially heightened in the case of the emerging markets. International markets have posted high returns from time to time. The real question is whether these returns warrant the risks inherent in all international investing. In examining these risks, let's look at the more-developed markets first.

Recently, we got a call from a friend of ours who works in an investment house in Frankfurt, Germany. He was thinking of coming back to the States and wanted a few leads on possible employers.

Since we knew our friend had some kind of relationship with the German firm, Metallgesellschaft, we pressed him for details about the high drama that had surrounded this company. Metallgesellschaft was the 14th-largest company in Germany with some $15 billion in revenues from metals, mining, and other industrial operations. Recently, Metallgesellschaft went virtually bankrupt from a combination of derivative mismatches involving short-term futures positions taken to hedge its long-term oil contracts. When the price of oil went against the company's positions, the whole thing had to be bailed out by massive loans from the company's lenders—all in all, a messy affair that could have happened anywhere. But our friend had something else to say that was interesting.

It seems that accounting rules in Germany make it impossible to monitor the downward slope of a company's finances. That's how Metallgesellschaft went so long without attracting attention to its declining fortunes. German accounting rules are complicated. They seem to be designed so that only insiders can know what's really going on. A good example is that German accounting conventions allow a company to hide its profits in special accrual accounts during good times and to release these hidden profits to dampen poor performance during bad times. This makes financial analysis difficult, if not impossible. Knowing of the tremendous interest in international investing, we asked our friend if his experiences living and working in Germany qualified him to manage a portfolio of German securities. At least he had the uncommon humility to admit the truth. No, he said, all he could promise someone is that he could help a portfolio manager avoid some of the more obvious stinkers. That's because only the insiders really know what's going on. He went on to remind us that Daimler-Benz had to write off $548 million to qualify under SEC accounting rules and get listed on the New York Stock Exchange.

As investors rush to pour billions of dollars into the international capital markets, they would do well to examine the risks as well as to drool over the potential rewards. If German rules and requirements are stacked against the investor, then what about Mexican rules? Or Indian rules? (Would you believe Sri Lankan rules?) This is not to say that international investing should be off limits to retirement investors. Global investing is here to stay. However, don't be so disingenuous as to believe that foreign markets operate on the same rules as domestic markets.

Let's not forget the risks associated with foreign exchange differentials over time. When you purchase securities in the local currency, there is always a chance that the value of that currency will fall relative to the dollar, thus endangering the value of your investment. Currency risks cut both ways for the international investor. Sometimes they add value to a positive rate of return on the underlying investment, and sometimes they can subtract value. Conversely, currency fluctuations can make a bad investment less painful or deepen a loss. As is always the case in the capital markets, nobody knows how to predict future events, and currency movements are no exception. Even the most-developed international markets have risks inherent in currency movements. At last glance, the yen was a little more than 108 to the dollar. So what happens to yen-denominated investments if the rate of exchange goes to 120 over the next few years? Some international investors hedge their currency risks through the use of derivative securities. They seek to protect their underlying investments from currency fluctuations in this way. However, nothing is foolproof, and this extra layer of derivative investing can represent just one more thing that can go wrong.

For all the risks associated with the capital markets of the more-developed countries, there are even more problematic risks associated with the smaller, less-developed markets. One of the more prominent of these problems involves the effects of the huge inflows of capital from investors in the more-developed countries, particularly from American retirement investors. These relatively huge transfers of capital will often have a self-fulfilling impact on many of the smaller markets.

Last September, we took three days off to go fishing at Opinicon Lake in Canada. The annual trip is sponsored by a fishing club that started some 30 years ago. Every September since, these fellows go fishing at the same place. Opinicon Lake is the largest in a chain of lakes that sit at different elevations. To facilitate the passage of fishing boats from one lake to another, there is a system of canals and locks. Each lock has its own name, with the deepest one being known as Chaffey's Lock.

Going through Chaffey's Lock in a small fishing boat is quite an experience. First you pull your boat into and through a canal that leads you to the open lock itself. The lock doors close slowly, and as you sit in your small boat at the bottom of the lock, you feel like you are sitting in a deep hole. But before you can get too claustrophobic, your attention is diverted by the loud and steady rush of water flowing into the lock from the higher lake. Your boat begins to rise, the far lock gate opens, and you motor into the next body of water. On the return trip, you do just the reverse: You get in the lock at the top level and sink down to the level of the lower canal.

Chaffey's Lock got us thinking about the impact of liquidity on illiquid markets. After the lock closes for the first time, you find yourself sitting in the boat in what amounts to a deep container with sheer stone walls on either side. As water comes rushing into the closed lock, the water (and the boat along with it) have only one direction they can go—up.

You don't have to go far in the capital markets to see that a similar condition exists among buyers and sellers as they exchange money for securities. There is no better example of this phenomenon than what happened a few years back when the smaller emerging markets first became fashionable for American investors and capital poured in. So what is wrong with investing in the emerging markets? In the first place, nobody can really be certain when emerging markets will actually *emerge* to become what we could call a market in any real sense of the word. Put in another way, are these emerging markets really full and liquid capital markets that are ready for absentee investment by American retirement investors? The answer is: probably not.

Yes, there have been unrealized capital gains registered from time to time in these markets. The question is: Have investors been able to freely sell their investments and repatriate their gains on a reasonably consistent basis? The answer is unclear. Certainly, emerging markets have done both well and poorly over the last few years. However, although they did so in the past, will that happy condition continue into the future? When it comes to local laws and regulations, the answer will vary from market to market. But when it comes to questions of liquidity, all we can say is that, on a net basis, the capital has been flowing out of the pockets of the developed-country investors and into the emerging markets in many areas of the world. However, the real test of liquidity in any market comes when it is time to sell. Until an outflow of capital becomes more common in most of these emerging markets, we simply will not know if there will be any buyers to match the sellers.

We suspect that the prices of these securities are rising quickly mainly because there are more buyers than sellers, but might there be more-fundamental forces at work that give rise to extra value in these securities? One answer suggested by those who promote investing in the emerging markets is that certain foreign economies have higher growth rates, and thus rising tides will raise all ships. Market sages extrapolate this observation to the capital markets and conclude that the prices for securities in these markets have nowhere to go but up. The recent numbers do tend to bear out this view. Many emerging markets are in countries whose economies are rapidly growing when compared to that of the United States. It is also true that 10 percent of a billion is one hundred million, while 10 percent of a million is only one hundred thousand. Growth rates can mask the maturity of emerging economies and give rise to optimism that is out of proportion to the opportunity for prudent investing.

In the long run, those who favor emerging market investing might be right someday, but not just yet. As market economies begin to replace the less effective centrally controlled economies, foreign capital markets all over may provide appropriate places for pensions to invest substantial assets. The trouble is, who knows how long the "long run" will be? Will it be 10 years? 20 years? 50 years? A century or two? There is a variety of reasons to be careful about pouring money into the emerging markets. Timely and reliable information may be difficult or impossible to obtain about securities traded in emerging markets. There is also the lack of antifraud laws and regulations to worry about. Nepotism and bribery are honorable and time-tested ways of life in many countries. Next, there are all sorts of unproductive government interference and regulation that stack the deck against foreign investors. Language and cultural difficulties are another problem. While many language and cultural issues are obvious, others are subtle.

Finally, for a variety of reasons, one thing seems obvious: Even if you put aside the other problems faced by investors in the emerging markets, most of the world's capital markets are far too small to absorb significant amounts of capital from America's mutual funds without severe price distortions taking place. These markets (if they have actually emerged enough be called "markets") are a lot like Chaffey's Lock. You go into the lock, and the water either rises or falls, depending upon which direction you are going. When the dollars rush in, there are often more buyers than sellers, simply because the aggregate market capitalizations of these markets' securities are so small.

A surge of money has been flowing into international markets. This tide has increased the level of water in the locks that stand between capital markets that are wildly different in size and liquidity (for example, Argentina and the United States). The bottom line is that most of the world's capital markets have yet to prove themselves as more attractive than the domestic markets over the long haul. Global change often takes place over relatively long periods of time, even during modern times when the pace of change is faster than it has ever been in recorded history. For example, you may remember during the late 1980s all the fuss over the unification of Europe that was to take place in 1992. Needless to say, reports of the demise of nationalism in Europe were wildly exaggerated. This situation may change as emerging market structures mature and grow. A process is likely to take place at a far slower rate than is assumed by many.

However, as with investing your retirement monies in small-cap stocks, investing in international stocks must be strictly a secondary priority. Only after you have established a firm and well-funded foundation of large-cap domestic dividend-paying stocks should you consider investing in any international equity markets. Better yet, a safer way to participate in foreign economies is to invest in U.S. multinational corporations. Most large companies in the United States have extensive foreign operations, often deriving from 20 percent to 30 percent or more of their earnings from abroad. This allows you to participate globally without directly assuming all the risks specific to international investing itself.

DERIVATIVE SECURITIES RISK

Derivative securities are derived from either debt or equity securities. They often have exotic names, terms, and conditions. Options, futures, strips, swaps, and similar devices are all considered derivatives. The responsible purpose of derivatives is to control the risk of an invested position by holding a security that, in theory, will stabilize or prevent losses beyond certain predetermined boundaries. The ill-advised and inappropriate use of derivatives has created a complex, fast-moving gambling-like arena. This speculative derivatives activity is so complicated that it cannot be undertaken without heavy dependence on computers. Humans are relegated to secondary status. The purpose of derivative speculation is not to control risk, but to beat other participants in the market.

One phenomenon associated with derivatives is that, for each and every trade, there is a distinct winner and a distinct loser. Every trade has to have somebody on the other side, wagering that the counterpart will lose. This type of activity is known as a *zero-sum game*. The implication for most investors is clear: Stay away from this kind of gambling. In a game where even the pros get whacked regularly, this is no place for the retirement investor.

One reason for caution is that many of the newer nonstandard derivative products are extremely complicated. This can be especially dangerous for retirement investors. So exactly what are those risks? Unfortunately, we don't know and neither do their creators. Many derivative gurus are primarily mathematicians and computer geniuses with far too little grounding in the real world. They are usually intensely concerned with the risks inside the derivative operation and don't always perceive the underlying practical risks involved. On paper, most derivatives work just great. But the hidden and unpredictable risks of these products are just that—hidden and unpredictable. That these doggone things are hard to understand should spell caution for retirement investors. And if you don't fully understand the risks in something, then don't do it.

Not all derivatives are inappropriate. When a corporation wants to protect itself from currency swings in its foreign operations, it can attempt to use derivative securities to lock in a currency price, thus making their operation more stable and predictable. Farmers use derivatives to lock in prices for their crops, giving them the stability and predictability of revenues necessary for smooth operations. Farmers don't really care whether soybeans will go up or down once they have hedged their crops with soybean futures. The important thing is that they know what their crops will bring once it comes time to sell them. Manufacturers and other companies can also stabilize the prices of the materials they need for production through the use of derivatives. The company that controls the costs it must use in production is seeking stability, not speculative profit. Finally, banks and insurance companies sometimes improve their asset-liability management through the use of derivatives. They want to make sure they can pay their obligations when due, not make a killing on the derivatives they use.

But it is far too easy to move from these mission-critical derivative strategies into the realm of speculation for its own sake, where derivatives are used to make huge bets on the movements of securities, currencies, or capital markets. Often, this speculation is made even more dangerous through the use of borrowed money, which magnifies gains or losses.

Derivative positions often stray so far from reality that there isn't a liquid market for them. For that matter, even when the market is running smoothly, the reliability of the investor on the other side of a nonstandard derivative trade can be called into question. There's no problem when everyone makes good on their promises. But what happens under less than favorable conditions if one side of the trade is unwilling or unable to fulfill its end of the bargain? To take the situation one step further, you never know who the other side of your derivative trade has hedged with. As in the insurance business, where insurers may lay off risk to a reinsurer, so, too, derivatives players may lay off risks to unrelated third parties in many nonstandard derivative operations.

Many pension funds, investment managers, and mutual funds use derivatives in their portfolios. Some of these derivative activities are clearly speculative in nature. Unfortunately, it is difficult for individual retirement investors to get their hands around the derivative question when they are investing in mutual funds or other professionally managed investment products. Not all derivatives are created equal, and certain types are definitely dangerous, while others may have redeeming features when used properly. So be sure to ask plenty of questions when you invest in portfolios with derivatives. The best rule is that if you do not understand something, then don't invest.

MORTGAGE-BACKED SECURITY RISK

There are a lot of computer eggheads on Wall Street today. It used to be that all you found lurking among the caverns of Broad and Wall in Lower Manhattan were bond men and stock jocks with the odd technical chartist thrown in for good measure. But no more. The Street has been given over to mathematicians and computer gurus. So, in an odd twist, the real action is now among the nerds. These propeller-headed people love statistics and probability theory, and while they used to make their homes in the universities, they seem to have found an ideal playground on Wall Street. Nowhere are the techies more in evidence than in mortgage-backed securities.

In the days before mortgages were pooled together for sale to investors around the globe, community bankers knew many of their borrowers. The relationship between borrowers and lenders was reasonably simple. The advent of mortgage-backed securities changed all that, carrying with it the promise of a more liquid market for these debts, with benefits accruing to borrowers in the form of lower interest rates. Institutional investors in these securities also got a good deal, because they could participate in the mortgage market much more easily.

But the simple sale of assets and the pass-through of interest and principal left the mortgage bondholder unusually exposed to prepayment risk. This occurs when interest rates fall and homeowners refinance their mortgages at those new, lower rates. Prepayments give bondholders their principal back when they really don't want to get it because proceeds from refinancings can be reinvested only at lower rates of interest than those paid on the original bonds. But, since interest rate movements cannot be forecasted, prepayments due to refinancings are difficult to predict. Worse, if a bondholder purchased the bonds at a premium, prepayments result in a capital loss, because the mortgage principal amounts are repaid at their face value, not at the premium value. When interest rates drop steadily, mortgage brokers become a growth industry and urge people to refinance their home mortgages. Increasingly, the pace of prepayments will rise sharply when interest rates fall.

In the early 1980s the *collateralized mortgage obligation* (CMO) was introduced into the mortgage securities market. With CMOs, the issuer of the mortgage-backed security itself (usually a large Wall Street investment bank) acts as principal in the issuance of bonds backed up by mortgages. This arrangement allows the issuer to create all types of hybrid bonds with differing maturities, interest rates, and other features.

About 70 percent of CMOs are packaged into what are known as *planned amortization classes* (PACs). These PACs each have specified maturities and are relatively tame, even though they are quite complex to construct. Usually, PACs are constructed to make the cash flows attributable to each maturity more predictable than is the case with ordinary pass-through mortgage-backed securities. But the increase in predictability for some comes at a steep price for others. Like some wild genetic experiment gone awry, the techies tinkering with mortgage pools have spawned all sorts of strange fungi and beasties that grow from the nooks and crannies of the housing market. And, while the mortgage geneticists gave us some valuable innovations, they've also given birth to freaks and monsters every bit as weird as trapezoidal tomatoes or 15-legged goats.

To understand these bizarre securities, we have to look at the remaining 30 percent of CMOs, a group of securities that are devilishly complicated. A good example of these complex CMOs is *principal-only* bonds (known as POs), others are *interest-only* bonds (known as IOs), and still others are some of each in varying proportions. Put simply, IOs pay only interest from mortgages, no principal. When refinancings occur, interest payments stop. That means that these perverse bonds act the opposite of other bonds. When interest rates rise, so do the IOs. But, when rates fall, watch out below!

During the past few years, a number of sophisticates have been caught in the IO vise. At one point, the father of the mortgage-backed bond business itself, believing rates had bottomed out, placed huge bets on IOs, only to see their value fall precipitously when rates rose. A large public pension fund got tagged for huge losses when its chief investment officer tried to sell his IO portfolio. J.P. Morgan & Company took about $200 million of IO-related losses in 1992, and Salomon Incorporated posted $173 million of trading losses.

Clearly these securities are speculative in nature. IOs and POs are packaged and sold in a variety of combinations, depending on the investor's appetite for risk. However, no combination of these types of securities is appropriate for retirement investing portfolios. PACs, on the other hand, parcel out much of the prepayment risk to those who want to make those bets. Given their premium to Treasuries, their low default rate, and their relative stability, PACs are acceptable in a retirement portfolio (in modest proportions), even if their riskier cousins are not.

NINE

Putting It All Together

EXPECT ADVERSITY—PREPARE TO OVERCOME

The town of Wilton, Connecticut, has its share of beautiful country roads lined with stone walls and colonial houses. In the early 1960s, right off Olmstead Hill Road was a small dirt path that gave access to Pope's Pond, the prettiest little reservoir you ever saw. More than a mile and a half long and maybe a half a mile wide, Pope's Pond was a source of drinking water for nearby Norwalk. On maps, for some strange reason, Pope's Pond was known as Street's Pond, but you never heard anyone refer to it that way.

Pope's Pond had been created by damming up a stream. The original dam was a 30-foot-high stone affair that, by the late fifties, had become completely overgrown with trees, grapevines, and moss. Though the area was supposed to be off limits for fishing, you could regularly catch bigmouth bass, perch, and catfish from off the dam. It never occurred to any of the kids that Pope's Pond had ever been anything but Pope's Pond.

One summer during the sixties, there was a long, hot drought. During that summer, Pope's Pond was reduced to a mudhole, revealing its history for all to see. Stumps with ax marks poked out of the mudflats, showing the remnants of the forest that had grown up in what was now the reservoir. But the trees had been cut down late in the game, because stone walls were also visible. That means that before it had been reforested, earlier settlers had used the land for grazing. There was even an old fireplace foundation in the middle of Pope's Pond. Perhaps 150 years ago, some farmer had lived next to the stream that was now Pope's Pond.

The stumps and stones made it all but impossible to continue to fish in Pope's Pond during the drought. The fish must have all gone to the center of the pond, seeking deeper water. The fishing hole at the base of the dam was ruined. When you tried to get out to the deeper water, the stumpy mudflat made the going tough, and your fishing lines would get snagged on stumps and debris with every cast.

When the water was high, you couldn't see the stumps, stone walls, or the fireplace foundation. And you can't see them today. After the drought, the reservoir company came in and tore down the old dam, replacing it with a bigger one made out of concrete. After the new dam was built, and once the drought was over, the water level rose in Pope's Pond by six feet or more, once again covering all the stumps and stone walls and creating an entirely new shoreline.

We never see underlying problems beneath the surface until there is a drought. In retirement investing, you could say that well-funded and carefully invested retirement accounts have ample water behind their dams. That is, when there are sufficient assets of the right type, you can cover up many of the capital market–related stumps and debris. It is important to save enough to put plenty of water behind the dam before the drought, because when a drought hits it is too late to do much.

In the capital markets context, there are plenty of stumps and rocks just under the surface of a liquid market. When you drain liquidity, all kinds of problems can crop up. There was a nifty financial service set up prior to the crash of 1987. It was called portfolio insurance. The "insurance" component depended on a liquid market of willing buyers and sellers ready to settle all their derivatives trades. It looked great on paper, but as soon as frantic sellers blew past the normal trading mechanisms, there wasn't a chance of getting all pieces of the "insurance" executed properly. Sell! To whom? Many so-called derivatives contracts work like this. You can buy 'em just as easy as pie—but just try to sell the damned things under adverse market conditions.

Aggressive growth or value investing, particularly in the so-called micro-capitalization arena, can also present numerous problems when it comes time to sell. Emerging market securities are another example of securities that can run up against stumps when you drain the pond. Easy to buy, hard to sell if there's a drought. There's a long list of investments that are hard to sell when the markets are dry. And, even if you can find buyers for marginal securities, they probably won't be willing to pay the price you need.

Difficult times test how adequately we have prepared for adversity. The larger our margin of safety, the more likely we will be able to ride out the problems. This concept of a margin of safety was put forth vigorously by Benjamin Graham, the father of security analysis. He argued that every facet of an investment operation must include a margin of safety. A bond should be purchased only if the issuer has more than enough to make all interest and principal payments. The amount of extra principal- and interest-paying capacity is the margin of safety. In buying stocks, there is a margin of safety to the degree that the intrinsic value of the stock exceeds its market price.

The concept of a margin of safety is important in retirement investing, too. Selection of investments must be made carefully. In stocks, large, solid, domestic dividend-paying companies offer a greater margin of safety than small, untested micro-cap stocks. In bonds, credit quality and maturity selection should always have plenty of attention from the safety-minded retirement investor. In the allocation of investments, it is better to err on the side of conservatism. Money set aside for retirement is difficult enough to get and must be invested as prudently as possible. Careful preparation for adversity helps ensure that we will "arrive alive" when it comes time to retire.

AGE IS THE COMMON DENOMINATOR

As anyone who has even a few tomato plants knows, tomato season comes but once a year. Three or four plants put into the ground at the right time of the year will provide enough tomatoes to satisfy even the most voracious tomato-lover's appetite. In our backyard, we usually set out a few plants in late spring. By August, at least two new large tomatoes ripen each day, with plenty more on the way. Each year, the cycle is the same. Small yellow flowers appear; then tiny green tomatoes grow steadily, turn red, and are finally ready to eat. In February, we have to buy those rock-hard supermarket tomatoes (grown who knows where), knowing full well they've probably been ripened with ethylene in some boxcar during shipping. But by mid-September tomato time comes to Pennsylvania.

One May a few years back, a 13-year-old boy we knew brought four small peat pots home from school. Each pot held the results of some now-forgotten biology experiment in plant cultivation. According to the boy, the pots held seedlings purported to produce the hottest peppers on earth. We told the boy he would have to plant the peppers himself if he wanted to have any by September. But kids will be kids, and the small plants languished in the peat pots on a deck in the hot sun of early summer. After a couple of days, the boy's mother took pity on the poor things and put them into an old pan filled with a couple of inches of water. And there the hottest peppers in the world sat and baked for weeks.

One day in July, we were watering our tomato plants. Spying the old pan on the deck, we looked inside, and there were the four small pepper plants. Not only had they not grown, but two had died and two were close to death. Without much thought, we put the two that were alive into the tomato garden next to the tomatoes. There they got plenty of water, fine soil, and good sun. Still, they refused to grow much larger than they had been in the peat pots. When the tomato plants erupted into a small jungle of vegetation, the two surviving chili pepper plants appeared healthy enough, but surely never produced any peppers before frost that year.

Natural rhythms impose themselves on every nook and cranny of our world. Farmers have known forever that you have to make hay while the sun shines and milk the cows every morning come hell or high water. In farming, an unquestioned acceptance of the natural order of things is not only necessary, it is vital. There is a time when things will work and a time when they won't. It may not have been only poor timing that ruined the hot pepper plants, but it sure didn't help them. In late spring, when they should have been growing a strong root system and putting up stems and leaves, they sat on a hot deck in a pan of water.

Human activities have natural rhythms, too, even though we struggle like the dickens to deny it. As a reflection of the human aging process, retirement investing has an undeniable rhythm as well. We start work, start families, continue working, age, and finally stop working full-time and retire. The natural human life cycle cannot be denied. A farmer can't wait until winter to put up hay for the cows. Neither can he wait until fall to plant the crops. Similarly, retirement investors must recognize what crops to plant, how long to cultivate them, and when it is wise to sow and reap. We must deal with natural rhythms as they are and not as we might wish them to be. We must bend our wills to them and not the other way around.

For retirement investors, a recognition of the natural rhythms of life is an essential component of success. Without the patience to await the outworking of events, actions taken will be taken too soon. Without the courage to decide and then to act, nothing ever gets done. But in either instance, whether waiting or acting, there are rhythmic imperatives that will determine much of the success or failure in getting the job done. In other words, if you want to harvest fresh tomatoes or hot peppers in September, you have to plant them appropriately in the springtime.

It has long been a practice in the financial services industry to stress the unique nature of each person's circumstance. And it is true that every human being does have a unique circumstance. We earn different amounts, have different financial obligations, and approach our financial problems differently. Yet, for all our differences, when it comes to retirement investing, we remain remarkably similar with respect to the human cycles in retirement investing.

What binds us together in this area is age. Here, too, there are differences, but these differences are largely a matter of degree. In general, younger people are not good candidates for retirement. The young usually lack the resources, and the applicable laws and regulations do not encourage retirement before the age of 60. And, while older people may retire at different ages, it is a matter of degree. As a rule, younger people do not retire, while older people usually do.

Understanding this common denominator is important for understanding how to put together a rational plan for retirement investing. What is exactly right for a 30-year-old is exactly wrong for a 70-year-old. What's more, there are times when only certain things can be done successfully. Every human being matures and ages. Successful retirement investing must mesh age-related elements together into a seamless approach to solving the problem. So what are those fundamental elements of age that condition the retirement investing portfolio over time? Let's summarize a few of the more important age-related issues we covered earlier:

- The sooner people start to invest for retirement, the more successful they are likely to be. An early start allows the magic of compounding to work for you. The later you start, the harder it becomes to generate sufficient assets to support your retirement needs.
- Social Security will not provide the level of benefits in the future that it does today. Unless Social Security is overhauled radically, it will not be able to support the baby-boom retirees. Given the misinformation on this subject, it seems likely that Social Security taxes will have to be raised, initial retirement ages will have to be extended, and Social Security benefits will not be as large as they are for current retirees.
- Company-sponsored pension plans have shifted the responsibility of retirement investing from the employer to the employee. This makes it more important than ever to take charge of your own retirement investing earlier rather than later. Company-sponsored defined-contribution plans are full of pitfalls. Daily valuation and switching assets, borrowing against retirement accounts, as well as the inexperience and emotional instability of many investors all stack the deck against the average investor.
- It is important to take full advantage of all tax-deferred retirement investing vehicles available to you. Taxes can wipe out a large portion of your retirement investments. If you have a lump-sum payout from one tax-deferred retirement account, roll it over into a tax-deferred account. Do not spend it. Do not pay taxes on it until you begin to withdraw monies during retirement.
- Most people wait until they reach the retirement window some five years or so before retirement to confront the problem of shifting their retirement investments to generate cash to pay for retirement living expenses. This may be too late in the game. The capital markets are notoriously unpredictable.

One cannot afford to take the chance that a retirement portfolio is in a slump just when it is most needed to pay retirement expenses.

- Young people have the time to compound their investments
  before retirement but usually do not have much money to
  invest. Having time in their favor, younger people can afford
  to withstand a certain amount of temporary loss in their
  investments. However, they must be careful not to speculate
  and thereby take permanent losses when there is so little capital to replenish their retirement accounts.

- Older people may have more money to invest but do not
  have as much time or income to recover from losses. Because
  they usually have less time to wait out bad markets, older
  people must be more conservative and cannot afford excess
  volatility. Because they have little or no outside income, older
  people cannot afford to take permanent losses, because once
  the money is gone, it is gone forever and cannot be replen-
  ished.

- People are living longer and, as a consequence, will need to
  save and invest more wisely for their retirement. It is important to save and invest sufficient capital for an extended
  period of retirement. If you do a poor job, you will not be
  able to retire on your own terms and might even have to continue to work to earn money for a reduced lifestyle. Extended
  life spans also heighten inflation-related risks. Older people
  must be careful to protect themselves from inflation, while
  not unduly exposing themselves to other risks in the process.

These common age-based elements form the foundation for
approaching the retirement investing problem. When these factors
are taken together, we can see that age-specific retirement investing
exists on a continuum, stretching from the day we begin work as an
adult to the day we retire and beyond.

IT IS ESSENTIAL TO BEGIN EARLY, BUT IT IS NEVER TOO LATE TO CLIMB ON BOARD

It is not easy to save for retirement. It always seems like there are
other, more pressing needs for your money. The car breaks down,

the clothes dryer dies, a child needs braces, and so on. Many people don't even begin the process until they get into their fifties and their child-related obligations are fully discharged. What's more, there is some evidence that many Americans are having their children later in life, pushing the starting date for retirement investing even further into the future. These trends have important implications.

It is true that the earlier you start saving and investing, the better the outcome you are likely to have. The simple fact is that time and patient compounding will outperform even the most brilliant investment minds. But, for many people, their early years are filled with lost opportunities and missed chances. This leads many to believe that they can make up for lost time by investing more aggressively, even though they are beginning much later in life.

The capital markets are fickle. They can go great guns or stagnate for years at a stretch. This means you can't always fine-tune your expectations around the historic averages. You have to prepare for adversity, because the consequences of guessing wrong can be devastating. Beginning your retirement investing program late in life does not increase your life span. If you begin late, the only sensible remedy is to save and invest more rather than to become more aggressive in your investing. Becoming more aggressive as you get older is, in reality, an effort to cheat time. You may win, but if you lose, you will not be able to recover financially from the decision. We hasten to add that it is important to become more conservative as you get older, regardless of when you begin to invest for retirement. It is sad to see people like Jim and Edith Iazzi end up with little to show for their many years of saving and investing, but there are no guarantees in the investing world.

There is a way to cheat time on behalf of your children, however. Under current law, there is a nifty way to do this with an individual retirement account in your child's name. To set up an IRA in your child's name, the child must have taxable compensation. Taxable compensation includes wages, salaries, tips, commissions, fees, and bonuses. Children can contribute $2,000 or 100 percent of their taxable compensation, whichever is less, each taxable year. Naturally, when children get jobs and receive this compensation, they are not likely to be inclined to invest it for their retirement. This is where you, as a parent, can intervene. You and your spouse can each make a gift of up to $10,000 a year to any recipient without adverse tax consequences. If your children earn at least $2,000 in compensation in a tax year, then you can make a gift to each of them of $2,000, which they can turn around and invest into IRAs in their own names. That way, they can spend amounts equal to their after-tax compensation and invest your gifts in their own IRAs.

Though small, these gifts can make a huge difference to your children's retirement investing program. The reason is the power of compounding. Assume for example, that your children start work when they get out of school. Say you were to invest $2,000 a year on their behalf for, say, five years and then stop giving them any money whatsoever for their retirement accounts. After 45 years of compounding at 8 percent per year, each child would have an enormous account worth some $254,898. That's right—by investing a total of $10,000 over a five-year span, by the time your child was ready to retire, 45 years from when you started, he or she would have an account worth over a quarter million dollars! Figure 9.1 illustrates this example dramatically. Remember, only $10,000

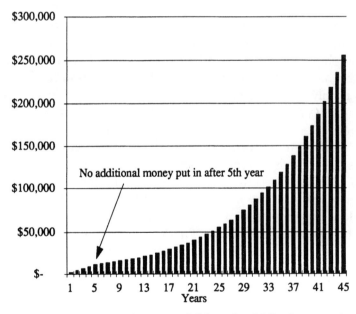

Figure 9.1 How to give your child an "unfair" advantage in retirement investing.

is put into the account over five years, no additional money is placed into this IRA account after the fifth year, and the average rate of return is 8 percent.

There would be one additional benefit from the gift you would be providing to your child. Many people never experience first-hand the magic of compounding. They simply do not save and invest enough money for a long enough period of time for the effects of compounding to become obvious. By setting your children up with modestly funded IRAs of their own, you will be making an example for them to see the effect of compounding first-hand. The impact of this lesson will not be lost on your kids. Once they have experienced the magic of compounding, they are not likely to forget the lesson it offers. This should make your children into better savers and investors than any amount of lecturing on the virtue of thrift.

YOUR FIRST JOB IS TO BUILD AND MAINTAIN A BASE RETIREMENT BENEFIT

Some kids can climb trees like squirrels and have absolutely no fear of heights. They are always testing the limits of their athletic ability, the recuperative power of their bodies, and their capacity to go to new heights. One ten-year-old we know climbs trees all year round. His yard has a number of large trees. The pin oaks would be great to climb if only you could get up the first 30 feet of limbless trunk. The silver maples have plenty of low branches but aren't very challenging to climb. However, the eight or nine mature apple trees are an entirely different matter. At a certain time of the year, there are always apples to eat. This gives any kid a good reason to climb the trees.

One year, the Macintosh apple tree on one side of the house bore a fantastic crop. At the start of the season, you could pick them right off a low-hanging branch. However, as time wore on, all the low-hanging apples disappeared. This meant our apple scavenger was forced to climb the tree in search of better pickings. Late one afternoon, the boy had an itch for an apple and stepped out to his favorite produce department. Scanning the Macintosh tree, he saw a big red fruit halfway up the tree, hanging from a branch that stuck out over the side porch roof. This was the snack he was looking for. He started up the tree as if the devil were in hot pursuit. It didn't take him long to get to the branch that held his prize.

Once there, he began the "coconut waltz," dancing out on the limb. Three-quarters of the way down the branch, life became a bit uncertain. It seems the branch was beginning to bend under his body weight. Just then, a strong wind kicked up, making the tree pitch and roll. Moments later, he met his reward as the branch broke and our boy was inspecting his brushburns from the shingles on the porch roof.

It is a given that ten-year-olds can be reckless. And, it's OK to go out on a limb. That's part of life and everybody does it now and then. But before you go out too far, you should ask whether the branch will support your weight. The same rule applies to retirement investing. There are times when you are tempted to make a retirement investment because of the allure of its potential returns. But before you take the plunge, make sure your retirement portfolio can support the gamble. You must first build a solid base of retirement investments before you go out on a limb for a speculative investment. This brings us to a central question of how to invest our money so that it will work for us when we are no longer able to work to support ourselves. The first task is to establish a *base retirement benefit* for ourselves.

What is a base retirement benefit? It is the amount of money necessary to support an individual's essential living requirements in retirement. These are the things that every individual must have to keep the wolf away from the door. The first objective in retirement investing must be to ensure the certainty of meeting those needs. For many people, a base retirement benefit will be all they can reasonably expect to accomplish. That's because their incomes and responsibilities won't allow much more. But everyone, whether rich or poor, must take responsibility for the establishment of a base retirement benefit for themselves. How much of your pre-retirement income will you need to generate your base benefit? The answer varies with every individual. Many estimates are that you will require some 70 percent of your pre-retirement income to create a decent base retirement benefit for yourself. But this number is an approximation that won't fit everyone's circumstances. The point is that provision for the basic retirement living expenses is the essential and primary objective of any retirement investing program.

Even though the size of the base retirement benefit will vary depending on individual circumstances, the concept applies equally to all. Remember, you cannot expect an employer to accomplish this on your behalf. And we really don't know what we can expect from the government. So establishment of a base retirement benefit is an imperative for each and every person.

Once you have established a base retirement benefit for yourself, then you may begin to go farther out on a limb and invest for a supplemental retirement benefit. This is where you might stretch for a bit of additional total return, short of actual speculation. The supplemental retirement benefit is created by investing in, for example, small-cap stocks or perhaps even a few international investments. The whole point is to take care of your base benefit first. Then and only then should you think about taking less-liquid and risky investments into your retirement portfolio.

The base benefit is created from a solid foundation of investments. The purpose of those investments is to create the required income streams that an individual will need to maintain a base-case retirement. The object of the concept is to get retirement investors to focus on that job first and to stay focused until that job is accomplished. The vast majority of people will find it difficult to provide for their own base retirement benefit, much less being able to stretch to finance a supplemental retirement benefit.

Figure 9.2 illustrates how the concept of a base retirement benefit fits into the investing triangle introduced at the beginning of the book.

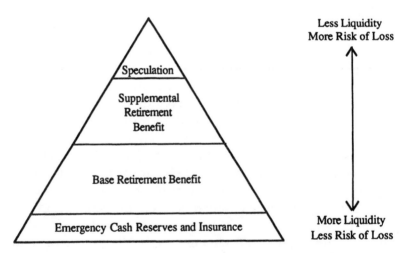

Figure 9.2   Investing triangle with illustration of a base benefit.

The base retirement benefit embodies the old philosophy that you should crawl before you walk and walk before you run. It means the primary goal in retirement investing should be to establish a portfolio built from conservative investments that are capable of providing the replacement income needed by retirees. As you go about this job of ensuring the creation of a base benefit for yourself, remember that it is not about trying to see if you can make money in the market faster than your neighbor. You are preparing a livelihood for yourself when you are no longer able to work. This is a serious job, and because we have only one life to work with (that we know of), you get just one shot at it. This means you have to focus money and see that it is invested with the correct job in mind. The best way to do this is by accumulating sound financial assets that produce dividends and interest that will build wealth through patient compounding. So let's turn to the creation of the portfolio. Which securities are appropriate for the job of building a base benefit for yourself?

BETTER SAFE THAN SORRY—APPROPRIATE SECURITIES FOR RETIREMENT INVESTING

Not all types of securities are appropriate to build a base benefit retirement portfolio. We have seen how risk control is linked with the ability to save and with the time available until the portfolio must be put to its intended use. This interrelationship between risk management, savings ability, and time creates a powerful argument against speculative securities in the retirement investing portfolio. Therefore, to properly control risk as you construct a base benefit, it is necessary to invest in only the highest-quality securities. It is one thing to have to accept the uncontrollable capital market risks inherent in any investment. It is another thing entirely to accept the controllable risks presented to an investor in poor-quality securities.

Only stocks from the highest-quality companies with long and successful track records should be included in the well-designed retirement portfolio. Moreover, the long-term evidence shows that purchasing high-quality stocks that make consistently high dividend payments have the best long-term rates of return and the lowest risk of loss. Conversely, over the long haul, growth stocks have demonstrated a greater degree of risk with a smaller likely return. Similarly, smaller-capitalization stocks have proven themselves to be more likely to create losses for the retirement investor than the larger-capitalization stocks. International stocks carry their own set of risks and problems. Neither should have a place in the creation of the portfolio that helps you build a base retirement benefit.

Bonds used in retirement investing should be of the highest quality to ensure steady and consistent cash flows of interest and principal payments to the bondholder. Municipal bonds should be avoided in the retirement account because you do not need double protection from taxes. Junk bonds should be avoided because their issuers have not proven to have sufficient creditworthiness.

The proper use of bonds of differing maturities can also be used to manage risk and income. In the young person's portfolio, short- and intermediate-term bonds can be used to help stabilize the account's value during difficult periods in the stock market. In the older person's portfolio, bonds must be selected to maximize interest income without getting maturities that are too long. Longer maturities tend to fall more in value when interest rates rise, and exposure to this risk must therefore be controlled.

LIFE-CYCLE ASSET ALLOCATION STRATEGIES

In the sixth century B.C., a Chinese philosopher, Lao-tzu, had a knack for finding wisdom in the rhythms of daily life. One day Lao-tzu called on his friend, Li Quan, a furniture craftsman. When Lao-tzu stopped by, Li Quan was deeply absorbed in carving an elaborate design into the leg of a heavily ornamented chair. Gradually, the chair leg took the shape of a dragon's foot. But, since the rest of the chair was decorated with lacy vines, Lao-tzu wondered why Li Quan had not also carved vines on the chair's legs. When Li Quan looked up and saw Lao-tzu, he put his chisel down, and the two men talked.

Lao-tzu asked, "I was wondering, my friend, why didn't you carve vines on the dragon legs that support the chair?"

Li Quan replied, "To make the dragon legs pleasingly proportional with the rest of the chair, I had to make them thin. But the more wood I carve from the legs, the less support they give the chair. You cannot take too much wood away without the chair breaking when somebody sits on it. If you try to over refine things, even in the name of beauty or fashion, frailty is substituted for strength."

There is an important message here for retirement investors. The two main types of asset classes are stocks and bonds. However, many other asset classes have been categorized over the years. Much of this categorization appears to be done in the attempt to apply the statistics of modern portfolio theory to every facet of investing. Thus, domestic stock investing has been divided into large capitalization, small capitalization, micro-capitalization, growth stocks, value stocks, and all manner of equity-based derivatives. International investing carries these distinctions as well as others. Then there is real estate, venture capital, precious metals, and commodities. Since asset allocation is the process of dividing your investment portfolio between assets of different types or classes, it is no wonder that people's eyes tend to glaze over when they hear about all the choices available for investment.

Things have been made one heck of a lot more complicated than they have to be. The issue is really rather simple. There is equity and there is debt. Stocks and bonds. And once you control for quality and risk, the field narrows even further. The secret to retirement investing is to know when to use how much of what kind of asset to accomplish what you need to get done. As with the wooden chair legs, you should emphasize strength in place of an overrefined approach. But how do we begin?

Last week it came time to take the car into the shop. The tires were wearing unevenly, and the front end needed alignment. We dropped the car off and told the service manager to give us a call later in the day. That afternoon, the service manager called to report the inevitable—more work had to be done, and we needed two new tires. As he went through the list of parts and labor needed to finish the job, we could see dollar bills flying out of our wallet as if they had wings. To fix the front end, we needed new tie rods, bushings, and other parts. Then we got to the tires. How much did we want to pay? How many steel belts did we need? What about the blowout guarantee? We wouldn't want to put on new tires without balancing the wheels, right? This was the last straw—balance the wheels! You buy a new pair of tires, and they make you pay to balance the wheels. Finally we said, "Yeah, sure, of course you've got to balance the wheels," and hung up the phone.

But there was something about that word *balance* that hung in the air. When you go rooting around the retirement investment world looking for the things that don't seem to make sense, balance is not the first thing that comes to mind. After all, the art of successful living requires finding the proper balance between extremes. Balance is as indispensable a part of wisdom as any quality we know. But when you apply the conventional meaning of balance to the investment world, things start to get confusing.

Ever heard of a balanced account? Not the checkbook kind, but the sort handled by a mutual fund that manages a single portfolio with both stocks and bonds. Then there's the concept of rebalancing a portfolio itself. This has to do with selling one investment and buying another to obtain a desired mix. In a car, you balance the wheels by attaching small weights to the wheel rim. This balances the spinning wheel to the axle which is the center of rotation. But in the investment world, what are we trying to balance things to? To what center point is a balanced mutual fund managed?[1] How about rebalancing a portfolio? What are we rebalancing it to? These are slippery questions that don't yield their answers easily.

There's a problem implicit in the contemporary notion of balance in the investment world. The current motive behind balancing an investment portfolio appears to be to manage a group of stocks and bonds to satisfy an investment objective. That objective usually relates to maximizing income and capital gains, while minimizing volatility. But for a retirement investor, management of a portfolio to satisfy this type of an investment objective solves only part of the problem. As they are presently understood, investment objectives relate almost exclusively to the capital markets. But capital markets don't give a fig about paying you a base retirement benefit. And there is an even thornier issue. How does balancing an investment portfolio to capital market objectives help us in the seamless and disciplined creation of a base retirement benefit?

The balanced account has an alluring and almost seductive name. The word *balance* itself has a nice, responsible ring to it. Most folks like to think they are balanced in their approach to investing. But we have to look beyond the name to understand how to balance an account to our needs rather than to the capital markets. That's why the balance between stocks and bonds in retirement investing has to be designed with the evolving needs of the individual in mind. This places the human investor at the center of the investing universe. Let's see how we can balance human needs over time with the realities of the capital markets over time.

We have seen how, over the long term, stocks have had higher total returns than bonds. Since young people must build retirement assets, they need to have high concentrations of stocks. The other side of these higher returns is periods when stock values drop, causing temporary losses that can last for years. However, since younger people do not have a current need for their retirement money, they can afford to bear this temporary risk of loss that a larger allocation to stocks implies.

Older people need to generate income, preserve their capital, and attempt to protect their assets from the ravages of inflation. Because older people have less time to make up from losses, they cannot afford as much principal risk, income risk, or inflation risk as younger people. This means that older people must have less of their money (but not too much less) invested in the stock market and more money (but not too much more) invested in high-quality bonds that will protect their principal and pay regular income. It is important for older people to continue to be partially invested in stocks to generate the higher long-term returns that come from stock prices and stock dividends to help protect the value of their assets from the erosion of inflation.

In general terms, asset allocation for retirement investing is all about having more stocks when you are younger and more bonds when you are older. But this is not the only factor in understanding the process that must accompany age-based asset allocation. This process requires an understanding of both the age-based needs of the retirement investor as well as the historic realities of the capital markets.

Controlling investment risk and return requires an assessment of the time each investor has to recover from losses and of the ability to save enough money to replenish lost funds. It also requires an understanding of the changing investment objectives and needs of all retirement investors—both young and old. The one constant in every person's retirement account is time. As such, how much of your retirement portfolio should be in stocks and how much in bonds depends on your age and stage in life. What is appropriate for the 30-year-old is inappropriate for the 70-year-old, and vice versa. But because we all age, any time-based factors must change along with us as we grow older.

We have seen how there have been ten-year periods when domestic stocks have had small negative returns. When the same test is applied to bonds, we see that there have been five-year periods when bonds have registered small negative returns. When this knowledge is coupled with the impossibility of forecasting movements in the capital markets, we can understand why it is imprudent to rely on your ability to sell securities whenever you want, both quickly and painlessly.

The unpredictability of movements in the capital markets implies that the conversion of your assets from stocks to bonds must be accomplished gradually over time. If you begin this process too soon or convert too many of your assets too quickly, you may lose valuable compounding available to you in the stock market. If you begin the process too late or do it too slowly, you may find that the stock market is in one of its periodic slumps just when you need to convert your assets to bonds to produce cash for your retirement living expenses.

The appropriate asset allocations for creation of a base retirement benefit should become an annual target. This means that each year, you should rebalance your portfolio to your age-specific asset allocation. This accomplishes two important tasks. First, and most important, the allocation that is appropriate for your age is maintained, so that your retirement account is always on target to generate the planned results. Second, the process of annual rebalancing has been shown to be important in enhancing the chances for a higher overall rate of return. This is because, all other things being equal, when the bond allocation becomes too high, it will be the result of bond prices moving up more sharply than equity prices. This fact allows you to sell bonds at a high point and purchase equities at a relative low point. Conversely, when stock prices have moved up sharply, annual rebalancing allows you to take some profit and protect a portion of your gains. The longer-term forces at work will continue to operate, but annual rebalancing will tend to enhance the rate of return in your portfolio. Figure 9.3 illustrates the life-cycle retirement investing process.

Figure 9.3 shows the process from a conceptual perspective. Although not indicated in this figure, rebalancing should occur each year. Table 9.1 shows specific allocation targets that were developed by considering mortality rates, as well as historic inflation rates and rates of return in the stock and bond markets.

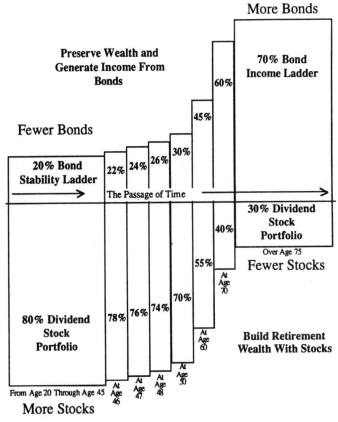

Figure 9.3 The life-cycle retirement investing process.

Appropriate asset allocation targets depend on a number of factors. In general, when you are under the age of 46, an allocation of
approximately 80 percent of your assets to dividend-paying large-
cap stocks and 20 percent to a stability-seeking bond ladder will
produce both good returns as well as a reasonably smooth path.
The 20 percent of the portfolio devoted to fixed income will tend to
smooth out the bumpy ride you will have in your stock account,
because this type of bond ladder is almost always more stable than
stocks.

Then, once you turn 46 years of age, it is a good idea to begin to
slowly reduce your exposure to the stock market and slowly increase
the bond exposure. This move should be done very gradually, so

Table 9.1   Age-Specific Asset Allocation Targets

Investor Age	Dividend Stock Portfolio (%)	Stability or Income Bond Ladders (%)
To age 45	80	20
At age 46	78	22
At age 47	76	24
At age 48	74	26
At age 49	72	28
At age 50	70	30
At age 51	68	32
At age 52	66	34
At age 53	64	36
At age 54	62	38
At age 55	60	40
At age 56	59	41
At age 57	58	42
At age 58	57	43
At age 59	56	44
At age 60	55	45
At age 61	54	46
At age 62	53	47
At age 63	52	48
At age 64	51	49
At age 65	50	50
At age 66	48	52
At age 67	46	54
At age 68	44	56
At age 69	42	58
At age 70	40	60
At age 71	38	62
At age 72	36	64
At age 73	34	66
At age 74	32	68
75 and over	30	70

that year by year, you shift a small percentage of your assets over from stocks to bonds. By age 65, provided you have the right kind of stocks, it is a good idea to be at approximately 50 percent in stocks and 50 percent in bonds. This relatively high exposure to the stock market will help protect the value of your retirement portfolio from inflation.

As you approach retirement, you should continue to reduce your exposure to the stock market as well as increasing the income component of your bond portfolio. This will enable you to gradually convert your assets into a more reliable stream of cash to fund your retirement expenses. This means that by the time you enter your 60s, you should be shifting the construction of your bond ladder to emphasize more income, as shown earlier. By age 75, provided your equity portfolio is properly constructed, you should still have 30 percent of your assets invested in it, with the balance of your assets invested in an income-producing bond ladder.

Please note that these target allocations take into account the probable demographic realities that are likely to face retirement investors over the next 15 or 20 years. By having a gradual process of asset conversion through age-specific targeted allocations to conservative equity and fixed-income portfolios, we attempt to protect ourselves from the possible downturns that could take hold of the equity market as a result of persistent selling to fund baby-boom retirement expenses.

LIFE-CYCLE MODEL PORTFOLIO RESEARCH

Earlier, we looked at how to construct a high-quality dividend-oriented stock portfolio and how to construct high-quality bond ladders that provide portfolio stability and income. We have also set forth an age-specific asset allocation table that takes into account mortality rates, the first principles of each type of investment class, the historic capital market rates of return, and the historic record of inflation. We took the stock and bond research and applied it to the asset allocation model shown in Table 9.1 to give an interesting glimpse at the big picture. We took the results of this research and applied the data to the construction of model life-cycle portfolios. Each portfolio was set in historical context for either 5, 10, or 15 years, ending December 1994. We started with a hypothetical $10,000 investment and tracked the value of the investment for various starting and ending ages across each of the three time periods studied. Each model portfolio was tracked across a timeline for investors of all ages, assuming account rebalancing to have taken place at the beginning of each year. No withdrawals are assumed to have been made. All interest and dividends are assumed to have been reinvested, and no allowance has been made for expenses of any sort. We also compared our recommended age-specific asset allocations to what would have happened if we applied the historic results using indexed portfolios instead of the research portfolios.

These model life-cycle portfolios are shown in Tables 9.2, 9.3, and 9.4 for the 5-, 10-, or 15-year periods ending December 1994, respectively.

Table 9.2 Five-Year Total Annual Return—
Life-Cycle Model Portfolio versus Indexed Portfolio

Model Portfolio Used	Total Return, 1990–1994 (%)
Model dividend portfolio	12.10
Model stability bond ladder	8.33
Model income bond ladder	9.66
Indexed Portfolio Used	
S&P 500	8.73
U.S. Intermediate Government Index	7.46
Government Index and Mortgage-Backed Index	6.65

Starting Age in 1990	Ending Value Model Portfolio, 1994	Ending Age in 1994	Model Total Return, 1990–1994 (%)	Indexed Total Return, 1990–1994 (%)
40 and under	$17,297	45 and under	11.58	8.50
41	17,337	46	11.63	8.47
42	17,330	47	11.62	8.45
43	17,298	48	11.58	8.43
44	17,189	49	11.44	8.35
45	17,141	50	11.38	8.33
46	17,092	51	11.32	8.31
47	17,042	52	11.25	8.29
48	16,992	53	11.19	8.27
49	16,941	54	11.12	8.24
50	16,890	55	11.05	8.22
51	16,819	56	10.96	8.21
52	16,770	57	10.89	8.20
53	16,734	58	10.85	8.19
54	16,736	59	10.85	8.21
55	16,709	60	10.81	8.20

Table 9.2   (*Continued*)

Starting Age in 1990	Ending Value Model Portfolio, 1994	Ending Age in 1994	Model Total Return, 1990–1994 (%)	Indexed Total Return, 1990–1994 (%)
56	16,694	61	10.79	8.23
57	16,736	62	10.85	8.12
58	16,882	63	11.04	8.09
59	16,958	64	11.14	8.06
60	17,043	65	11.25	8.04
61	17,043	66	11.25	8.01
62	17,021	67	11.22	7.99
63	16,991	68	11.18	7.96
64	16,921	69	11.09	7.90
65	16,882	70	11.04	7.87
66	16,843	71	10.99	7.84
67	16,802	72	10.94	7.81
68	16,761	73	10.88	7.78
69	16,719	74	10.83	7.75
70 and over	16,677	75 and over	10.77	7.72

It is important to recognize that these are idealized returns that would have been lower in the real world due to expenses associated with managing the portfolios over time. And we have to remember that the 15-year period from 1980 through 1994 was especially kind to stock and bond investors. Remember that Jim Iazzi had also seen a terrific period for investing just before he began his retirement in 1969 and proceeded to lose most of his carefully accumulated nest egg. The capital markets can be fickle, and there is nothing that will necessarily protect you from all losses or reversals. But if you stick to your guns, select conservative securities, and carefully balance your portfolio to reflect your age, you will go a long way to funding your base retirement benefit. That said, however, you can get a good idea of the kinds of returns that life-cycle retirement investing can produce.

Once retired, the asset allocation targets should be maintained, even in the face of withdrawals. If you are retired and withdrawing

Table 9.3 Ten-Year Total Annual Return—
Life-Cycle Model Portfolio versus Indexed Portfolio

Model Portfolio Used	Total Return, 1985–1994 (%)
Model dividend portfolio	18.22
Model stability bond ladder	9.13
Model income bond ladder	10.54

Indexed Portfolio Used	
S&P 500	14.40
U.S. Intermediate Government Index	9.40
Government Index and Mortgage-Backed Index	8.53

Starting Age in 1985	Ending Value Model Portfolio, 1994	Ending Age in 1994	Model Total Return, 1985–1994 (%)	Indexed Total Return, 1985–1994 (%)
35 and under	$ 46,272	45 and under	16.56	13.45
36	46,377	46	16.58	13.43
37	46,359	47	16.58	13.42
38	46,275	48	16.56	13.41
39	45,982	49	16.48	13.37
40	45,853	50	16.45	13.36
41	45,542	51	16.37	13.31
42	45,127	52	16.26	13.25
43	44,710	53	16.16	13.18
44	44,124	54	16.00	13.10
45	43,464	55	15.83	13.01
46	42,764	56	15.64	12.92
47	42,128	57	15.47	12.82
48	41,528	58	15.30	12.73
49	41,031	59	15.16	12.65
50	40,467	60	15.00	12.56
51	40,020	61	14.88	12.51
52	36,016	62	13.67	11.29
53	35,996	63	13.66	11.21
54	39,642	64	14.77	12.25
55	39,595	65	14.75	12.20
56	39,517	66	14.73	12.13
57	39,469	67	14.72	12.10
58	39,368	68	14.69	12.03
59	39,133	69	14.62	11.91
60	39,197	70	14.64	11.84
61	38,810	71	14.52	11.76

Table 9.3 (*Continued*)

Starting Age in 1985	Ending Value Model Portfolio, 1994	Ending Age in 1994	Model Total Return, 1985–1994 (%)	Indexed Total Return, 1985–1994 (%)
62	38,384	72	14.40	11.68
63	34,531	73	13.19	10.44
64	29,951	74	11.59	9.06
65 and over	28,799	75 and over	11.16	8.69

Table 9.4 Fifteen-Year Total Annual Return—
Life-Cycle Model Portfolio versus Indexed Portfolio

Model Portfolio Used	Total Return, 1980–1994 (%)
Model dividend portfolio	18.22
Model stability bond ladder	9.13
Model income bond ladder	10.54

Indexed Portfolio Used	
S&P 500	14.40
U.S. Intermediate Government Index	9.40
Government Index and Mortgage-Backed Index	8.53

Starting Age in 1980	Ending Value Model Portfolio, 1994	Ending Age in 1994	Model Total Return, 1980–1994 (%)	Indexed Total Return, 1980–1994 (%)
30 and under	$143,103	45 and under	19.41	13.79
31	143,426	46	19.43	13.78
32	143,373	47	19.43	13.77
33	143,110	48	19.41	13.76
34	142,204	49	19.36	13.74
35	141,806	50	19.34	13.73
36	140,845	51	19.28	13.70
37	139,562	52	19.21	13.66
38	138,270	53	19.14	13.61
39	136,460	54	19.03	13.56
40	134,420	55	18.91	13.49

Table 9.4   (*Continued*)

Starting Age in 1980	Ending Value Model Portfolio, 1994	Ending Age in 1994	Model Total Return, 1980–1994 (%)	Indexed Total Return, 1980–1994 (%)
41	132,278	56	18.79	13.45
42	129,978	57	18.65	13.38
43	127,800	58	18.51	13.31
44	125,417	59	18.37	13.29
45	122,297	60	18.17	13.21
46	119,576	61	17.99	13.16
47	117,448	62	17.85	13.08
48	116,065	63	17.76	13.02
49	114,435	64	17.64	12.96
50	112,984	65	17.54	12.91
51	111,447	66	17.44	12.85
52	110,166	67	17.35	12.81
53	108,781	68	17.25	12.76
54	107,208	69	17.13	12.65
55	106,752	70	17.10	12.60
56	105,817	71	17.03	12.53
57	104,357	72	16.92	12.47
58	103,293	73	16.84	12.40
59	81,388	74	15.00	10.63
60 and over	77,923	75 and over	14.67	10.33

money, and you turn, say, 70 years old, and your life-cycle retirement account has drifted from where you set it at age 69 (i.e., 58 percent bonds and 42 percent stocks), you should use your withdrawals to rebalance your account to meet your 60 percent bonds and 40 percent stocks allocation appropriate for a 70-year-old.

HURDLE RATES CAN REDUCE RISK AND FUND YOUR BENEFIT

All human activity has limits. Investing is no exception. We have discussed how fickle and erratic the capital markets can be, especially the market for stocks. This is why it is helpful to consider the concept of a hurdle rate for your stock investments. A hurdle rate is a target rate of return that can be used to preserve exceptional gains.

For example, suppose you invested $1,000 in 100 shares of an individual stock selling for $10 per share. When you purchased the shares, you made a decision that you would consider anything over $16 a share as an unusual return. In effect, you say to yourself that if the shares sell for over 60 percent of your cost, they will have produced such unusual profits for you that anything more is unlikely to be sustainable. That 60 percent target becomes your hurdle rate of return.

Let's suppose that, over the course of a year, the stock's price climbs to $20, an exceptional return by anyone's standards, but an excessive return by the standards you set when you first bought the shares. The $4 excess return ($20 minus $16) is like found money. You didn't anticipate making that much from the stock, and you decide that you do not want to tempt the fates and leave the entire $2,000 worth of stock sitting in your stock account. Thus, you decide to sell 20 shares for $400 and put it into your money market fund to preserve this exceptional gain. This is what is known as *hurdle-rate harvesting*.

On a portfolio basis, hurdle-rate harvesting works in the same way, but with a different kind of target. This is because, when you add up all the gains and subtract out all the losses in a diversified portfolio, the net overall portfolio rate of return will fall in between the highs and the lows. This means that if you were to select a hurdle rate for an entire portfolio, it will have to be lower than the hurdle rate set for any given individual stock.

A hurdle rate will allow you to preserve an incremental portion of the unusual gains you might be able to rack up during a set period, usually one year. In this fashion, it will tend to reduce your risk of loss. It also allows you to reinvest the amount you "harvested" if the value of your equity portfolio falls below a certain target limit. Thus, a modest incremental hurdle-rate harvesting process will tend to lower the average cost of your equity holdings in a way similar to dollar-cost averaging, while helping to protect a portion of your gains from the risk of principal loss. This effect will diminish most of any incremental equity return you might have earned had you left the entire account untouched. Remember, most of the gains from your equity account should remain in the account to compound for you over time. It is only the incremental gains over the target hurdle rate that are subject to harvesting.

A hurdle rate of return is an incremental risk management device during your pre-retirement years. However, as you get older, your risk tolerance will decrease. This is because you must become more conservative as you approach and enter into retirement. This is why, over time, your hurdle rate should be set at a lower and lower target. Eventually, when you retire, hurdle-rate harvesting allows you to actually fund a portion of your own retirement benefit from slightly higher than average gains you might make in your equity account. This will allow most of the gains and the principal to continue to work for you while you skim off the excess to help fund your benefit.

FINAL THOUGHTS

Retirement investing has been made needlessly confusing. There is no good reason for such confusion to exist. Investing is mostly a matter of common sense and understanding the basics.

Many people believe they have to chase every rainbow in a search for the highest return. The problem is that they almost never get the highest return by chasing it. This is because you will never know where the highest return will be by looking where the highest return used to be. Last year's hottest investment is not likely to be next year's. It also means that the stock you thought was destined to multiply your money many times over could very likely end up a loser.

Instead, patient compounding along with a regularized savings program will always win out against the frenetic attempt to find the next sure thing. To be sure, this careful and conservative method is not as exciting as chasing every hot tip, but it is a lot more likely to succeed.

The important thing is to start now and invest regularly, carefully, and with discipline. Procrastination is the retirement investor's biggest enemy. Be determined that nobody is going to do this for you, so you will have to do it on your own. Good luck and God-speed.

To the reader:

More information about life cycle retirement investing
may be obtained from the authors by calling
1-800-266-5240, and selecting option #5.
Or, if you wish, you may write us at:
Benson White & Company
656 East Swedesford Rd.
Wayne, PA 19087

Notes

CHAPTER 2

1. Benjamin Graham, David L. Dodd, Sidney Cottle, and Charles Tatham, *Security Analysis,* 4th ed. (New York: McGraw-Hill, 1962). Italics and boldface in original.
2. Ibid.
3. Most Americans would not have it any other way. Imagine what would happen if the United States government were to invest Social Security taxes into the private economy. In this event, politicians and bureaucrats would control the debt and ownership of America's corporations. This method of economic organization proved to be disastrous when attempted in the former Soviet Union, North Korea, Cuba, China, Poland, East Germany, and other communist countries.
4. *1994 Annual Report to the Trustees of the Social Security Administration.*
5. The Vanguard Group of Investment Companies, *Vanguard Retirement Investment Guide* (Homewood, Ill.: Irwin Professional Publishing, 1995), 5.
6. Thomas G. Donlan, *Don't Count On It!* (New York: Simon & Schuster, 1994), 137.
7. Andrea Knox, "Firms Are Replacing Traditional Pensions," *Philadelphia Inquirer,* June 30, 1996, E-1.
8. Employee Benefits Research Institute, "Current Population Survey," 1993.
9. The notable exception to this rule involves the ability to replenish savings in the event of a permanent loss in the retirement investment portfolio. This ability, when considered

in conjunction with a person's age, will constrain design of the retirement portfolio. Because, for all but the wealthiest of people, the ability to replenish savings is limited, the appropriate portfolio design for most people will tend toward the conservative.

10. Federal Reserve Bank of New York and Benson White & Company.

CHAPTER 3

1. The "Inflation" category represents the Consumer Price Index (CPI) as calculated by the Bureau of Labor Statistics. The "Short-Term Government Bills" category represents Treasury securities maturing in 30 days, used as an approximation of representational returns one might expect from an invested cash account. The category labeled "Long-Term Corporate Bonds" was constructed from the Salomon Brothers Long-Term High Grade Corporate Bond Index and tracks bonds that had an approximate maturity of 20 years. The category of "Large Company Common Stocks" tracks the total return of the S&P 500 Composite with dividends reinvested from 1957 through 1994, and the so-called S&P 90 from 1926 to 1956. The category of "Small Company Common Stocks" tracks the results of the New York Stock Exchange (NYSE) fifth quintile of stocks ranked by their market capitalization for the period from 1926 to 1981. For the period 1982 through 1994, the category tracks the total return of a market weighted index of the ninth and tenth deciles of the NYSE plus American Stock Exchange and OTC with market capitalizations no larger than the ninth decile of the NYSE and no smaller than $10 million.

2. See, for example, Gary Brinson, Brian Singer, and Gilbert Beebower, "Determinants of Portfolio Performance II: An Update," *Financial Analysts Journal,* May/June 1991, 40–48.

CHAPTER 4

1. Lipper Analytical Services.
2. Cited by John Train in *Money Masters* (New York: Harper & Row, 1987).

3. Dividends and reinvestment of dividends have provided approximately 48 percent of total long-term annual return of large-cap stocks. Data taken from Ibbotson Associates, Inc., *Stocks, Bonds, Bills and Inflation, 1995 Yearbook* (Chicago).
4. David Dreman, *New Contrarian Investment Strategy* (New York: Random House, 1982), 161.
5. "Chronically Clouded Crystal Balls," *Forbes*, October 11, 1993, 178.
6. *Present value* is the value today of a future payment or stream of payments discounted at some level of compound interest. Present value operates on the notion that a dollar in the hand today is worth more than a dollar promised in the future. Today's dollar can be invested to generate additional income, while the future dollar cannot be invested and, in fact, may never arrive.
7. Ibbotson Associates, Inc., *Stocks, Bonds, Bills and Inflation, 1995 Yearbook*.
8. Graham, et al., *Security Analysis*.
9. More properly put, the customers of the corporation pay taxes on the profit. Corporations do not really pay taxes; they only collect them. Taxes become merely another expense that must be figured into the purchase price of the goods or services sold by the corporation. An argument can be made that it is shareholders who pay the taxes because they own the corporate profits. However, since profits are ultimately derived from revenue collected from customers, the customers are the true source of the tax payment.
10. Maggir Mahar, "Caught In The 'Net," *Barron's*, December 25, 1995, 25.
11. Randall Forsyth and Sandra Ward, "Watch Out! Do American Households Have Too Many Eggs In The Market Basket?," *Barron's*, September 4, 1995, 26.
12. Ibid., 27.
13. Roger G. Ibbotson and Rex A. Sinquefield, *Stocks, Bonds, Bills and Inflation: The Past (1926–76) and the Future (1977–2000)* (Chicago: Financial Analysts Research Foundation, 1977).

CHAPTER 5

1. " 'Growth and Income' Can Be a Misnomer," *Wall Street Journal Mutual Fund Quarterly*, April 5, 1995.

2. In its simplest form, *book value* is the total value of a company's assets minus its debts and liabilities. It treats all debts and liabilities as if they have already been paid to determine what would be left over to split up among the shareholders in the event of a liquidation of the corporation. *Cash flow* is the cash earnings of a company. It is calculated by taking the company's earnings, and adding back the noncash expenses such as depreciation. Earnings are always calculated after all expenses have been paid, including taxes and noncash expenses such as depreciation.

3. Clay B. Mansfield and Timothy W. Cunningham, *Pension Funds: A Commonsense Guide To A Common Goal* (Homewood, Ill.: Irwin Professional Publishing, 1992), 72–74.

4. "The Value Stock Question: Study Attempts to Identify Reasons for Outperformance," *Pensions & Investments*, July 11, 1994, 35.

5. Ibid.

6. Dreman, *The New Contrarian Investment Strategy*, 181.

7. "BARRA Creates Equity Income Index," *BARRA Newsletter*, no. 195, Winter 1994, 25.

8. Ibbotson Associates, Inc., *Stocks, Bonds, Bills and Inflation, 1995 Yearbook*.

9. Interview with Meyer Berman, "Still Alive and Kicking," *Barron's*, December 25, 1995, 20–23.

10. Frank Russell Co., Russell Universe Performance System.

11. John Rekenthaler, "Where Have All The Top Value Funds Gone?," *5 Star Investor*, April 1995, 40.

12. The Dow Jones Industrial Average is better known, but, with only 30 stocks, it is far too small a universe to use in the search for high-quality, high-yielding stocks that offer both superior income and capital gains.

13. We should note that we use operating earnings as the figure for earnings. This is due to the large number of extraordinary one-time earnings charges that often have little to do with a company's ability to sustain and grow its dividend, particularly if it passed the other screens as well. A negative price-to-earnings ratio indicates that the company lost money from operations. In this event, it would be eliminated from further consideration.

14. For an approximation of a high-dividend portfolio's performance in the nine-year period from August 1968 through August 1977, please refer to David Dreman's research summarized in Table 5.6.

CHAPTER 6

1. Sydney Homer and Richard Sylla, *A History of Interest Rates,* 3d ed. (New Brunswick, N.J.: Rutgers University Press, 1991), 18–26.
2. Benjamin J. Stein, "Junk Revisited," *Barron's,* November 20, 1995, 42–43.
3. Noah benShea, *Jacob The Baker* (New York: Villard Books, 1989), 20–21.
4. Ibbotson Associates, Inc., *Stocks, Bonds, Bills and Inflation, 1995 Yearbook.*
5. Total return Salomon High Grade Long-Term Corporate Bond Index versus the Ibbotson data for total return of long-term government bonds.

CHAPTER 7

1. Gustov LeBon, *The Crowd: A Study of the Popular Mind* (London: Unwyn Hyman Ltd., 1977, originally published 1895), 23–24.
2. *The Wall Street Journal,* April 20, 1995, 1.
3. "Big Investors Suffer as Foreign Markets Sour," *The New York Times,* March 4, 1994, sec. D, 1.
4. *Ibid.*
5. "Stock Market Extremes and Portfolio Performance," a study commissioned by Towneley Capital Management and conducted by Professor H. Nejat Seyhun, University of Michigan, 1994, 11.

CHAPTER 8

1. Ibbotson Associates, Inc., *Stocks, Bonds, Bills and Inflation, 1995 Yearbook.*
2. Alan Yuhas, "Arbitrage Pricing Technique—Slow and Steady Wins the Day," *The Trustee's Journal,* September/October 1993, 7.
3. From 1926 through 1994, the standard deviation of total returns of small-cap stocks was 34.6 percent, while that of large-cap stocks was 20.3 percent.
4. Rex A. Sinquefield, "Where Are the Gains from International Diversification?" *Financial Analysts Journal,* January/February, 1996, 8–14.

CHAPTER 9

1. Mutual fund companies have offered "balanced" mutual funds
for years. Many mutual fund companies have cleverly renamed
these funds to take on the appearance of solving the retirement
investing problem. *Lifestyle funds,* as many of these financial
products are known, are balanced funds composed more or less
aggressively in the attempt to market to investors of differing
ages. The more conservative mixtures are for the older customers, and the more aggressive mixtures are for the young.
These funds do not provide the ideal environment for the creation of a base retirement benefit for a variety of reasons. First,
they are not targeted or structured for the individual investor.
Second, they are not seamless in their approach, so they do not
evolve along with their shareholder. Third, they have not adequately defined the retirement problem and do not have a clear
path to create a retirement benefit. And, finally, they are typically not well disclosed in terms of how their investing philosophy actually applies to the problem at hand.

Glossary

accretion. Adjustment of the difference between the price of a bond bought at a price lower than par value and par value itself.

accrued interest. Interest that has accumulated between the most recent payment and the sale of a bond or other fixed-income security.

active bond management. Management of bonds in the effort to generate rates of returns that are higher than the returns calculated from a relevant bond index.

active equity management. Management of equities (stocks) in the effort to generate rates of returns that are higher than the returns calculated from a relevant equity index.

active manager. Financial services professional who actively manages a portfolio of securities in the attempt to generate rates of return that are higher than a relevant index. As opposed to a passive manager.

actuary. Mathematician employed to calculate insurance premiums and pension contribution rates using risk factors from experience and other statistical data.

agency bonds. Bonds issued by an entity associated with the U.S. federal government. Agency bonds have either an implicit or explicit guarantee of timely payment of interest and principal from the federal government.

aggressive growth investing. Subset of growth investing in which an active equity manager attempts to identify companies predicted to grow much faster than other companies in the economy.

American Stock Exchange. Stock exchange based in New York City where shares of stock are bought and sold. Sometimes known as the AMEX.

amortization. Adjustment of the difference between the price of a bond bought at a price higher than par and par value itself.

analyst. Financial professional employed by brokerage and asset management firms to study a group of companies and make recommendations to buy or sell securities issued by those companies. Most analysts specialize in companies in a single industry. Also known as a *financial analyst* or *securities analyst*.

annual compound return. Average compound rate of return expressed on an annualized basis.

annualized return. Compound rate of return generated over a multiyear period and expressed as an annual average.

arbitrageur. Financial professional who attempts to profit by exploiting the differences that may arise when the same security, currency, or commodity is traded on two or more markets.

asset. Anything having a marketable, commercial value that is owned by an individual, corporation, government, or other entity.

asset allocation. Division of invested assets among different types of asset classes.

asset class. Broad groups and subgroups of investable assets that have similar risk and return attributes. The two principal asset classes are stocks and bonds. Other asset classes include cash, real estate, commodities, venture capital, and foreign currencies. Sub-asset classes include small company stocks, international stocks, junk bonds, and mortgage-backed bonds.

average weighted maturity. Average maturity of a bond portfolio weighted by the proportion of dollars invested in bonds of each specific maturity relative to the total number of dollars in the portfolio.

baby boom. Demographic group of approximately 76 million people born in the United States between 1946 and 1964.

balance sheet. Financial statement that shows the value of assets, liabilities, and owner's equity as of a specific date.

balanced account. An investment account holding both stocks and bonds.

balanced mutual fund. Mutual fund that invests in common stocks, preferred stocks, and bonds in an attempt to lower the overall risk versus a pure stock mutual fund, yet improve the long-term return versus a pure bond mutual fund.

base retirement benefit. Amount of money necessary to support an individual's essential living requirements in retirement.

benefit. Cash derived from a retirement account to support retirement expenses.

blue-chip stocks. Generally, stocks issued by large, well-recognized companies.

bond. Interest-bearing or discounted corporate or government security that obligates the issuer to pay to the holder of the bond specified sums of money at specific intervals. Payments include both interest amounts in excess of the principal value of the bond as well as repayment of the principal at maturity. Bonds are debts of the issuer to the holder and do not represent ownership interest in the issuer.

bond default. Failure to pay interest or principal in accordance with the terms of the bond's issuance. Default may also occur upon the failure to fulfill other terms agreed to by the issuer of the bond.

bond ladder. Bond portfolio built using bonds of different maturities, with each maturity forming a rung on the ladder of the portfolio. Laddered bonds are generally held to maturity. Interim trading is not done unless necessary to generate additional liquidity for the bond investor.

bond mutual fund. Mutual fund that invests in bonds in accordance with the terms of its prospectus. Bond mutual funds are categorized by the types of bonds they usually hold, as differentiated by average maturities, types of issuers, and types of credit quality.

bond risk premium. Component of the interest rate on a bond. It is the amount by which a bond's coupon exceeds the riskless coupon on a U.S. Treasury obligation of like maturity. The risk premium includes an assessment of credit risk, (the risk of non-payment of interest or principal), interest rate risk, (changes in the price of a bond because of shifts in interest rates), reinvestment rate risk (the rate at which a bond buyer can reinvest interest and principal as cash payments are received), and perceived inflation risk (the rate of inflation).

bond yield. Bond coupon rate of interest divided by the purchase price of the bond, also known as the *current yield*.

bondholder. The owner of a bond.

book value. Balance sheet entry derived by subtracting all liabilities from all assets. Also known as *shareholder's equity*. Represents the net aggregate value of shareholder ownership as measured by a company's balance sheet. Often expressed on a per-share basis.

call risk.   Risk inherent in a bond that can be called or redeemed by the issuer prior to maturity. Most corporate bond issuers reserve the right to call their bonds after a preestablished period of time by repaying bond principal and thus shortening the maturity of the bond. A corporation does this when prevailing interest rates have declined. Then they can issue new bonds at lower coupon rates to save money on interest expenses. Because the bondholder will receive money back when rates are lower, reinvestment of called bond principal amounts will almost certainly yield less than the original bond. This makes call risk a type of **reinvestment rate risk.** Bonds issued by the U.S. Treasury are usually not callable.

callable bonds.   Bonds that can be called or redeemed by the issuer prior to maturity.

capital appreciation.   Increase in the value of an asset.

capital gain.   Difference between the purchase price and the selling price of an asset when that difference is positive.

capital loss.   Difference between the purchase price and the selling price of an asset when that difference is negative.

capital market financial objective.   Financial objective related to the capital markets. Generating an investment rate of return that exceeds a capital market benchmark such as an index is a capital market financial objective. Distinct from a **human financial objective** that seeks to solve a human problem such as financing a retirement income.

capital markets.   Markets where capital assets—debt and ownership—are traded. Includes organized stock exchanges, computer trading systems, and privately negotiated purchases and sales of capital assets.

cash flow.   In investments, cash earnings of a business. Derived from net income plus all noncash expenses such as depreciation and amortization.

cash flow ratio.   Share price divided by the cash flow per share.

cash-matched bond ladder.   Laddered bond portfolio where the interest and principal payments to the portfolio owner are sufficient to meet a specified series of liabilities such as pension benefits.

collateralized mortgage obligations.   Mortgage-backed security in which the issuer (usually a large Wall Street investment bank) acts as principal in the issuance of bonds backed up by mortgages. This arrangement allows the issuer to create various types of hybrid bonds with differing maturities, interest rates, and other features. Also known as CMOs.

common stock.   Unit of ownership of a corporation.

compounding.   Growth in a rate of return that includes the increase in the rate of return due to returns earned on previously earned returns.

corporate bonds.   Debt instrument issued by a private corporation, as distinct from a bond issued by a government or governmental agency.

coupon.   Stated rate of interest on a debt security expressed as an annual percentage of face or principal value and payable on a regular basis established by terms set at the time of the debt security's issuance.

coupon risk.   Increased volatility of the coupons on shorter-term bonds when compared to coupons on longer-term bonds. Investments into short-term bonds face less certainty of maintaining any given size of coupon than investments into long-term bonds. When this investment is made with cash flows from other bonds, coupon risk becomes a special form of reinvestment risk.

credit markets.   Markets where debt capital assets are traded. Includes computer trading arrangement, and privately negotiated purchases and sales of debt and loans.

credit quality.   Rating given a bond as judged by a rating agency based on a bond issuer's perceived ability to pay all principal and interest on a timely basis.

credit risk.   Risk that a bond issuer will not have the ability to pay all principal and interest on a timely basis.

cyclical stocks.   Stocks issued by companies whose earnings fall in recessions and rise during expansions.

debt-to-equity ratio.   Company's debt, divided by the value of its shareholders' net ownership in the business (or equity).

declining interest rate environment.   Economic environment where interest rates in general are declining for bonds and debts of most maturities.

defensive stocks.   Stocks issued by companies that provide basic goods and services such as food or electricity. Said to be defensive because they are supposed to defend the investor from some measure of loss during a poorly performing stock market.

defined-benefit pension plan. Type of pension plan that promises to pay specified benefit payments to plan participants upon retirement. The risk of making these specified benefit payments falls on the plan sponsor, usually a corporation, union, or governmental entity. Contributions are usually made by the employer, although employees will sometimes contribute into the plan as well.

defined-contribution pension plan. Type of pension plan that does not promise to pay a specified amount to a plan participant. The amount of the retirement benefit available to the defined-contribution plan participant depends on the amounts both invested and earned in the participant's account prior to retirement. So named because contributions by the plan sponsor are defined, but the pension benefit to the participant is not.

demographic twilight zone. Years from approximately 2006 to approximately 2023 when there will be more U.S. investors reaching 65 years of age (retirement) than reaching 45 years of age (investing for retirement).

demographics. Study of population statistics and trends.

derivative, or **derivative security.** Security created from another security or set of securities. Derivatives are created from stocks and bonds. Stocks and bonds derive their value solely from the financial characteristics of their issuers. Derivatives are designed to yield returns that depend on other factors beyond the characteristics of the issuer and that may be related to the prices of other assets. Examples of derivatives include options and futures. An *option* is the right to buy or sell property (such as common stock) at an agreed-upon price for an agreed-upon period. A *futures* contract obligates a trader to buy or sell assets at an agreed-upon price on a specified future date.

discount. (1) Difference between a bond's market price and its face value or principal value at maturity. (2) Relationship between two currencies. (3) Assumption that the market price of a security reflects all available information about that security. (4) Method of selling bonds that are issued at less than face value (i.e., their principal value) and are redeemed at face value. (5) Method of estimating the present value of an asset based on a predicted future cash flow and an assumed rate of interest used to derive that present value.

dispersion. Observed discrepancies of a set of data points from the average value of those data points. In investments, dispersion is often measured by standard deviation of annual returns, sometimes called **volatility.**

dividend. Earnings distributed to the owners of an entity. In the case of a corporation, the amount of a dividend is decided by a board of directors and may be made in the form of cash or shares of stock (known as *stock dividends*).

dividend discount model. Formula used to estimate the intrinsic value of a share of common stock by calculating the present value of all expected future dividends.

dividend yield. Dividends per share divided by the price per share.

dollar-cost averaging. Method of accumulating assets by investing a fixed amount of dollars in securities at set intervals, regardless of the price of those securities at the time of purchase.

Dow Dogs. Those 10 of the 30 stocks in the Dow Jones Industrial Average with the highest dividend yields as of each January 1.

Dow Jones Industrial Average. Price-weighted average of the actively traded stocks of 30 large companies as prepared and published by Dow Jones & Company.

earnings. Net after-tax profit of a corporation as expressed for a certain period such as a quarter or a year. Calculated by subtracting all costs and expenses from revenues.

earnings estimates. Forecasts of future corporate earnings made by stock analysts. Also known as *earnings projections*.

earnings growth. Rate of growth in corporate earnings over a given period of time, such as a quarter or a year.

efficient markets hypothesis. The prices of securities fully reflect all available information. Under this hypothesis, it is asserted to be unlikely that an investor can analyze available information to determine which securities are "undervalued," and thereby earn a higher-than-average rate of return.

emergency cash reserves. Reserve of cash saved by an individual to meet unforeseen emergency financial needs. To qualify as an emergency cash reserve, cash must be invested in a safe and liquid form.

emerging market. Relatively small capital market domiciled in a less-developed country.

equity security. Ownership interest, usually possessed by shareholders of common stock in a corporation. Often used interchangeably with the term *stock*.

FDIC. Federal Deposit Insurance Corporation, a federal government agency founded in 1933 that guarantees funds (within limits) on deposit with member banks.

FHLMC. Federal Home Loan Mortgage Corporation, publicly chartered agency that buys and pools certain residential mortgages from lenders, packages them into new securities backed by those mortgages, provides certain guarantees on the new securities, and then sells the securities in the capital markets. FHLMC securities are not guaranteed by the federal government, but they have certain borrowing rights from the U.S. Federal Reserve, creating an implied guarantee whose effectiveness has never been tested. FHLMC is sometimes known by the nickname "Freddie Mac."

fiduciary. Person, company, or association that holds and manages assets in trust for a beneficiary. A fiduciary must act in the best and highest interest of the beneficiary at all times.

financial services industry. Industry serving customers with financial assets. Examples include banks, brokerage companies, insurance companies, mutual funds, investment advisors, and consultants.

first principles of investing. Concepts and principles that serve as the root basis or foundation for the theory and practice of investing.

fixed income. Securities that pay a fixed rate or return. Often used interchangeably with the term **bond.** Sometimes refers to preferred stock with a fixed dividend payment.

foreign bonds. Bonds issued by a foreign government or by an entity such as a company domiciled in a foreign (non-U.S.) country.

foreign exchange differential. Difference between the rate of exchange of two currencies as measured over a set period of time. For example, if the U.S. dollar is worth 100 Japanese yen on one date and 105 Japanese yen on another date, the difference in the two rates of exchange is regarded as a foreign exchange differential.

401(k) plan. Retirement plan sponsored by an employer. In a 401(k) plan, an employee may elect to contribute pretax dollars into a retirement account. A 401(k) plan is a defined-contribution retirement plan.

fundamental analysis. Form of securities analysis that attempts to establish a range of intrinsic value for a given security. Usually based upon examination of the current and forecasted future financial condition of the issuer of the security.

fundamental ratio.   Ratio calculated on the basis of a fundamental value per share of common stock. Examples include the **price-to-earnings ratio,** price–to–book value ratio, **price–to–cash flow ratio,** dividend payout ratio, and **debt-to-equity ratio.**

fundamentals.   Set of financial characteristics of the issuer of securities. Most often refers to a single company or industry grouping.

global manager.   Asset manager that buys and sells securities issued by entities without regard to domicile. Distinct from international manager in that a global manager will consider securities issued by both U.S.-domiciled issuers as well as foreign issuers, whereas an international manager will consider only non-U.S. issuers.

GNMA.   Government National Mortgage Association. Publicly chartered agency that buys and pools certain residential mortgages guaranteed by the Federal Housing Authority (FHA) or the Veterans Administration (VA), packages them into new securities backed by those mortgages, provides certain guarantees on those new securities, and then sells the securities in the capital markets. GNMA securities are guaranteed by the U.S. federal government insofar as they use FHA and VA mortgages to back up their securities. The GNMA is sometimes known by the nickname "Ginnie Mae."

growth and income mutual fund.   Mutual fund that purchases mostly equity securities and pursues an investment strategy that includes growth stocks and dividend-paying stocks.

growth investing.   Investing style that focuses on the identification of companies that are predicted to grow faster than the economy as a whole and other companies in a given industry.

growth stocks.   Stocks issued by companies that are predicted to grow faster than the economy as a whole and other companies in a given industry.

human financial objective.   Objective related to the solution of an individual's financial problem, such as financing a retirement income or paying for a college education. Distinct from a **capital market financial objective,** such as outperforming an index.

hurdle rate.   Rate of return applied to an investment account and used as a minimum or maximum acceptable return.

hurdle-rate harvesting. Investment technique using a **hurdle rate** as an equity profit-taking device. Amounts earned in excess of a hurdle rate of return are sold.

Ibbotson-Sinquefield research. Research performed by Roger Ibbotson and Rex Sinquefield into the rates of returns of U.S. stocks, bonds, Treasury bills, and inflation. First published in 1977, it concluded that equities outperform fixed income over long periods of time.

illiquidity. Condition of an investment that is not easily and quickly able to be sold for cash. Assets for which there is little or no actively traded market.

income investing. Investing style that focuses on the identification of securities forecasted to produce income for the investor. Often used in reference to investing in companies that pay steady dividends.

income loss. Loss of income that occurs when a fixed-income security matures after a drop in interest rates. The income able to be earned by reinvesting the principal amount received will be lower than in the previous investment due to the drop in interest rates.

income-oriented bond ladder. Bond ladder that is dollar-weighted skewed to longer-maturity bonds.

income-producing asset. Productive asset that produces regular cash payments to an investor.

income stocks. Stocks that pay dividends.

index. In investing, a statistical composite that measures the fluctuations in the returns from a given set of securities. Examples include the Dow Jones Industrial Index, the S&P 500 Index, and the Wilshire 5000 Index. In economics, a statistical composite that measures the fluctuations in a given set of economic data such as the prices of goods and services.

indexing. Investment style where investments are made in a portfolio of equity or fixed-income securities that provide returns that closely resemble the composition of an index. Also known as *passive investing*.

individual retirement account. Individual, tax-deferred retirement account that can be used by employed persons. An IRA is not an investment or a security. Instead, it is an account that holds securities selected by the account holder.

inflation. Rate at which the general level of prices for goods and services is rising.

inflation loss. Loss in purchasing power over time due to inflation.

inflation risk. Risk that an investment will not offset the loss of purchasing power due to inflation.

interest-only strip. Derivative security that gives holders the interest portion of the monthly payments on a group of mortgages. These securities lose value quickly if mortgages in the underlying pool are refinanced, a trend that takes place after interest rates have declined.

interest rate anticipation. Active bond management style that attempts to improve the rate of return on a portfolio of fixed-income securities by forecasting the magnitude and direction of changes in interest rates.

interest rate risk. Risk of loss in price of a fixed-income security caused by an increase in prevailing interest rates.

interest rates. Rates of interest charged for debt obligations of all types and maturities within a given capital market.

intermediate bond. Bond with a maturity in the two- to ten-year range.

international investing risk. Risks of international investing compared to U.S. investing. Includes political, economic, currency, regulatory, and trading risks unique to international capital markets and securities.

intrinsic value. Value of a stock independent of its market price. Determination of intrinsic value attempts to calculate what a stock is worth if it were properly valued in the market.

investing triangle. A triangular representation of an individual's investment portfolio. The base of the triangle consists of safe and liquid investments. As you move higher in the triangle, the investments get riskier. The apex of the triangle is represented by speculation.

investment-grade bond. Higher-quality bond issued by an entity rated to be of higher creditworthiness as rated by an independent bond-rating agency.

investor. A person or institution that, after careful consideration and analysis, purchases, holds, and sells assets in the belief that the activity will provide a return of principal and generate a satisfactory rate of return while maintaining mindful acceptance of the potential consequences that might arise from loss of principal, income, or purchasing power.

junk bond. Lower-quality bond issued by an entity rated to be of lower creditworthiness as rated by an independent bond-rating agency.

large-capitalization stock. Companies with a market capitalization generally larger than $750 million or $1 billion. Also known as *large-cap stock*.

leverage. The proportion of debt to equity on a company's balance sheet or in the financing of an investment position.

liability. Balance sheet entry representing an amount owed.

life cycle. (1) *Corporate* life cycle refers to the series of stages companies evolve through, including a struggle to start up, success and prosperity, and a leveling-off of their growth rate. (2) *Human* life cycle refers to the normal process of human maturation, employment, family formation, aging, and retirement.

liquidity. Condition of an investment that is easily and quickly able to be sold for cash. Assets for which there is an actively traded market.

listed stock. Stock traded on the **New York Stock Exchange** or the **American Stock Exchange.**

long-term bond. Generally, bonds with maturities longer than ten years.

margin of safety. In bonds, the excess ability to pay interest and principal on a timely basis, given the cash flows and senior payment obligations of the issuer. In stocks, the excess of a calculated intrinsic value over the market price of a stock.

marketable securities. Securities that are easily sold in the capital markets.

market capitalization. Value of a corporation determined by multiplying the number of common stock shares outstanding by the market price per share. Also known as *market cap*.

market-cap weighting. The weighting within a portfolio or an index based on the market capitalization of each security relative to the market capitalization of the entire portfolio or index.

market price–to–book ratio. Market price per share of common stock divided by the book value per share.

market share. Percentage share of total share revenue garnered by a participant in a given market.

market timing. Investment management method that allocates assets into and out of various asset classes in anticipation of broad market movements.

maturity. Date upon which the principal value of a debt instrument becomes due and payable.

micro-cap. Companies that range in market capitalization from approximately $10 million to approximately $100 million.

mid-cap. Companies with a market capitalization greater than approximately $250 million, but less than approximately $750 million.

mission-critical derivatives. Derivatives whose function is related to the nonspeculative business objective of the holder.

modern portfolio theory. The application of probability theory to the patterns of historic rates of return in an effort to predict future patterns of return. Inherent in this theory is that investors must have a higher expected return to compensate for a higher degree of uncertainty about that expected return.

momentum stock investing. Stock investing style that ignores fundamentals and invests based on the rate of acceleration in the price of a stock.

money manager. Professional who manages assets on behalf of individuals or institutional clients such as mutual funds, insurance companies, or pension funds. Sometimes referred to as a **portfolio manager.**

money market mutual fund. Mutual fund that invests in highly liquid debt securities of very short maturity.

money market security. Short-term debt, sometimes with a one-day maturity.

money supply. Total stock of money in the economy. Includes currency and deposits with banks.

mortgage-backed securities. Security backed by a pool of mortgages where interest and principal payments made on the underlying mortgages are passed through to the holders of the security. Sometimes known as *pass-through mortgage-backed securities.*

mortgage-backed security risks. Risks unique to mortgaged-backed securities, the most prominent of which is the risk that the underlying mortgages will be paid in full prior to maturity. This is known as prepayment risk.

municipal bonds. Debt obligations issued by state and local entities. Interest is free from federal taxes and often from state and local taxes as well.

mutual fund. Investment company that raises money from shareholders and invests that money into securities.

NASDAQ system. National Association of Securities Dealers Automated Quotation system. A network of computer-linked brokers and dealers that buy and sell stocks.

net spread. Net difference between two interest rates, two prices, two rates of return, or two exchange rates.

New York Stock Exchange. Large stock exchange located in New York City. Stocks must meet stringent requirements to be traded on the New York Stock Exchange.

nonlinear. A system that does not evolve in a straight line, and thus whose behavior cannot be predicted. In a nonlinear system, each event leads to an outcome that conditions the beginning of the next event.

OTC stock. Over-the-counter stock. Stock not listed on an exchange and that trades either by computer network or over the phone.

par value. In common stocks, a virtually arbitrary assigned nominal value. In bonds, the principal value, also known as the *face value*.

passive bond management. Investing style that seeks to match the investment performance of a bond index.

passive equity management. Investing style that seeks to match the investment performance of an equity or stock index.

payout ratio. Percentage of a company's after-tax earnings paid out to shareholders in the form of dividends.

permanent loss. Realized loss of principal arising from selling a security at a price lower than cost.

planned amortization class bond. Type of mortgage-backed security where payments of interest and principal on the underlying mortgages are packaged by maturity and coupon rate into predictable cash flow to the bondholder. Also known as a PAC.

plan sponsor. The organizer of a tax-qualified retirement plan, almost always an employer.

portfolio. Combined holding of more than one stock, bond, commodity, real estate, or other financial asset by an individual or institution.

portfolio diversification. Spreading a portfolio of assets among many different types of investments to avoid the concentration of risk in any single investment.

portfolio effect. The minimization of risk associated with holding any single security by instead holding a diverse portfolio of invested assets.

portfolio insurance. The practice of using derivative securities in the attempt to protect the value of a portfolio from loss.

portfolio management. Process of combining securities in a portfolio to meet the needs of the investor.

portfolio manager. Professional who manages assets on behalf of individuals or institutional clients such as mutual funds, insurance companies, or pension funds. Sometimes referred to as a **money manager.**

preferred stock. Nonvoting shares in a corporation that pay a fixed or variable dividend.

premium. Extra payment made as an incentive to buy or sell. In bonds, when prevailing interest rates fall, bonds with existing lower coupons will sell at a premium to equalize the yield with prevailing rates. Also, the amount exceeding par value that a bond issuer will pay a bondholder to call (or repay) a bond before maturity.

prepayment risk. Risk that mortgage holders will prepay mortgage principal before maturity, and mortgage-backed security holders will be forced to reinvest at a lower rate of interest than that on the original pool of mortgages.

prevailing interest rates. Interest rate environment for debt securities of all maturities.

price–to–cash flow ratio. Price per share of stock divided by cash flow per share of stock.

price-to-earnings ratio. Price per share of stock divided by earnings per share of stock.

principal. In general, the major party to a transaction buying or selling for their own account and at their own risk. In investments, the basic amount invested, exclusive of any earnings. In bonds, the face value or amount to be paid to a bondholder at maturity, exclusive of interest.

principal-only strip. Derivative securities that give holders the principal portion of monthly payments on a group of mortgages. These securities are sold at a discount and increase in value quickly if mortgages in the underlying pool are refinanced, a trend that takes place after interest rates have declined.

probability distribution of returns. Set of data points representing rates of returns from a specific asset class as measured on a consistent basis over a specified period and organized to illustrate the frequency of representation that each data point has relative to the average for the entire set.

productive asset. Invested asset that produces cash flow payments to its owner as a consequence of ownership. Distinct from nonproductive asset that must be sold to realize a cash payment to its owner.

profit. Money left over after paying the costs and expenses associated with the generation of revenue.

prudent man rule. Rule governing investing behavior of a fiduciary or a person in a position of trust. This rule requires that the fiduciary act as an informed person would with their own affairs—that is, with prudence and discretion, paying close attention to the preservation of capital and avoiding speculation.

publicly traded company. Corporation whose shares of common stock are offered for sale to the public and become available for subsequent sale and purchase as market conditions allow. As opposed to a privately held corporation whose shares are more highly restricted by law as to their sale and purchase.

quality risk. Risk that the issuer of securities has a poor financial condition. In bonds, related to the issuer's ability to pay all interest and principal in a timely manner. In stocks, related to the sustainability and growth of an issuer's profitability.

quarter. One-fourth of a year. Most companies use calendar quarters as financial reporting periods (ending March 31, June 30, September 30, and December 31).

rate of return. In bonds, same as current yield, coupon rate divided by the purchase price. In stocks, same as **dividend yield,** annual dividend rate divided by purchase price. Sometimes refers to **total return,** which equals income plus capital appreciation.

rating agencies. Independent companies engaging in assessment of riskiness of debt securities. Major rating agencies include Fitch, Moody's, and Standard & Poor's.

real interest rate. Current interest rate minus inflation rate. Sometimes includes a premium for perceived credit risk, but often does not.

realized gain. Capital appreciation resulting from the sale of an asset for a higher price than the purchase price.

realized loss. Capital loss resulting from the sale of an asset for a lower price than the purchase price.

rebalancing. Adjustment made to an investment portfolio to bring it into line with a solution-based target.

regression to the mean. Statistical function used to predict values of a random variable, given the values of a known variable or variables. Returns from a defined-asset class are thought to tend to revert to the average return over time. This implies that higher-than-average returns will be followed by lower-than-average returns, and lower-than-average returns will be followed by higher-than-average returns.

reinvestment rate risk. The risk associated with reinvesting the principal and interest payments received from a bond. Shorter-term bonds have a greater reinvestment rate risk than longer-term bonds because they mature faster, placing reinvestment of the principal at a greater risk of earning a lower rate of return than it did while working within the original bond itself. Also known as *reinvestment risk.*

retirement assets. Assets invested for the purpose of providing retirement income to their holder.

retirement benefit. Cash used to pay for retirement expenses and generated from invested retirement assets.

retirement savings period. Portion of the human life cycle during which an individual is not retired and is thus able to save and invest money earned from employment.

retirement spending period. Portion of the human life cycle during which an individual is retired and thus uses invested retirement assets to provide a retirement benefit.

return on equity. Amount earned by a corporation expressed as a percentage of the value of its shareholders' equity. Calculated by dividing common stock equity as it appears on the balance sheet at the start of a period by the earnings of the corporation (before common stock dividends) over the entire period.

rising interest rate environment. Economic environment in which interest rates in general are increasing for bonds and debts of most maturities.

risk. Investment loss. The degree of risk is a function of the consequence of the loss. Losses arise from three sources: loss of principal (both temporary and permanent), loss of income, and loss of purchasing power due to inflation.

risk management. Effort to minimize the consequence of loss.

Russell 1000 Index. Index of the 1,000 largest-capitalization domestic stocks, published by Frank Russell Co.

Russell 2000 Index. Index of the 2,000 smallest-capitalization domestic stocks in the Russell 3000 Index, published by Frank Russell Co.

Russell 3000 Index. Index of the 3,000 domestic stocks ranked large to small for inclusion by their market capitalization, published by Frank Russell Co.

sales revenues. Money received for the sale of goods or services during a given accounting period.

Salomon Long-Term Corporate Bond Index. Index of representative bonds with maturities generally longer than ten years. Prepared by the investment firm of Salomon Brothers.

S&P/BARRA Growth Index. Stocks representing that half of the market capitalization of the Standard & Poor's 500 Index with the highest market price–to–book value ratios.

S&P/BARRA Value Index. Stocks representing that half of the market capitalization of the Standard & Poor's 500 Index with the lowest market price–to–book value ratios.

satisfactory return. Return that satisfies an investor's financial need.

savings. Personal income in excess of expenses.

seasonal stocks. Stocks issued by companies whose earnings rise and fall with the seasons.

SEC. Securities and Exchange Commission. Federal government agency created by the Securities and Exchange Act of 1934. Statutes administered by the SEC are intended to promote full disclosure of information and protect the investing public from fraud and malpractice.

sector mutual fund. Mutual fund that concentrates on one sector of the economy.

security. In investments, a financial instrument that is the evidence of an ownership position in an enterprise (for example, stock), or a creditor relationship with a public or private entity (for example, bonds), or ownership of the right to buy and sell other securities (for example, options).

security-specific risk. Risk of loss unique to a specific security.

serious money investment. Concept used in the **investing triangle.** Invested monies that are riskier than emergency cash reserves but less risky than speculation. Generally, investment used for a serious life purpose such as retirement, educational expenses, or housing purchases.

short-term bond. Bond with a maturity of one year or less.

small-cap. Generally, companies with market capitalizations between approximately $100 million and approximately $250 million.

small-cap effect. Observation that rates of return on stock investments increase as the size of the market capitalization decreases.

small-cap risk. Additional risk of loss borne by holders of small-capitalization stocks.

solution-based investing. Method of investing concerned with the solution of human financial problems instead of being solely focused on the capital markets. Can be applied on both institutional and individual levels. Examples of individual financial problems include investing for retirement, education, or housing. An example of an institutional problem for a pension fund is paying all benefits affordably to the contributors and without fail to the plan participants.

speculative discount. Reduction in the market price of a security to adjust for negative perceptions about the present and future financial condition of the issuer.

speculative premium. Addition to the market price of a security to adjust for positive perceptions about the present and future financial condition of the issuer.

speculative value. Degree of uncertainty in the market price of a stock.

speculator. An investor who assembles a portfolio of individual investments that cannot reasonably be expected to return at least the original outlay in accordance with a need for a satisfactory return and liquidity. The more speculative an activity, the less valuable, and the more difficult it is to analyze the chances for success or failure.

stability-oriented bond ladder. Bond ladder that is dollar-weighted skewed to the shorter-maturity bonds.

Standard & Poor's 500 Index. Five hundred mostly large and mostly domestic companies deemed by Standard & Poor's to be most representative of publicly traded domestic equities.

standard deviation. Statistical measure of the degree of variation from the mean in a probability distribution. In investments, used to measure how widely dispersed a set of investment returns are from the average return of the entire set. Also known as **volatility.**

stock dividend yield. Annual dividend per share divided by the current market price per share, expressed in a percentage.

stock market. General term used to describe the purchase and sale of stocks either by computer or on an exchange. In popular media, sometimes used interchangeably with the Dow Jones Industrial Average.

stock mutual fund. Mutual fund that invests in stocks in accordance with the terms disclosed in its prospectus. Stock mutual funds are categorized by the types of stocks they usually hold, for example, by growth stocks, income stocks, small-cap stocks, and foreign stocks.

supplemental retirement benefit. Amount of money in excess of what is necessary to support an individual's essential living requirements in retirement.

tangible value. Component of the market price of a stock represented by a conservatively calculated discounted present value of expected future dividends.

tax-advantaged retirement account. Government-defined and -regulated retirement account where earnings are allowed to compound without being subject to taxation until taken out of the account. Examples include the IRA, 401(k) plans, 457 plans, 403(b) plans, deferred-compensation plans, Keogh plans, profit-sharing plans, and ESOP plans. One insurance product, the variable annuity, may also be considered as a tax-advantaged retirement account. Some tax-advantaged retirement accounts allow for pretax contributions, while some do not. Also known as a *tax-deferred account.*

temporary loss. Unrealized principal loss in an investment expected to recover its value over time.

total return. Capital appreciation plus income, expressed as a fraction of beginning value. For a given period, equal to the current value of an asset plus its income minus its value at the beginning of the period. The resulting remainder is then divided by the value at the beginning of the period.

trader. Individual who buys or sells securities or commodities in anticipation of a quick profit.

trading costs. Costs associated with the purchase or sale of securities.

Treasury obligation.   A direct debt obligation of the U.S. Treasury.

U.S. Treasury bill.   Direct debt obligations of the U.S. Treasury with maturities under one year.

U.S. Treasury bond.   Direct debt obligations of the U.S. Treasury with maturities ranging from 10 to 30 years.

U.S. Treasury note.   Direct debt obligations of the U.S. Treasury with maturities ranging from one to ten years.

value investing.   Investing style that attempts to purchase securities with a market price less than a calculated intrinsic value.

volatility.   Statistical measure of the degree of variation from the mean in a probability distribution. In investments, used to measure how widely dispersed a set of investment returns is from the average return of the entire set. Also known as **standard deviation.**

zero-sum game.   Activity where for each and every winner there is an identical loser.

INDEX